Writing
A Great Movie

*Four Advanced Tools
for the Dramatist*

by Jeff Kitchen

Acknowledgments

I'd like to thank my wife, Hope Mineo,
for all her help in bringing this book to completion,
and my editor, Cheri Smith, for all her long hard hours,
clear thinking, insights and encouragement.
Thanks also to Steven Deitz, Irving Fiske
and William Thompson Price.

CONTENTS

PART ONE -- LEARNING THE TOOLS

1. Some Preliminary Nuggets..................... 1
2. Dilemma.. 17
3. Crisis.. 33
4. Decision & Action............................ 37
5. Resolution.................................... 41
6. Theme... 47
7. The 36 Dramatic Situations.................. 57
8. The Enneagram............................... 97
9. Research and Brainstorming................. 115
10. The Central Proposition...................... 127
11. Sequence, Proposition, Plot.................. 145

PART TWO -- DEVELOPING A SCREENPLAY

12. Utilizing Dilemma............................. 171
13. Utilizing Crisis.............................. 181
14. Utilizing Decision and Action............... 185
15. Utilizing Resolution.......................... 189
16. Utilizing Theme.............................. 191
17. Utilizing the 36 Dramatic Situations....... 195
18. Utilizing the Enneagram...................... 225
19. Utilizing Research and Brainstorming..... 233
20. Utilizing The Central Proposition.......... 239
21. Utilizing Sequence, Proposition, Plot...... 253
    Epilogue.................................... 287

1

SOME PRELIMINARY NUGGETS

I always start my seminars asking why we go to so much trouble writing a screenplay. It all comes down to one word: Audience. It's all about the audience. And for them it's all about two words: Great Movie!

This book is a practical manual on how to write a great movie. I teach the craft of the dramatist, focusing on four tools for the screenwriter and presenting a complete working technique. Included is the real-time development of a screenplay, built from scratch, to give a clear picture of how to actually use these tools on your own scripts. Any level of writer can learn this material, and the intention is to be as useful as possible so that you can take what you have learned here and be able to consistently create, develop and construct a wide variety of screenplays.

The four tools that I teach come from different sources. The first is from observations that Aristotle made about what tends to be common to those dramas that grip an audience; the second is a powerful brainstorming tool called the Thirty-Six Dramatic Situations; the third, called the Central Proposition, works with the logic of argumentation to tie a script together into a coherent whole; and the fourth, a three-step process called 'Sequence, Proposition, Plot' is a remarkable tool for actually constructing the plot.

Before we get into the process of writing a screenplay, I'll lay out some useful concepts born of my experience as a writer, script consultant and teacher for fifteen years. I was classically trained as a playwright in the work of William Thompson Price, a turn of the century playwriting teacher. Price founded the American School of Playwriting in New York in 1901 and of his twenty-eight students, twenty-four had hits on Broadway. I worked in the New York theatre as a dramaturg and taught playwriting for several years before I started teaching screen-writing. All the tools from playwriting were perfectly applicable to screenwriting because it's really the craft of the dramatist. It's about making a story work dra-matically, it has to be actable—and it has to grip an audience.

IT'S ALL ABOUT THE AUDIENCE

When you go into a movie with major expectations, what *specifically* do you expect? You've heard this movie is great, that it will rock your world, and you're in a charged state. Can you put your finger on what you expect from it? Obviously this will vary with different genres because you expect one thing from a romantic comedy and another from an action thriller, but it's interesting to examine your expectations as specifically as possible. It's your job as a screen-writer to satisfy audience expectations.

Anyone who's ever done live performance knows intimately that it's all about the audience. Some screenwriters who sit in their rooms trying to come up with a wild story aren't necessarily trained to think in terms of the audience. But that's what this medium is all about. A movie playing to an empty theatre has no power—it's just shadows on the wall. The power of the film resides in the re-sponse of the audience.

I would urge you to make a professional study of the audience—your audience. You're doing all this for them. Pay attention to the way in which people get excited about an upcoming movie. Study audiences on your way into the theatre. Look at your own expectations as you go in. Gauge the electricity in the air. Feel the prelude. While the movie is playing, feel the ride, feel the audience response. Are they thrilled, scared, let down, intoxicated, bored, electrified? When the movie is over, stand outside the theatre and watch the people come out. Study the expressions on their faces. Listen in on how they're reacting. I'm always pas-sionately curious about how my fellow moviegoers are reacting to the movie we've just seen together.

When *Star Wars I* came out, people camped out at Graumann's Chinese theatre six weeks in advance. On opening night I went there and hung out with them, specifically to study audience expectations. They *really* had it—audience expectations, that is—and I wanted to stick my finger in that electric socket. I interviewed them, asking "What are you expecting?" They were pumped! I'd get answers like, "Oh man, I saw the first one when I was seven years old and it was the greatest movie ever! I'm expecting a ride to the moon. I'm so psyched!" I was there when they let the first couple hundred people into the theatre and they ran screaming inside, jumping and whooping it up. You could measure the electricity in the air that day with a voltmeter.

Study your own reactions. Make yourself your own guinea pig. You're an audience member and you can see right into your own deepest responses. Look at your body chemistry afterwards. Are you tripping on adrenaline? What is your physical response? Is your gut churning? Are you in shock? Look at your moods. Are you giddy and in love? Do you feel energized, infatuated, distressed, inert, crazed, pissed off, silly, serious, demonic, transfigured? How did the movie match up to your expectations? Are you on the phone to your friends right away, telling them to see it? Or warning them to run in the other direction? Look at how the best movies impact you. Look at how you feel when you come out of a truly great film. Look at the various levels of exhilaration, satisfaction, intensity, adrenaline, happiness, clarity, fury, energy or love that you're feeling. As a screenwriter, this is what you want to do to an audience.

If I'm walking down the street and there are people lined up around the block for a movie, I'll look each one of them in the eye as I walk by and ask (in my mind), "Why are you here? What do you need out of this movie? What are you hungering for? What are you paying $10 for? What are your hopes, your dreams, your ambitions, your desires?" I'm studying this group of people who are there to get something special. They're not lined up at the checkout counter of a supermarket. They're there to sit in the dark and experience the thing that I spend my time writing. I'm observing them with the passionate curiosity of a writer, a scientist, a student of human nature and a fellow moviegoer who loves a great movie. I'm trying to get an ever deeper, more complex, but also clearer and simpler understanding of the audience. I consider it part of my job, because the audience is who I'm writing for. I'm not writing for readers, agents, studio execs, directors or actors but for each and every person who comes in on Saturday night and wants a great movie.

WHY DO PEOPLE LOVE MOVIES?

Another good question is "What's special about a good movie?" It's a simple enough question, but it's literally the sixty-four million dollar question these days. If everyone knew what's special about a good movie, then each movie you see would be the best movie yet made. Certain movies have a 'magic something' and it's your job as a screenwriter to put that magic something into the script. The more you can put your finger on that magic something, the more you'll tend to be able to either recognize it when you stumble over it in your material, or create it. The more you ask what's special about a good movie, the deeper and clearer your own understanding will become of what the best movies have going for them.

"Why do you love movies?" is another good question. Again, it's a simple question, but ask it of yourself and over the years you will get deeper and deeper levels of understanding. What is this creature, the movies? Why do you love it? What does it do for you? Why do you crave it? What hunger does it satisfy? It's interesting to think about the movies that stick in your brain, to look back at scenes you'll never forget, to remember the first time you saw one of your favorite movies. Sit down and make a list of the movies that changed your life, gave you a new outlook on life, awakened you to something. Then look at why they had this effect. See if you can articulate specifically what they did for you.

Another question is "In real life what transports you?" What puts you over the moon? What puts you in a wildly altered state? To be really *transported* is an astounding experience. It is to be swept into a different dimension, to be taken to an exalted place, to feel a wildly energetic freedom. It's interesting to look at the absolute peak experiences in your own life—the ones that you can count on one hand, the ones that stand out far above all the others. If you can isolate one of them, you can look at the confluence of powerful emotions around it, the intensity, the exhilaration or the pain (a peak experience can be intensely painful as well). Why will you never forget it? Bring this level of intensity to your writing and it will help you create a great movie. Not that you're replicating this specific event, but that you're bringing that intense energy into your script. The audience wants your movie to be one of the absolute peak experiences of their lives. As a storyteller and a dramatist, you are working with the elements of magic, transformation, rekindling dreams and changing people. Throughout history, the storyteller has traditionally been a bringer of fire, of life, energy, healing, freedom, fun, action, insight, beauty, intensity, focus, clarity and so on. You have a wonderful job, bringing powerful transformative energy and a full spectrum of emotions into people's lives.

THE CORE OF YOUR SCRIPT

Part of the definition of dramatic writing is that it's a fight to the finish. Conflict is to drama as sound is to music. Conflict or opposition is central to what makes a story compelling to an audience. A fight to the finish is two people in a knock-down, drag-out fight and only one of them is going to walk away. Two dogs fighting over a bone. This is true whether it's a fight over the fate of the world or over where to go on the family's Christmas vacation. Conflict makes comedies work dramatically as well—it's just within a different context.

If you go back to the earliest Greek theatre, there were only two characters onstage. The introduction of the third character by Sophocles was considered a major dramatic innovation. This ability to see two main characters in conflict helps you get down to the absolute core of your material. Once you strip it down to your protagonist and antagonist, then you're right at the nucleus of your plot. If this works then the rest of your script will tend to work. If it doesn't, then whatever you add to the plot probably won't help.

UNITY OF ACTION

Aristotle noticed that those dramas that grip an audience tend to consist of one complete action. He talks about it as the telling of a deed—a hero's deed. The ability to find one main action at the core of a script can help unify it. For instance, even in a script as complex as *The Godfather*, there is one main action at its heart and it's that Michael defeats Barzini and saves the Corleone family. Can you find the one main action that constitutes the heart of your script? Is there one main deed that the hero performs? Part of what we're dealing with is that you have a two-hour window in which to tell your story. Movies are this length and it's rather inflexible, unless you're hugely successful and you're allowed to make a three-hour film. Having that limited amount of time forces you to focus your resources. It's like being in a fight where you only get one punch. You really want to make that one punch count. Find the main action of your script and build everything around it. The four tools presented in this book will help guide you through doing just that.

Unity of Action is a concept that is not well understood in either the film or theatre industries. This simple definition of Unity of Action has held up well for me over the years. Unity of Action consists of:

1. A Single Action
2. A Single Hero
3. A Single Result

You have one main action happening, one main person doing it and one main result springing from it. This means that all the parts of the film serve the one main action that the script revolves around. A good example of Unity of Action is a symphony. All the different instruments in the orchestra are each doing different things, but they all work together to create this one piece of music. In drama you have powerful ideas operating together as a unit—operating together to achieve a specific goal. You see this in the military or sports. Everybody is doing different things, but they're all working toward the achievement of one thing. In drama, we're talking about structural unity. Coherence. If it's not part of the one main action, then it doesn't belong in the script.

THE CRAFT OF THE DRAMATIST

A big part of your job as a screenwriter is to dramatize your script. To dramatize a story means to make it gripping to an audience, to create continuous and coherent and compelling dramatic action. Essentially what we're talking about is turning mere 'Story' into Drama. Mere Story is a term that a script doctor would use to describe a weakness in the material, in the sense of it being merely 'episodic.' Mere Story means that there are unconnected episodes that don't really go anywhere and don't build much tension. A simple example of mere Story is: Joey wakes up in the morning, has some orange juice, ties his shoes and walks his dog. It's a mere succession of events that doesn't necessarily engage the audience. It's flat dramatically and has to be dramatized or it probably won't work as a performance medium. There's a huge difference between narrative and drama. What I teach are the habits of mind of a trained dramatist and part of your job as a dramatist is to be able to recognize mere Story when you see it and to be able to dramatize it. And believe me, it's like turning water into wine.

You want your whole script to be Drama and not Story. You want each act to be dramatic and not mere Story, and the same goes for each sequence and for each scene. You never want to revert to mere Story. How you do this? The short answer to this question is read this book. In other words, there's not one magic button that you push to suddenly turn Story into Drama. There are a combination of interlocking steps and processes to take to help render every part of your script dramatic.

You definitely need a good story as the basis of your script, but mere Story is not enough. In the same way, you need life in your script, but mere life is not enough. You need character, but mere character is not enough, and you need action, but mere action is not enough.

There's an important distinction here, because you need storytelling skills as big as you can get them. A movie is a story rendered into the dramatic medium. You need imagination, a sense of adventure and fun, an ability to weave a story together and to spellbind an audience—and you need all these things as big as you can get them. It's important to bear in mind that even the most advanced structural tools applied to bland material simply don't work. Well-structured crap is still crap. It may run like a formula one race car, but it's still not a movie that anyone wants to pay good money to see. To compete as a screenwriter you need a healthy and vigorous imagination and it's hard to stress this enough. But however creative your story is, it still has to be dramatized if it's going to work in this performance medium. It has to be actable and it has to grip an audience.

Perhaps the single biggest misconception is that a good story automatically makes a good film. There are many excellent novels that don't lend themselves to being movies. In theatre there's a saying: "It may sound great around a campfire but it's not stageworthy. Yes, it's a good story, but we can't act it out in a way that will grab an audience." Essentially your job as a screenwriter is to create compelling dramatic action. By compelling, I mean that at the high point of suspense you couldn't pay the audience to leave. They are compelled to stay and see how it   turns out.

DRAMATIC ACTION

This brings up the concept of Dramatic Action. Dramatic Action is not car chases and shoot outs. It's a state of action you put the audience in, a state of subjective excitement that a movie creates in the audience. You've probably seen movies in which they're blowing up half the world and you're nodding off in your seat, and you've seen movies in which two people are fighting it out in a living room, and you're riveted. It is in the latter that you are truly in a state of action. This is the real meaning of Dramatic Action. You want to get them on the edge of their seat and keep them there.

It is generally acknowledged that 90-95% of all scripts submitted in both film and theatre are atrocious. And I've often heard, don't kid yourself, it's 95%. Script readers at studios tell me that it's 98%. And when they say atrocious it's not just a figure of speech. These scripts are so bad as to be unreadable. This means only 2 to 5% of them are even worth reading. Is it surprising then how many mediocre movies get made? Writing a screenplay is much harder than most people imagine. What is the problem? Many of the people writing these scripts are intelligent and often have good stories to tell, but they have yet to grasp the craft of the dramatist.

ENGINEERING YOUR SCREENPLAY BEFORE YOU WRITE IT

Price said that you can take all the energy that goes into rewrites and engineer your screenplay properly before you write it. This is what this book is all about. What I'll be showing you is how to build a script—plot construction—and a big part of this is knowing how to structure coherent compelling Dramatic Action. It's a lot of work, but so is fifteen rewrites. I'll teach you how to do it up front. Listen to what David Mamet, a fellow Vermonter, has to say on the subject in his great book *On Directing Film* (Penguin Books, New York, 1991):

It's very difficult to shore up something that has been done badly. You'd better do your planning up front, when you have the time. It's like working with glue. When it sets, you've used up your time. When it's almost set, you then have to make quick decisions under pressure. If you design a chair correctly, you can put all the time into designing it correctly and assemble it at your leisure. (p. 58)

DRAMATIC WRITING IS A SLIPPERY CREATURE

Dramatic writing is generally considered the most elusive of all the literary disciplines. *Elusive* is an interesting word, meaning hard to pin down, slippery, tricky and unpredictable. In my experience as a script consultant, I've found that it's tricky figuring out why something looks good on paper and fails onscreen. It can be hard to figure out why something worked most of the way through and then falls apart. It's clearly hard to predict whether a script will work onscreen or onstage. It's mysterious how a movie with all the top people and big money loses a bundle on its opening weekend and the same basic plot shot for a pittance goes on to make a fortune. The producer of the big movie may never know why the little one worked and his didn't.

Writing a script is a lot like building a car from scratch. You're literally manufacturing the entire vehicle from the ground up, building tires out of rubber, stretching out your own brake lines and building your own carburetor. You can end up with a vehicle, but it may not run. It may have a number of compound, complex problems and fixing any one of them still doesn't make the damn thing run. A screenplay can be just like this. It may never work no matter what you do, and you may never know why.

One of the things I'll be urging you to do with these four tools is to use them as precisely as possible. The tools and techniques create certain distinctions that help you cut through the natural elusiveness of dramatic writing. They give you a set of talons that help you grab onto this slippery thing, dramatic writing, stop it in its tracks and make it do what you need it to do. You don't want to muddy the distinctions every time they become inconvenient. This is a central part of the craft of a dramatist. As William Thompson Price says in his book *The Philosophy of Dramatic Principle and Method* (W.T. Price Pub., New York, 1912): "In dividing the drama into distinct principles or elements we get at the function of each. By this means we are enabled to make an implement of a principle. We do not confound the uses of each." (p. 1) Again, what I teach is the habits of mind of a trained dramatist. You can train your mind to think in certain ways that will help your stories work dramatically. Not that you are a slave to these tools, but your goal is to be extremely skilled with each of them.

As an artist, you will use the tools to help you make your script work, but you want to be the master of these tools, not their servant. The power saw doesn't dictate how the house will look. Solid craft will help you be consistent as a writer—your material will more consistently work and you'll be able to tackle a broad spectrum of plots and genres successfully. Even though I teach classic structural technique—and this is extremely useful for you to have as second nature—it's important to note that literally *anything* can work. And either it works or it doesn't. A movie is two hours of entertainment, period. It can be someone onstage shouting at a wall for two hours, and if they line up around the block for six months, then it works. So learn the craft, but don't worship it, and don't limit yourself to how you apply it. Also bear in mind that precision of technique doesn't negate the need for deep intuition as an artist, explosive creativity and dynamic storytelling. These are absolutely crucial things to have as a storyteller and should not be underestimated, but if you combine them with substantial craft as a dramatist, then you can have a complete package as a screenwriter—and that is rare indeed.

WHAT ARE YOU TRYING TO DO TO YOUR AUDIENCE?

How do you want the audience to feel? Specifically, what mood do you want them to be in at the end of the movie? As the dramatist, you are sculpting the mood in which they will leave the theatre. It's like a magic spell or hypnosis, where it all comes together at the end, "When I snap my fingers you'll feel light and refreshed." It's all about transforming the audience, so what do you want to transform them into? The more specifically you can pinpoint the mood that you want the audience to leave the theatre in, the clearer your focus will be as a writer.

I had a clear experience of this a few years ago when a friend came back from seeing the band, the Moody Blues and he was in a fabulous mood. He was telling me how phenomenal it was and how I had to go the next night. I'd had my fill of the Moody Blues years before and I said, "Sure, it sounds great" but I wasn't getting very fired up or even pretending well. He got frustrated and said, "No, you're not getting it!" He had something inside him that he really wanted me to have. This is what I'm talking about. What do you have in you that you really want to transfer into your audience? What, specifically are you trying to do to them? The more you can pinpoint this, the more focused you will be as a writer and the more clearly you will see your intention for the whole movie.

THE STAGE AND THE ALTAR

At one time in history, the stage and the altar were the same thing, for example in Druid times. The altar would be used as a stage, with religious dramas enacted upon it. Generally they were about the transformation of the hero and were for the benefit of those gathered there. They were used as a way to show those watching how to transform themselves.

From its earliest days drama has served a shamanistic function. People need help and often seek guidance getting through life's normal problems, especially during transitions: from childhood into adulthood, marriage or its dissolution, having children, growing old and death. Think about the great movies that have given you a direction in life or helped you understand something key about yourself or the world. It may sound strange to think of movies having a religious function but, again, it's about transforming an audience. As Gandhi said, "I can show you a way out of hell." In this context I often remember Martin Luther King saying that a powerful emotional experience can be the first step on the road to commitment.

Comedy is about transforming an audience as well, and clowns have their ancestry as priests. Laughter is very transformative. Many comedians take their job very seriously. They know it's crucial to laugh, especially to be able to laugh at yourself. Groucho Marx once inscribed a book, "They'll never know how necessary our insanity is to their sanity."

AUDIENCE DEMAND

People expect a lot from movies. Audience Demand is a very important thing to understand because it's so powerful, even if audiences are often unaware of it themselves. It's like a river that looks lazy on the surface but has a fierce undercurrent. Audience Demand is definitely there and it's your job as screenwriter to satisfy it. So get in touch with it. A great way to get in touch with Audience Demand is to remember the last time someone told you that you *have* to go see a particular movie, it will rock your world and change your life. You go and the movie is very disappointing. Look at your response. It isn't "Oh jeez, that's too bad. It was lame." It's more like, "DAMN IT! I didn't get what I was promised and I'm mad. I *needed* that!" The mark of a great artist is that they give the audience what they want even if the audience itself doesn't know what it wants. So penetrate down to what audiences want and demand, and get as much in touch with it as you can. It's your bread and butter. Locating it is like digging up the street and finding the giant electric line that powers the whole city, and tapping into that. Audiences bring a lot of energy to the theatre and if you can tap into it, then it will multiply the power of your movie.

Why does an audience bring such a powerful set of demands to a movie? It's because in real life our own demands often go unmet. Notice in your own life the myriad demands that you place on your friends, your spouse, your parents, your children, your neighbors and politicians. How many of them are likely to be met or can ever be met? Look at the demands placed on you. Movies are an arena in which magical things can happen. It can be a fairy tale arena and that's part of the magic of movies—the things that could never happen real life *can* happen in film and theatre, even if it's only for a few special hours. Many of us have what could be called chronic avoidance, in which we tiptoe around tricky or difficult issues. Say, in a dysfunctional family there may be an unspoken contract that a certain issue will not be broached, so everyone tiptoes around it. There can be a tremendous hunger for resolution. If someone *does* tackle this tricky issue it may blow up in their face, making the problem a thousand times worse and still leaving it unresolved. The hunger for resolution is still active. People seek closure and meaning in life.

Another important question is, "How do you intend to penetrate the indifference of the audience?" Audiences at the beginning of the 21st century are very jaded. From their point of view they've seen everything and they know everything. This isn't true, of course, but they can genuinely feel that way. Plus, anyone entering into a new experience will tend to have a certain degree of insulation. This is natural, but it's something you have to overcome to get the audience into your world. It's very much akin to an electrician stripping the rubber coating off a wire in order to get a live connection.

Drama is often compared to a crucible. You may know that in chemistry a crucible is a ceramic pot used to contain a powerful chemical, or that in steel making it's the container that holds the molten steel. Look at the drama as a crucible in which we can experiment with radical solutions, powerful chemicals, explosive reactions and forbidden ideas. People often need radical solutions in their lives, but these can be very tricky to experiment with. What if your marriage is falling apart and you need a radical solution? You don't want to go home and just try one out, because if it doesn't work then there goes the rest of your marriage. But you can engage in a movie or play that does it, and thereby get a feel for how it might work at home. The movies are a 'let's pretend' arena in which we can engage in an experiment at a safe distance. We can put out our feelers or do a taste test to see how it would work in our own life. Some of the best medicines are poisons in the right dosage, in the same way that radical insights in life, properly used, can liberate people. The healing power of art is something that people continually seek out and has always been a central part of civilization itself.

TRANSFORMING THE AUDIENCE

Part of the fun of being a dramatist is being a bull in a china shop, going after the sacred cows, going where it's *verboten*. The key word in the entertainment industry is 'outrageousness.' You can describe your job as a screenwriter as a cross between a bombmaker and a poet. You're blowing up ideas and doing it all through language. The audience seeks a profound transformative experience, so as a dramatist you're working with elements of great change, radical transformation and powerful resolution, with the possibility of powerful, cataclysmic, permanent change. It's a chance to really rewire the brain of the audience, to permanently change the way they think. And the audience is up for that. They come in, open their minds and say, "Come on. Do something, anything. Let's party. Change things."

Catharsis is an emotional release, a cleaning out of the system, a fresh start. Aristotle described it as a cleaning out of the undesirable emotions, a purging of the system. Think about how a great movie can make you feel cleansed or new or energized or inspired. Sometimes you just need to have the normal day-to-day banter that rattles around in your brain burned clean. David Mamet, in *Three Uses of the Knife* (Vintage Books, New York, 1998) says: "The purpose of theater, like magic, like religion—those three harness mates—is to inspire cleansing awe." (p. 69) Catharsis is like an oil change. Thinking about it should bring up the question, "What do you periodically need to have cleaned out of your system?" It's been proven by behavioral scientists that people need to change states at least once a day. You see people coming home, having a beer or going jogging or going to the movies—to shift into a different state.

What I teach is classic structural technique for the dramatist. It's a good thing to have under your belt. Not that you want to rely on it for everything, but in my experience it will cover about 85% of the scripts you work on. Tim Robbins, the actor, writer and director said in an interview:

> I respect the classical form of film and storytelling. I've done experimental, absurdist and dadaistic theatre and there are ways to incorporate those styles into storytelling, but you've got to go to the classical structure of storytelling. I don't believe in indulgence for the sake of indulgence. I believe in the audience. I think they're central to what we're doing. That's why we're doing it. I'm always aware that an audience will be watching

this. I don't want to get too esoteric or intellectual with something I'm doing because it really is entertainment we're doing.

My playwriting teacher, Irving Fiske, did a translation of *Hamlet* into modern American English in 1946 and in his introduction he said: "The profoundest hunger of the modern audience is not for an escape from reality, as is commonly thought, but for an escape *into* reality from much of the meaninglessness of their everyday lives." Certainly, escape from reality is a perfectly valid form of entertainment, but escape into reality is a more interesting concept. A solid jolt of reality can connect an audience with what really matters to them in their lives.

PRINCIPLE AND METHOD

The two main things that I teach are Principle and Method. There are certain principles that tend to make drama work and there are certain methods that embody those principles. If, for instance, you're learning how to fly an airplane, it's not enough to know which buttons to push at what time. You have to understand the principles of flight, and your understanding of the principles will inform your application of method. Then you know *why* you're pushing this particular button at this time and what it does to the vacuum above the wings. The same thing is true in acupuncture. There are certain principles behind why acupuncture works—you're balancing meridians and opening flow, etc., and there are certain specific methods that embody those principles—exactly where you put the needles and for how long.

Your understanding of the principles informs your application of the methods. I've had students who understood the underlying principles, but didn't have a good grasp of the actual techniques, and that only gets them so far. I've also had students who were good at the tools, but didn't know why they were using them and that's working in a limited and blind way. You want to know both of them inside and out. Essentially, the principle becomes an implement. The more you understand the principle behind a tool, the more you can adapt the tool as needed because you understand its function.

THE PURPOSE OF THIS BOOK

This book is an attempt to put in writing what I've taught professionally for fifteen years. People have been asking me to write a book for a decade now and I finally have been able to turn my attention to it. I submit four tools for your toolkit as a dramatist within the context of a complete working process. Everything will work equally well for both screenwriters and playwrights. I teach my classes in a hands-on format to bridge the gap between having an understanding of the tools and actually being able to use them in the field. I remember that gap very distinctly when I was first learning. After some substantial study, I began to truly grasp the tools and techniques but still couldn't use them for a while longer. Countless times in my classes, I'll explain a tool clearly and fully and everyone says, "Yes I get it," but when I say, "OK, now let's do it on your script," they fall apart. Obviously, part of that is just the panic of confronting something new, but part of it is that it genuinely takes some real *doing* to gain a working knowledge of something.

In the class we work with script analyses of *The Godfather*, *Tootsie* and *Blade Runner*, and these films make screenwriting look easy, the same way that Tiger Woods makes golf look easy. I would recommend watching these films again, as well as *Training Day* (which I use in this book), because if you're fresh on them you'll get more out of this book. We're studying acknowledged masterpieces as illustrations of the tools that I teach, but we're doing so in order to be able to apply them to unformed scripts that are in the beginning phases of creation and development. So I try to provide real experience in building a script from scratch, or from whatever level of development my students are at with their own material. My primary concern is that you are able to really use these tools on however wide a variety of scripts you're developing.

These four tools have served me well over the years and I find them quite suitable for a complete working process. One of the benefits of teaching them for so long and using them hands-on with each student is that I have acquired more and more expertise in their use. A friend of mine who has been a martial arts teacher for years said because teaching forced him to stick to the basics it solidified his foundation as a martial artist in a profound way. He said he realized that they're basics or first principles for good reason. All mechanics are based on the simple machines: the lever, the inclined plane, the pulley, and the wheel and axle. Everything else is built from various combinations of them. David Mamet talks about this in *On Directing Film*:

> It's good, as the Stoics tell us, to have tools that are simple to understand and of a very limited number—so that we may locate and employ them on a moment's notice. I think the essential tools in any worthwhile endeavor are incredibly simple. And very difficult to master. The task of any artist is not to learn many, many techniques but to

learn the most simple technique perfectly. In doing so, Stanislavsky told us, the difficult will become easy and the easy habitual, so that the habitual may become beautiful. (p. 106)

I had first thought to entitle this book *How to Write a Great Movie* because instruction in the use of the tools here is like handing a journeyman a toolbox, taking each tool out and insuring that it's properly understood, handled, and demonstrated. With them and with practice you will be able to construct a finely crafted piece of dramatic work. But a dramatic work, a play, a movie is a work of art and art demands originality, inspiration, imagination, all rather mysterious entities and it's a question whether these can be taught. While we court the favor of the muses, there is the solid fact that craft can definitely be learned. The more diligently you apply yourself to becoming master of these tools and developing your own feel for them and making them your own, the better you will become as a dramatist. In the end, however, craft is in the service of art, the art of writing a great movie, and the foundation of the art of writing is your discipline and dedication to writing, pure and simple. Just keep writing is ultimately the best advice to give to any writer.

In writing this book, I try to demonstrate this process by developing a script from scratch using the tools. I start with an utterly raw idea and build it up, with you watching over my shoulder as I wrestle it into shape. I try to leave the process as unvarnished as possible, because that's what *you've* got to deal with as a writer. How do you handle the little bumps and wipe outs and puzzles and black holes that constitute the daily grunt work of building a script? So this is a manual of plot construction as well as a full explanation of four remarkable tools for the dramatist. I sincerely hope that it gives you several dependable and well regarded tools to add to your screenwriter's toolkit. It is not meant to displace other techniques, but to complement them and round out your abilities as a dramatist. Best of luck, and please knock my socks off at the movies. That's what it's all about.

2

DILEMMA

Twenty five hundred years ago Aristotle made some very astute observations about drama, using his native Athens as a laboratory. Each year during a religious theatre festival a topic would be assigned to the playwrights and they would all then write on that subject, for example, on Oedipus. You can imagine what it would be like if every film at the Sundance Film Festival this year had to be about the Kennedy assassination. Aristotle thus had the chance to compare and contrast all these plays in very specific ways. He observed that some put the audience to sleep while others were intensely gripping. This made him wonder, "Is there anything in common among those dramas that grip an audience?" He studied them and found that they did tend to have several things in common—a good strong Dilemma, Crisis, Decision and Action, Resolution and Denouement.

It is important to note that these are just his observations. They're not rules or dogma or laws, they are merely observations. Aristotle was not a dramatist—he never wrote a play. Sophocles, Euripides and Aeschylus did not study with him; it was in fact he who studied them. If Aristotle had been around for early experiments in rocketry, he would have made the observation, "Hey, the rockets with fins tend to fly better." His observations do happen to be particularly astute and if you know how to use them properly, they can really help make a script work.

Let's start with dilemma. The dictionary defines dilemma as a situation with a choice to be made in which neither alternative is acceptable. Two equally unacceptable alternatives—two equally painful choices. The story of a person trapped in a good strong dilemma can be riveting. Say your brother badly needs an operation and asks to borrow money but the cash you have is earmarked to finally turn your business into a success and pay for a new home, thus saving your marriage and getting your kids out of a dangerous neighborhood. This is a dilemma to lose sleep over, to wrestle with, to debate with yourself in a gut-wrenching way. Or another one: say you get caught in a horrible situation with the police and are forced to either turn in your best friend or do the hard time in jail yourself? Or do you choose between your morals or your duty? Or between your survival and the life of another person? These are real dilemmas and they can stop someone in their tracks. Dilemma is a necessary and powerful thing to focus on in a screenplay because it will put your protagonist in a situation that will grip an audience intensely.

In *Training Day* Ethan Hawke's character, Jake Hoyt, is caught in a tough dilemma when Denzel Washington's character, Alonzo Harris, keeps crossing the line morally. When Jake challenges Alonzo for stealing the money from the Sandman's house, Alonzo tells him that this is what it takes to do the job. He tells Jake to choose between being a real player who gets things done or going back to cutting parking tickets. Jake is trapped, unable to go back to mundane police work, but equally unable to go along with Alonzo's criminal ways. Alonzo has taken drugs off college students, then made Jake smoke them (while lying about what it is), then won't lift a finger as Jake tries to stop a rape, even letting the suspects go afterwards. And yet Alonzo gets real results with his tactics. He forces information out of the Snoop Dogg dealer character, shoving a pen down his throat to make him puke up crack vials and bargaining with him for his freedom. Jake stands in awe of Alonzo, this seasoned hard core veteran in an elite anti-drug unit who takes no prisoners and has handed out 15,000 man-years of jail time. All this keeps Jake off balance. He's damned if he goes along with Alonzo and damned if he doesn't. Either bend the law a little to take down the big-time bad guys or go back to the cub scouts. Jake is trapped, and this trap is what the movie is about.

Two equally unacceptable alternatives. Being caught between the devil and the deep blue sea. Kill or be killed. You can't hang on and you can't let go. Trapped between a rock and a hard place. Damned if you do and damned if you don't. I've learned from working hands-on with thousands of screenwriters and playwrights in the last fifteen years that a dilemma of magnitude can always improve the plot. A writer comes in with a well-plotted story, but when we create a dilemma or strengthen one that already exists, it invariably improves the material.

Essentially, there is either a dilemma inherent in the plot or there isn't. When it is there, we identify it, build on it, complicate and dimensionalize it in ways that substantially develop the script. If it's not there, we experiment with the possibility of creating a dilemma, and this often leads to a set of intriguing possibilities that can enhance the material. This will create more Dramatic Action, engaging the audience much more in the character's fate. It puts the protagonist in a more complex and compelling situation. Also it makes the role a meatier one and that attracts top actors looking for roles with substance, complexity and challenge.

There's an excellent example of someone caught in a dilemma in the 1956 science fiction film, *Forbidden Planet*. Commander Adams has traveled to a ship-wrecked space colony to check on survivors and finds it inhabited only by two survivors, a scientist Morbius, and his daughter. Morbius has used alien technology found inside the planet to build Robbie the Robot, a very sophisticated robot. While demonstrating Robbie for Commander Adams, he has Adams give Robbie his ray gun. Morbius then orders Robbie to point the gun at Commander Adams. Morbius orders Robbie to fire, and Robbie starts to short circuit. Arcing electricity, he's frozen in place. Morbius says that Robbie is caught in a dilemma. He's been programmed on one hand to never disobey Morbius' orders, but he's also been programmed to never harm a human being. He says if he leaves Robbie like this he'll melt down, so he releases him from the command. This is an interesting look at how someone acts when they are trapped in a good strong dilemma. If you have to choose between whether to sacrifice your wife or sacrifice your son then you will be paralyzed—unable to send a command in either direction.

Catching a person in a dilemma is much like cornering a wild animal. Have you ever seen a cornered wild animal in real life? Perhaps a raccoon caught in your garage when you're taking out the trash? It's a fearsome scene, loaded with fierce energy. Think about great moments in film and theatre in which a character was essentially cornered like a wild animal.

I always find it interesting to look at the characters in my scripts as though they were animals, with the following in mind: Animals, you could say, have much more naked behavior, for instance in a territorial dispute. They don't have rationalizations about why they're trying to kill you—they just do it. Characters can have similar instincts beneath their complicated social behavior. Look at your protagonist and antagonist as two lions fighting over a carcass or two apes in combat. It's another way to help you see the reality underneath all their reasoning, posturing and clever rationalizations. A cornered wild animal is capable of phenomenal acts—like jumping extreme distances or attacking with astonishing strength. A person can do similar things when tightly cornered and this can be spellbinding onscreen. Think about when you have been badly cornered and remember that feeling, that desperate, tormented feeling of being trapped in a horrible way.

A good strong dilemma is important—a dilemma of magnitude. Magnitude implies significance. Is it significant to an audience? Look at the difference between the film *Dead Man Walking* and *Malibu's Most Wanted*. This is not a value judgment, but *Dead Man Walking* is a film of more magnitude. You can have a dilemma, say, that it's unacceptable to clean the house and it's equally unacceptable to wash the dog. That *is* a dilemma, but it's not a dilemma of magnitude. It has to pass the 'So What?' test.

The 'So What?' test is something with which to challenge everything that tries to work its way into your script. It is a gatekeeper. Harry Cohn, founder of Columbia Pictures ran his development process this way: he would sit his writers down at a conference table and ask what their ideas were. The first writer would lay out his idea and Cohn would retort, 'So what?' The next writer would pitch his idea and he'd shoot it down the same way. It had to pass the 'So What?' test if he was going to pursue it. A dilemma of magnitude means the dilemma must pass the 'So What?' test. Even in comedy, the protagonist will probably take the dilemma seriously himself, even though it's hilarious to us. Once you get a dilemma up and running, then you should experiment with magnitude. Is it as substantial as it could be? Is it as potent as it could be? Does it hit the audience where they live and resonate in their own lives? How much more intense could you possibly make it? You want to be extremely tough on your own material because everybody else is certainly going to be.

Let's look at the dilemmas for *The Godfather*, *Tootsie* and *Blade Runner*. Michael Corleone is caught in a substantial dilemma insofar as he's being drawn into the family business, even though he knows it will ruin him. His dilemma is that it's unacceptable to sacrifice his happy and peaceful civilian life by getting involved in the family crime business, but it's equally unacceptable to allow the family to be destroyed by his non-involvement, given that it has become increasingly apparent that he is the only one capable of running the family properly. At the wedding Michael tells Kay that he is not in the family business. It is even clearer in the novel, his father tells him not to get involved in the business because it will destroy him. Vito says he did all this so that Michael could be free from the Mafia. Michael is smart and he truly understands this. He stays well clear of the business, but once the assassination attempt is made on his father he is drawn in. Sonny is clearly not a good don and Fredo is much worse. If Michael doesn't get involved, the family will probably fall, and if he does then it will cost him a great deal. He's damned if he gets involved and damned if he doesn't. The dilemma in *The Godfather* is not at all transparent, but works powerfully beneath the whole to create a compelling drama.

In *Tootsie*, Michael Dorsey has a major dilemma once he becomes Dorothy. It's unacceptable to quit being Dorothy because he's finally got work, a fat paycheck, respect as an actor, and a growing relationship with Julie. It's equally unacceptable to keep being Dorothy because the job is proving to be a disaster at many levels. John Van Horn is French kissing him and wants more, his friendship with Sandy is falling apart and he can only go so far with Julie because he's dressed as a woman. He can't let go and he can't hang on. It's simultaneously the best thing that has ever happened to him and the worst. The job is creating him and destroying him at the same time and this dilemma is agonizingly funny. So you see dilemma works for all genres. Put Martin Short in an excruciating dilemma and the more excruciating it is for him, the funnier it is for us.

In *Blade Runner*, Rick Deckard is caught in a dilemma about the fate of the replicants. He is told they are slaughtering people and it is his job to take them out, but he has also seen how Dr. Tyrell treats Rachael. "Rachael is an experiment, nothing more." She is entirely disposable. But, Deckard is moved by Rachael's emotional discovery that she is not human. He sees that the replicants have a legitimate grievance and that killing them is murder. He's a good detective because he's perceptive and he sees them for who they really are. As he falls in love with Rachael he opens up emotionally, and his fascination with and feelings for the replicants grow. This is clearer in the version that has the voice-over in which Deckard ruminates about why replicants have emotions. He begins to question his own—blade runners aren't supposed to have emotions. And yet the replicants are still out there killing people; so his internal debate—his dilemma—goes back and forth.

Dilemmas are not only something that happens to movie stars in films. In real life you are surrounded by hundreds of dilemmas, large and small. Take some time and write about the dilemmas that you've been faced with. They don't have to be earthshaking for them to be real and intense to you. The purpose of this exercise is for you to see them in your own life and to see how prevalent they are. Did you ever have to choose between your best friend and your spouse? Between your marriage and your career? Or where someone's life hangs on your decision? Look at the most painful dilemmas you have ever faced in your life. Look at areas of intensity like loyalty, money, security, betrayal, friendship, politics, career, love, children. When in your life were you damned if you did and damned if you didn't? Try to articulate both sides of the dilemma. Write about it. Explore it. Then go ahead and fictionalize it. Experiment with making it worse. What's the most excruciating it could be?

One thing I have noticed about dilemmas in my own life is that it can be easy to avoid dealing with them. I may need to call someone for business but know that she's a real pain on the phone. My inner debate goes back and forth: "I want the work… but what should be a two minute conversation will likely go on for twenty without getting to the point. I need the business, but—" and I notice that I say, "Never mind, I'll think about this tomorrow." I don't want to have to decide about it. Even in this miniature dilemma I notice the tendency to want to put it off, to want to escape because there's no answer in either direction. Watch yourself as you deal with dilemmas, both big and small and see how you deal with them.

You will find that dilemmas are found anywhere that people have conflicting needs, conflicting ambitions, emotions, imperatives, desires, necessities or absolutes. The so-called sticky subjects are fraught with dilemma: politics, race, class, gender, marriage, children, justice, war, ecology, future planning, the stock market, pentagon spending, welfare, abortion, taxes, big business, health insurance, the list goes on and on. How do people get caught in dilemmas in these types of situations? Think about how you've been trapped in them. Think especially about the most extreme examples of people being trapped in dilemmas in these complex issues. Just taking one example, consider the issue of national security versus privacy. There are serious questions on both sides. No one wants the country to be vulnerable to attack, but most people don't want their privacy and personal freedoms stripped away to achieve that, otherwise the cure could be as bad as the disease. This is a significant ongoing debate and is a dilemma of magnitude.

In terms of using dilemma in a screenplay it is important to have a sense of proportion. A dilemma will tend to kick in after some set-up time, often about a quarter to a third of the way into a script. This set-up time enables us to get to know and care about the character. To identify with a character means that we are essentially pretending to be that person. We have to walk that proverbial mile in their moccasins, getting to know them, so the dilemma generally doesn't start right away.

The following diagram represents an entire script:

The first X indicates generally where the dilemma might kick in. The second X indicates roughly were Crisis often occurs and the third X is for Decision & Action. The fourth is for Resolution. This gives a rough sense of proportion, and does not mean page 30, 60, 90 or anything like that. The point is that it takes a bit of set-up time to get to know and care about the protagonist and for the situation to develop. A good example is that Michael Dorsey's dilemma doesn't start until he becomes Dorothy, because then he is trapped in a situation in which he's damned if he lets go of this great job and damned if he hangs on to it either.

An important point in terms of working this tool is that one good strong dilemma can carry the whole film. Once the protagonist gets trapped in it, the dilemma can build in intensity until it gets to what I call the Crisis point. This forces a Decision & Action about the dilemma. The dilemma is finally resolved at the point of Resolution (the ending). In other words, we can talk about one central dilemma forming the *engine* of the drama.

In *Training Day*, once Jake gets trapped in his dilemma, he is truly paralyzed by it all the way through until it comes to a make-or-break point. This happens when Alonzo and his crew rob and murder Roger, and Alonzo tries to force Jake to say he was the shooter who killed Scott Glenn. Alonzo puts it to him in no uncertain terms that he either becomes a player on this team or he goes home dead. Jake makes a Decision that he absolutely will not be a part of this and he takes an Action to back it up—taking the shotgun away from Alonzo and turning it on him. He has broken the paralysis of the dilemma, but has still not resolved it. Jake has taken the first step in trying to resolve it, but he is in very hot water now. He is no longer frozen, but he's got a tough fight to get out of this mess. He ultimately resolves the dilemma when he beats Alonzo in their fight to the finish, takes the money as evidence and leaves Alonzo to his fate. So the dilemma is active throughout the film once it appears. It builds in intensity and comes to a critical juncture at Crisis, forcing a Decision and Action about the dilemma, and then is ultimately resolved at Resolution. Later chapters will deal with each these in turn.

STUDYING DILEMMA IN MORE DEPTH

In order to learn how to wield dilemma as a dramatist, you should become a student of human dilemma. Look at those around you who are caught in dilemmas. Look at dilemmas in history. Look at them in the news. Dilemma makes headlines because moral dilemmas are newsworthy. The U.S. was stuck on one about whether to go into Bosnia or not. If we don't, then we're allowing ethnic cleansing, and if we do, we risk getting bogged down in another Vietnam. The exact headline (I collect them) was: **NATO Campaign Poses Moral Dilemma For Religious Leaders**. Politicians are always caught up in dilemmas because they try not to alienate various voting blocks by getting trapped on questions as potentially problematic as their stand on abortion, for instance.

Most importantly, again study the dilemmas in your own life. Look at the tough choices that have stopped you in your tracks, in both big and small ways. Are you trapped in a boring job that keeps you from doing your art? Do you really need to borrow money, but it risks ruining a serious friendship? Are you staying in a bad marriage because you're afraid of the unknown? Do you have to sacrifice something you love for something you need? Do you absolutely have to let an employee go, but cannot decide who? Do you have to put off health care so that your kid can go to a better school?

I saw a great quote in the *Hollywood Reporter* in an article on the show *Law and Order*. One of the staffers, Roz Weinman, said of the show, "You can embrace a gigantic array of social, moral, legal and ethical dilemmas inside this concept. My background in sociology helps in telling stories that raise those kinds of issues. It's a terrific platform for floating unique dilemmas and different points of view." She's clearly someone who knows human dilemma and brings that level of experience to her writing in a very substantial way. You can be sure that the writing staff on that show has turned over thousands and thousands of dilemmas in their quest for compelling dramatic action. That's the kind of work that gets you the gold. (There's a game on the Internet called *The Prisoner's Dilemma*, which can take you further into an understanding of dilemma. There are a number of websites for it, but they're too complex to list here so just go to www.google.com and do a search.)

Now take some time and isolate one of your own dilemmas. State it as, it's unacceptable to _____ and it's equally unacceptable to _____. Write an essay about it. Study the ramifications of how this dilemma impacts your world, paralyzes you, how it makes you feel, the inner debate that rages about it, the sense of frustration, the rage at being trapped in such an impossible choice. Then take it further. Think about how much worse it *could* be. What's the most excruciating form of this dilemma that you could possibly imagine? Write about it. Go off the deep end with it. Get creative. Think about all the permutations of this dilemma and how, at its worst, it could cripple someone with its crushing power. Find ways to complicate it, add layers to it, add dimensions, compound it. Think about people around the world who are caught in dilemmas that we can scarcely imagine—a family who might be forced to sell a child into slavery to keep the rest of them alive for another few months. People who are forced to join a revolution which will probably get them killed or have their farm burned and their livelihood destroyed for refusing. Press the limits of dilemma—see how far you can take it. This will help give you a substantial understanding of it, and will help train you work with it as a dramatist. You'll probably find great material for a movie in this.

A friend who took my course used to spend a lot of time in Internet philosophy chat groups. He said someone would describe a situation they were caught in, say at the office and my friend would say, "You're caught in a classic dilemma." He'd describe their situation to them as a dilemma and they would reply, "Wow, I never looked at it that way before." What's interesting is that he didn't solve their problem, but merely restated it in the form of a dilemma (which can open up a fresh point of view and be helpful in solving it). It's as though he had those special infrared glasses that enable one to see the red laser beams that protect a bank vault. He could perceive dilemma where the other person couldn't. This is one of the most crucial skills in terms of working with dilemma. Essentially there's either a dilemma in your script or there isn't. But if it is there and you can't see it, then you may be trying to create one, while it's sitting right in front of you, unrecognized.

The word dilemma is often misused, and therefore misunderstood. When Irving Fiske, my playwriting teacher, first explained Aristotle's observations on Dilemma, Crisis and so on, I misunderstood dilemma. I thought to myself, "Oh that's a situation, like somebody has to solve a problem." It wasn't until about a year and a half later that one night on a whim I looked it up in the dictionary. I still remember it *verbatim* twenty years later: "Dilemma: a situation with a choice to be made in which neither alternative is acceptable. Two equally unacceptable alternatives—two equally painful choices." It not only clarified my understanding of Aristotle but increased my ability to add power to a dramatic plot. People will often say, "I had a dilemma today, I lost my keys." But this is not a dilemma—it's just a situation. And yet, the word has devolved to mean just that to many. A few years ago I looked up dilemma in the dictionary again and it said that a new meaning is entering the popular lexicon through extensive misuse—it is almost becoming correct to say, "I had a dilemma today, I lost my keys." The more you use it properly, however, and see dilemma in action around you, the more you'll be able to wield it as a dramatist.

In using dilemma, it's very important for the average person in the audience to be able to connect with the dilemma of your protagonist. In other words, do they see themselves in it? Can they empathize with this dilemma? Does it have significance in their own world and their lives? Hollywood can miss the mark with the average person by assuming they are consumed with one thing, when actually they are compelled by something much deeper and more human. They might be losing sleep about their friend committing suicide, or how their kids are drifting away from them. If they see a protagonist caught up in something that hits them where they live, then they're drawn into the story and feel connected to it. They wonder if this character can find a way out of the dilemma that's torturing them. The deeper you go, the more universal you get—the more you reach everyone where they live. A movie about a salmon fisherman in Alaska with a good strong dilemma could impact, for instance, a banker in Tokyo who might say, "Hey, I'm caught in the same dilemma." Or a brick maker in Argentina can say, "Wow, that's my life up there." Neither one may know anything about Alaskan fishing, but at a deeper level, this fisherman's dilemma may be about honor and betrayal and duty and survival. These are universals in human life and you find them when you dig deeper into the ramifications of a dilemma.

One thing that I ask when I develop a script is: "Can the guy across the street, who I don't know, relate to the dilemma in this story?" He's my audience and, remember, it's all about the audience. Say that I'm writing about a king who has to give up his throne or sacrifice his family. Can the person across the street relate to that? The first thing I do is say, "OK, how can I relate to this king's dilemma? I'm not a king." But I do know about moving away from a family to pursue a career, so yes, kingdom versus family, I can relate to that. And if the king did it *this* way, I could relate to it even more. And if he did *that* I could *really* feel connected to this guy. I seat myself in this character and his dilemma first, and then from what I know about human nature in general, about the universals of human life I can indirectly study the guy across the street, tuning the dilemma of my protagonist to this person who is my audience.

A great way to work with dilemma is to polarize its opposite sides with a two-sided chart. This is a simple way to separate out the two halves of the dilemma. Let's look at it for *Training Day*.

HE CAN'T LET GO OF JOB	HE CAN'T KEEP DOING IT
Damned if he quits	Damned if he keeps doing it
Totally wants to be in squad	Alonzo's morals are freaky
Extremely ambitious	He could get arrested or even killed
Awed by Alonzo	Appalled by Alonzo
Alonzo is the god in this arena	Alonzo is the devil
Alonzo gets big results	Must be a criminal to catch criminals
Jake is totally dedicated	He's being drugged and shot at
Wants to do good	He's an accomplice in theft
Will not quit	He's violating his vows as a cop
Driven by his career	Headed for jail
Adventure	Destruction
Making a difference	It's costing him his soul
He's really learning the streets	He's becoming corrupt
Results	Morality
Freedom	It costs too much
Ambition	Danger
Investigation bearing real fruit	It's costing Jake his integrity
Alonzo is his guru	Alonzo is his enemy
Alonzo is persuasive	Alonzo is corrupt
Old job too boring	New job too risky
Power	Loss of soul

This two-sided list is a very handy way to clarify things for yourself because it's easy for elements of the dilemma to get muddled together in your brain. An important aspect of this type of list is to let yourself run with it, to not worry about being repetitive because you can find fresh ways of seeing aspects of the dilemma by hitting it from different points of view. The above list tends to have a back and forth interplay, in that both sides of the chart connect to each other, such as Ambition on the left and Danger on the right, but you can also just run down one side of the page without specific reference to what's on the other, and then go back and think though the other side.

USING DILEMMA AS A WORKING TOOL

Now let's begin to see how to actively use dilemma as a tool, and then we'll get you using it on your own script. The first thing to do in terms of working with dilemma is to see if there already *is* a dilemma inherent in your script idea. Is there a situation in which your character is damned if he does and damned if he doesn't? Is there a way that your protagonist is caught in something that traps her, squeezes her, paralyzes her with some hard choices? The more you understand dilemma the more you will recognize it or feel its presence when it's there. The main thing is that you're looking for something big, something central. It's not a peripheral dilemma, not a minor one, but a dilemma that can carry the film. You're looking for something as big as an elephant in the living room, or an engine in a car. You can certainly find other motors in a car, like the ones that work the windshield wipers or the electric windows, but they don't power the vehicle. Look at the choices that your main character faces and make a list of them. And recall, the more you can get in touch with what you feel like when you are trapped in a dilemma, the more you will be able to feel its presence in your story. Or there may not be a dilemma in your story at this point. That's fine. We can create one and make it more powerful.

Essentially what we're talking about is turning a situation into a dilemma. For example, 'a cop having to catch the bad guy' is a situation, but if he owes his life to the bad guy or the bad guy is his brother, then he's got a much tougher choice. Creating dilemma is about complicating choices, adding alternatives and making them painful. This may sound simple, and in many ways it is, but you will be surprised at how much dramatic horsepower you can add to a script by focusing specifically on the dilemma. You want to take a good hard look at the two equally unacceptable alternatives, and be as specific as possible. This cuts through what is non-essential in what you've already got, and forces you to pay attention to something that might otherwise be overlooked. I've found that a deep and complex exploration of dilemma can take you on a fascinating journey into the heart of the story and the character. It can open a script up in ways that you might never have imagined.

The other thing to pay attention to is the word *equal*, in the phrase 'equally unacceptable alternatives.' If they are *equally* unacceptable, you will have the true paralysis that a dilemma creates. If they're not, then there is an easier way out. It is like being given a choice of whether to jump in the lava or get burned with a match. They're both unacceptable, but not equally unacceptable. The more you pay attention to keeping them equal, the more you trap the protagonist. This is especially true as you begin to experiment with the dilemma in different ways, making plot choices and exploring extremes. As you move one leg of the dilemma, you can easily make one of them *more* unacceptable than the other. The cure for this is to keep track of whether they are equal, and if needed, to increase the intensity of the choice that has dropped down the intensity scale. You want to keep Robbie the Robot short-circuiting—the paralysis of being caught between two equally painful choices. So test and adjust as you go along.

Once you get a dilemma up and running, you then want to play with extremes. Go off the deep end. Take it as far as you possibly can, just to see how far it can go. How excruciating can this dilemma become? You don't have to keep it at that ultimate intense level, but it's good to know what its absolute limits are. Think about the movies you have seen that didn't go far enough. They had something there, but they failed to perceive where the story could go, what its potential was; or perhaps they chickened out. The process of going off the deep end gets you outside the box, keeps your material fresh and violates the homogeneity that plagues the film industry. There's a great quote in the James Bond novel, *Dr. No*, where Dr. No says to Bond, "Mania is as priceless as genius." You want to turn up the dilemma to the max, just to see what it's like at that level of intensity. Don't play it safe. Get crazy. IT'S THE MOVIES!! This is known as 'Attack as a Storyteller.' Having a sense of attack, going after the audience, giving them the ride of their lives. It works in any genre. How funny can you make it? How scary? How nerve wracking? How silly? How dangerous? How unpredictable? How disorienting? How beautiful? How disturbing? How moving?

Exploring the extremes can take you into uncharted waters, but this is a core part of the fun and adventure of screenwriting. Getting outside your safety zone. This process can plunge you into chaos. As an adventurous screenwriter, don't be afraid of it; chaos should be your ally. Most writers say they aren't doing their job right if they are *not* getting in over their head. The more craft you have as a dramatist, the less afraid you are of chaos. In fact, you will begin to revel in the chaotic process of creation. If it's neat and orderly and simple, then it will often turn out flat or lifeless or uninspiring, or worst of all—boring. Remember, it's the *entertainment* industry. The key word in the entertainment industry is *outrageousness*. Do you want to write the same old movie that everyone else is writing, or do you want to create something that blows the lid off everything? When I'm starting a script there's a point where I'm getting in over my head and part of me says, "Uh oh, I'm getting in over my head." Another part says, "All right! Now we're getting somewhere." Someone once said that a writer is like a show horse—they're not happy unless they're trying to jump over something that can kill them. My favorite part of the writing process is when I'm at the point where anything goes. It's all still wide open and there's a real sense of total possibility, adventure and raw excitement.

A good way to take the dilemma to its extreme is to think about someone you truly despise. Take this person and, as a thought experiment, place them in the dilemma your protagonist faces and crank it up to the most excruciating it can possibly be. Let yourself go with it—really take it to the limit! Imagine the dilemma as a torture hat and crank the screws tight so that your enemy is screaming. Now you've gone all the way. Then take this torture hat off, put it on your protagonist and set the screws *that* tight. You'll have your protagonist really screaming too. The more your protagonist screams because of the dilemma, the more you've got the audience on the edge of their seat. This creates Dramatic Action because what you've done is to take your kid gloves off with respect to your protagonist. You tend to like your protagonist, so you're treating her too well and letting her off too easily. The more you torture your protagonist, the more you grab your audience. The fact is that you want to torture your audience with this dilemma. Make it as inescapable for the audience as it is for their hero, the protagonist. Remember, the more they see themselves in it, the more it connects to them and hits them where they live.

Another good way to improve dilemma is to put yourself in the position of the protagonist. Be this person who is trapped in this dilemma. This forces you to experience it first hand rather than from an observer's point of view. Say to yourself, "OK, I am this person stuck in this particular dilemma. It's unacceptable to _____ and it's equally unacceptable to _____. I can't move in this direction because of _____, but there's no way I can _____ either. I'm so screwed. How did I get in a position like this? It's such an impossible choice, but there's no getting out of it. I tried to wriggle out of it, but it won't let me go." Really get in there and live it, hash it out as though it is happening to you. Wrestle with it, freak out, struggle, thrash, lose sleep, tear your hair. It's this kind of connection that helps you feel and understand the dilemma more deeply and from the inside. It will help you write about it and understand your character more fully.

It's also a good exercise to put yourself in the position of the antagonist and from that point of view examine the protagonist trapped in his dilemma. Now you have got the totally opposite point of view; you're the protagonist's enemy looking at how he's stuck and vulnerable because of this dilemma. You now have a great opportunity to see a chink in his armor, maybe even a gaping hole that you, as the antagonist, can take advantage of. This is all part of the process of turning the dilemma over in your mind and strengthening it.

One of the images that I like to use in terms of dilemma is the Jaws of Life. These are used in car accidents to rip open the metal and get the person out. I find that a compelling dilemma will pry a character open with a tremendous hydraulic pressure. There's no stopping these two horrible alternatives from ripping your character's life wide open. There's no hiding from it, no pretending it isn't happening and no wishing it away. It's like the Terminator coming after you—utterly relentless. And this can be equally true if the dilemma is funny. For our hapless comic hero, there is no escape from an excruciating situation.

Once you have gotten a dilemma up and running, you will find that you are creating Dramatic Action. You are turning Story into Drama. The audience is now much more drawn into the plot, thanks to your amplifying the existing story.

It's worth repeating that a good strong dilemma gives the actor a meatier role, because the material is more complex. And this is an important part of getting a film made, attracting talent. The level of complication that a dilemma of magnitude brings to a role is huge. From my experience talking to actors, I know that they are starving for complex, dangerous and challenging parts.

Another thing that I've found to be very important about dilemma is that it can give you a real handle on your protagonist. Imagine a big pair of pliers with each half of the dilemma representing half the pliers. Notice that the more you squeeze, the more of a brutal grip you've got on your main character. And because the audience identifies with the protagonist, you've also got a brutal grip on them as well.

Also, dilemma is a handle with which to grip your plot. You may have all this energy for your raw story, yet be not quite sure where or what to grab onto first. Dilemma is the handle to grab onto, then crank it up so that all your energy is translated right into the story. *Because the more powerful the dilemma is, the more powerful the script is.* I find that it takes me right to the heart of the plot, gets me working on aspects of the story that will help the entire script to become the movie that I see in my mind.

Finally, you want to examine the ramifications of the dilemma. At first you want to have a laser focus on the protagonist and his or her dilemma, but once you get that squared away, you want to take a step back and look at the protagonist's entire world. You want to see how his dilemma impacts that world and see the ripples of this dilemma. For example, imagine someone in the Mafia who is tight with his brother, the Don. Say the police pull him over and find lots of heroin in his car. They'd say to him, "Look, it's not you we're after. We want your brother, the Don. So here's what we're gonna do. You are going to turn state's evidence against your brother, or we will put you in the toughest federal pen available with the horniest 600 pound cellmate we can find. You've got forty-eight hours to make up your mind." This dilemma is going to impact his relationship with his brother, his ability to think clearly, his relationship with his gang, his ability to sleep, his relationship with his wife and kids, and so on. All these are substantially impacted by the dilemma. Your understanding of these ramifications is reflected in your ability to paint the whole world of your movie vividly and succinctly.

GETTING STARTED USING DILEMMA ON YOUR OWN SCRIPT

1. Does your story have a dilemma or potential dilemma inherent in it? Define it. Does your central character feel trapped by some hard choices? What are they? Does the presence of this pressure increase like walls closing in on your central character?

2. Is the dilemma big enough to carry the script? Does it embrace most of the story or is it quickly resolved and therefore vanish? Does the resolution of this dilemma constitute the ending of the plot?

3. Do we care about the protagonist and his or her dilemma? Are we riveted by it and thus by the protagonist? Does it pass the 'So What' test?

4. Can you frame it as "It's unacceptable to _____ and it's equally unacceptable to _____"?

5. Do the two-sided chart in which you polarize the two unacceptable alternatives to this dilemma. This will help you separate the two halves of it and get a solid grip on it. The less abstract you make it, the more easily you can work with it. Go ahead, get your hands dirty. Don't be afraid to make a mess.

6. Is this a dilemma of magnitude? If not, why not? What would make it more intense, more significant, more substantial? Would the average person in the street care passionately about in this type of story, this type of dilemma?

7. Have you found yourself in a similar dilemma in your own life? Does it hit you where you live? Having observed yourself in similar circumstances, write about what it's like to be trapped in such a dilemma.

8. Can you gauge how strangers might be impacted by this dilemma? Would they care? Would they feel connected to it? Would it move them? Why?

9. How can you make this dilemma more intense? What's the worst it could be? Does this radically expand your story? Are you in over your head? Are totally new possibilities appearing in the plot? Are you having fun?

10. How can you complicate this dilemma? How can you add new layers to it? Do you find that it is much deeper than you at first suspected? Is it universal? It takes a while for the obvious to become apparent. Do you continue to have new insights about this dilemma as your story develops?

11. Are you 'attacking' the story enough? Are you tapping into its true potential? Are you out to give the audience the ride of their lives? As you write are you limping through the process or charging through it?

12. Is it still a dilemma? If you make certain plot choices, you can sometimes undo the dilemma because there are no longer two equally unacceptable alternatives. Are the two sides still EQUALLY unacceptable? Has one side gotten less painful? How do you beef the other side up to make it equal?

13. As you begin to understand the dilemma at a deeper level, can you feel it in your bones? Do you carry it with you all the time? Do you see people around you or in the news who are trapped in similar dilemmas?

14. Can you articulate it more clearly? Can you see new and various levels and dimensions and aspects of this dilemma? Do all these still constitute one single major dilemma?

15. Write an essay about the protagonist's dilemma. This gives you a chance to explore its intricacies and hidden folds. The more time you spend with the protagonist's dilemma, the more fully and clearly you will be able to articulate it.

3
CRISIS

Crisis is the point at which the dilemma comes to a critical juncture. Crisis forces the protagonist to react immediately to his dilemma, without the 'luxury' of being able to contemplate it from a distance. Figuratively it's the gun to the head, the breaking point. While dealing with the dilemma, the protagonist is worrying, "What am I going to do when I must make a choice?" Crisis forces that choice.

In submarine terminology when the sub is sinking toward the bottom, it will hit what is called 'crush depth' where it implodes from the pressure. For the plot, crisis is that crush depth. A good strong dilemma will be intensely gripping to the audience, but now at crisis we are hyper-compressing all that, which amps the pressure so much more. It's the cornered wild animal now backed in to the corner and pushed to the limit. Watch out!

A few years ago I was explaining Crisis to a group of students in New York when one of then said, "Oh, I get it. A crisis is a *crisis!*" The whole class laughed, but I said, "No, he's got it. That's exactly right." Think about a crisis in your real life. Your wife's mad at you, the kids are sick, you're late for work, the car won't start, you may get fired from your job, and then something *really* bad happens. It's all the worst possible things happening at the worst possible moment. It invites up the question: "How many anvils can you drop on your protagonist's head at once?"

In *Tootsie*, Michael's Crisis is essentially when, dressed as Dorothy, he tries to kiss Julie and she freaks out. Their cozy relationship is over and he's stuck being Dorothy because they won't let him out of his contract. But notice how many other terrible things happen right when he's at his most vulnerable. When he tries to tell Julie that he's really a man dressed as a woman and that he's in love with her, the phone rings and it's her father, Les. Julie insists that Dorothy go out with Les, and let him down easy since Julie now believes Dorothy's a lesbian. Les then proposes marriage and, as Dorothy runs away from him she gets grabbed at home by John Van Horn who tries to rape her. As soon as John leaves, Sandy is at the door, chewing him out when he admits that he's in love with another woman. All the lies that Michael has been juggling during the entire movie come crashing down on his head, all at once. He has always been in deep water, but now he's drowning. Something drastic has to be done or he's finished.

Remember our line of proportion, where the Crisis and Decision and Action happen at about the two-thirds or three-quarter point.

The first X is generally where the dilemma kicks in and builds in intensity to the Crisis (the second X), followed immediately by Decision and Action (the third X); the fourth X is the Resolution. Again, this gives just a rough sense of proportion and is not meant to specify page 30, 60, 90 and so on. It's just intended to help those learning this process to understand that, for instance, the Crisis occurs out toward the end of the timeline as things come to a head. I've seen so many of my students have substantial misconceptions about this proportion that I mention it for clarity's sake.

The current Random House/Webster's Dictionary defines *crisis* as: *1.) A stage in the sequence of events at which the trend of all future events, esp. for better or for worse, is determined; turning point. 2.) A condition of instability or danger, as in social, economic, political, or international affairs, leading to a decisive change. 3.) A dramatic emotional or circumstantial upheaval in a person's life. 4.) Medical. The point in the course of a serious disease at which a decisive change occurs, leading either to recovery or to death.*

Here's their definition of *emergency*: *A sudden, urgent, usually unexpected occurrence or occasion requiring immediate action. Quick action and judgment are necessary.* Crisis is mentioned then in this definition of emergency: *A crisis is a vital or decisive turning point in a condition or state of affairs, and everything depends on the outcome of it.*

I address Crisis for *The Godfather* and *Blade Runner* in the next chapter because Crisis and Decision and Action go hand in glove and I find that it makes it easier to learn them properly if you see them working together.

GETTING STARTED USING CRISIS ON YOUR OWN SCRIPT

1. Does your story come to a critical make-or-break point roughly two-thirds or three-quarters of the way through? What does it consist of?

2. Does the dilemma really come to a head? Has the dilemma gotten so intense that both halves of it are at the breaking point? Does this point demand that the protagonist make a substantial choice?

3. How intense is it? Could it be more intense? Can you feel how this is 'crush depth' in your story? The submarine here is your protagonist and he or she can't take another pound of pressure; is he or she about to cave in from the pressure?

4. What are the wildest possibilities? The scariest? The most unpredictable? The most dangerous? The funniest? (All of this is obviously context-sensitive to your plot.) Have you really explored the extremes?

5. If you're looking at the possibility that the worst possible things are happening at the worst possible moment, then are there any other awful things that can be heaped onto this moment—things that might happen near it in the plot, but which could be moved to this critical moment?

6. Have you ever been caught up in anything in your own life that resembles this moment for the protagonist? Even if it was on a much smaller scale, can you remember how it felt? Does this enhance your understanding and ability to work with this crisis in your script?

7. Write an essay on a substantial crisis that you have faced in your life. Explore as many different facets of it as possible and try to get at the emotions in their full intensity.

8. Write an essay about your protagonist's crisis. Explore it as deeply as you can and look at all the stress points that are imploding.

9. Think about how the audience will be impacted by this crisis. Is there any way they can say, 'So what?' to it? Can they see their own lives in it? Is it universal?

10. Does wrestling with the crisis in your script give you new specific insights into dilemma? Do you understand your character better? Does it expose you to entirely new ideas for your plot? Are you flexible enough as a storyteller to incorporate them into the mix? Do you mind having your story shattered? How can you reshape everything into a better story?

11. Now can you articulate this crisis cleanly and clearly? Are you satisfied with what you've got?

4

DECISION AND ACTION

The Crisis forces the protagonist to make an immediate Decision and take an Action. Decision and Action in the face of Crisis reveals the true character of the protagonist. The mask is stripped off. The classic example is when the big strong guy jumps up and runs out screaming and the little guy jumps up and saves the day. Another way to think about it is from your own life experience and how you never know who your real friends are until you've been through a crisis with them. Someone you thought was your friend might desert you when things turn critical, while someone you didn't really know or like steps in and saves the day. The audience is fascinated by seeing the mask stripped off. Why? Think about how infrequently we see this kind of naked human reality exposed. Pretence, subterfuge, diplomacy, and layer upon conventional layer cover reality so that, in fact, it's a rarity to see the mask stripped all the way off.

Not only is character revealed in a crisis, but it can actually be formed on the spot. People are capable of phenomenal things when crisis erupts. You have heard about the little old lady who picks up a car off her grandson, or the laid back farm boy from Missouri in the Vietnam War who snaps and becomes a creature of the jungle. It was always there, but that aspect of his personality never had to come out before. This is the lump of coal that turns into a diamond under pressure. It's the make-or-break point.

The thing about Decision and Action is that it breaks the paralysis or stasis of dilemma. The protagonist can be fundamentally frozen by the dilemma, even as it escalates. The word Decision means to 'cut off from.' What we've done is to put the protagonist into a highly pressurized situation with dilemma and then make it a whole lot worse, hyper-compressing it at the point of crisis. Something has to give. *The protagonist is forced by Crisis to make a Decision and take an Action.* This heightens the Dramatic Action that much more, putting the audience right up on the edge of their seat.

Crisis often brings out the best in people, but it can also bring out the worst. In most instances your plot will either end with a creative resolution (a happy ending) or with a tragic resolution (a sad ending). If it's a creative resolution then, at the point of Decision and Action, your protagonist will probably begin to break out of the paralysis of the dilemma and kick into gear. A Decision has been made and an Action has been taken that launches things toward the conclusion.

Often the protagonist is in more trouble than ever before, once he makes this Decision and takes Action, but he is moving and active rather than paralyzed. Once Michael Dorsey in *Tootsie* makes his Decision to unveil on live TV and does so, Julie is furious at him. He has by no means resolved anything, he has merely gotten out of being Dorothy—at the cost of any connection to Julie. He's out of the frying pan and into the fire. It's not until he makes things right with Les, her father, and wins her back over in the end that he fully resolves his dilemma. I say this to show that there is a real distinction between Decision and Action, and Resolution. They're truly not the same. We'll see more of that when we discuss Resolution next.

If the Resolution is tragic, then the protagonist may well do the worst possible thing at the most critical moment and begin the downward spiral to failure. You have probably seen this in real life when you're trying to convince someone not to do something that is obviously wrong at a critical juncture in their life, but you simply cannot stop them and they rush off into failure. A bad choice at a crucial moment works in a comedy, by the way. The protagonist, maybe an Inspector Clouseau type, will get it catastrophically wrong at the crucial moment and still stumble into solving the case in a funny way.

In *Blade Runner*, Deckard's dilemma about the replicants comes to a head when Roy Batty kills Dr. Tyrell and Sebastian. It propels him into action against the replicants and he can no longer debate their fate. Roy has killed one of the top industrialists in the Solar System on Deckard's watch and he must act. He gets sent to Sebastian's apartment where he runs into Pris. His Decision is to go after the replicants, whether he wants to or not, and his Action is to kill Pris (however reluctantly) and then try to shoot Roy. He's still trapped in his dilemma about the replicants, but his hand has been forced and he has taken action. He doesn't like killing Pris—he's still a draftee doing an awful job that he's torn about—and he is not happy or eager to have to go after Roy.

In *The Godfather*, following the attempt on Michael's life which kills his Sicilian bride, he is thrust into a leadership crisis when he is put in charge of the family because Sonny has been murdered. The family is in trouble, Barzini is muscling in and Tessio and Clemenza want to break off. When Don Corleone puts him in the hot seat by making him the head of the family, it pushes everything to the next level. Michael's Decision is to move the family to Vegas and his Action is to essentially declare war on Barzini by going after his agent, Moe Green.

This may not be readily apparent, but let's look at that scene again, it's all there: Michael comes in and tells Fredo to get rid of the girls, that he's here to do business, then immediately goes after Moe Green, telling him that Moe is going to sell them his share of their hotel and casino (they're co-owners). Moe explodes on Michael, saying the Corleones are washed up in New York and were chased out of town by Barzini. He says he's talked to Barzini and can make a deal in which Moe can keep his hotel and casino. This is not a casual business meeting at all. Michael has thrown down the gauntlet to Barzini by going after his agent, Moe Green. This is highlighted in the next scene when Don Corleone says to Michael that now they'll come after him and that Barzini will set up a meeting in which someone that Michael absolutely trusts will guarantee his safety, and that he will be assassinated at that meeting. This is war. It may not seem like it, because it's indirect—Michael and Barzini never go head to head—but the point of no return has definitely been crossed.

Michael is a brilliant general and makes a very smart move, adhering to many of the principles in Sun Tzu's *The Art of War*. If you're strong, act weak. If you're about to attack, make it look as though you're running away. Never meet an enemy on a battlefield where they're prepared. Lure to them to a battlefield that you have prepared. Everyone keeps saying that Michael is weak and doesn't know what he's doing. He never contradicts this, never tries to prove he's tough or smart. He's content to have them all underestimate him—and that's why he's able to take them all out in the end—because none of them are worrying about him. If you look at that scene between Michael and Moe Green again, you'll see that Michael is white hot.

In *Training Day*, Jake's Crisis occurs when Alonzo and his crew of dirty cops have stormed into Roger's (Scott Glenn) house and dug up the millions of dollars under his kitchen floor. Then Alonzo kills Rogers and wants Jake to say he, Jake, was the shooter when they file their report. Alonzo threatens to kill Jake if he doesn't do it. Jake is on the spot. His dilemma has definitely come to a head. The question of whether to be in or out of Alonzo's operation has turned deadly— the fun is over—and it's life or death. Jake's Decision is that he *will not* have anything to do with this and his Action is to grab the gun away from Alonzo and turn it on him, threatening to kill him if he doesn't stop. Notice how he's no longer short-circuiting because of his dilemma. He has committed fully and he's now in big trouble. This is obvious when, two scenes later, Alonzo drops him off at the gang members' headquarters to have him killed. He's not out of trouble until he takes down Alonzo at the end.

GETTING STARTED USING DECISION & ACTION ON YOUR OWN SCRIPT

1. Does your protagonist have to make a crucial decision because of this crisis? Does he or she take a substantial action as part of it? Can you distinguish between the two? You should be able to put your finger specifically on the decision and also on the action.

2. Does your main character change at this point? Kick into gear? Begin to come together? Begin to fall apart (in a tragedy or wacked-out comedy)? This is not the complete transformation that comes at the ending, but the solid beginnings of this transformation.

3. Is the paralysis of the dilemma broken at this point? This is distinct from solving it at the end.

4. Could this decision and action be more intense? How much more? What's the most intense it could be?

5. Is the true character of your protagonist revealed at this point? What is revealed about him or her? Is something new emerging? Is something clarified? Is something crystallized? Will this electrify the audience?

6. Write an essay about your protagonist's character at this crucial breaking point. Explore it as deeply as possible.

7. Have you been in a similar situation in your own life? How did it feel? How intense was it? It may be smaller in scope, but remember it in as much detail as possible. How did you react? How much more intense could it have been? How different could your reaction have been? Write about what is was like. Can you translate this into your screenwriting? What if you had done something unbelievably catastrophic or incredibly heroic? Play with the possibilities.

5
RESOLUTION

Resolution is the protagonist actively and conclusively solving the dilemma. It should be done by the protagonist as opposed to someone doing it for the protagonist, or it just happening to fall together. We tend to want our protagonist to be the doer of the action. If someone else does it for him or her, this is called *Deus Ex Machina*, the god in a machine who appears unexpectedly and solves an apparently insoluble problem. This is not satisfying for the audience. The cavalry can show up and help John Wayne win, but they shouldn't do it for him. If things just *happen* to fall into place, that can be equally ungratifying.

Being caught on the horns of a dilemma can be actively resolved several different ways. One way is to pick one of the horns—one of the unacceptable alternatives. Michael Corleone does this because he's caught between being a criminal and being a respectable civilian. He chooses being a Mafia don in the end and this resolves his dilemma. He's out of his trap. He seems to be unaware at this point that it cost him his soul because he's become such a reptilian crime lord. That's the tragedy of the piece, that it did cost him his soul. He's a completely different person at the end of the film then he was in the beginning. Look at him when he shows up at the wedding and then at the end. It's day and night—but he's not wriggling on the hook anymore.

The other way to resolve a dilemma is to go between the horns. This means that by thinking on her feet, our protagonist is able to come up with a radical third alternative in which neither of the two equally unacceptable alternatives is taken. You see this often when there is a creative Resolution—our protagonist comes up with something unexpected and pulls it off. It's as though someone forces you to choose between two doors and you pull out a chainsaw and carve your own door. A great example of this is when Tom Cruise in *The Firm* is really stuck between the Mafia law firm and the crooked FBI agent. He comes up with a radical third alternative when he realizes that the Firm is systematically over-billing their clients, and doing it through the mail. He gives the FBI the mail fraud bust, satisfying the letter of their agreement, but he doesn't violate his client-attorney privilege which would have gotten him disbarred. Thus he skates free from a very sticky dilemma. The FBI wanted copies of the Firm's entire client files, which would have given them a string of high-profile busts, but Tom Cruise thwarts them as well as the Mafia firm.

The Resolution should tend to be fixed firmly in finality, that is, it should be irreversible. If the protagonist wins it should stay a victory, and if he loses, it should stay a loss. The audience tends to be gratified by something that sticks and doesn't backslide. So much in life never gets taken all the way to the end, never gets fully resolved, so this tends to be something that the audience craves. Think of all the things in life that are never conclusively resolved. Look at the dilemmas in politics, in relationships and so on that will never be fully resolved. The movies are one of the very few places in which we can look forward to a substantial resolution. This is not to say that you should never have an ambiguous ending. If you want to irritate or unsettle the audience then, by all means, have an ambiguous ending. But don't have an ambiguous ending just because you can't think of a way to end it. Remember, it's all about the audience, so pay attention to audience gratification.

The Resolution in *Blade Runner* is that Deckard drops out of the situation that he was trapped in and runs off with Rachael, one of the replicants he was ordered to 'retire.' In saving Deckard's life, Roy has shown him what it really means to live, and Deckard gets it. He begins living with everything he's got. He finds a radical third alternative in a dead-end dilemma, breaking free of the entire system in which he was trapped. In *Tootsie*, Michael Dorsey makes up with Les and then reconnects with Julie. He has grown and developed so much as a person that Julie is willing to let him back into her life—this time without the dress. He truly pulls it off and is a new man in the process. In *The Godfather*, Michael Corleone goes all the way as a criminal when he kills off all his enemies, including the traitors within his organization, to emerge as a soulless crime lord. He achieves total power, but also doesn't recognize his wife anymore.

In *Training Day*, Jake conclusively resolves his dilemma by beating Alonzo in a fight to the finish and going off to turn in the evidence of Alonzo's criminal activity. He destroys Alonzo, both legally (which is what matters to Jake) and criminally, because Alonzo won't be able to pay off the Russians. He has completed what he set in motion at the point of Decision and Action.

Aristotle points out how those dramas that grip an audience tend to have maximum Dramatic Reversal at the end, also known as Peripety (from the Greek *peripeteia*). The classic example of Dramatic Reversal is when the hunter becomes the hunted. Other examples include the king becoming a beggar, the master becoming a slave or the underdog triumphing. It's about things swinging around to their opposite, and is part of the kick of a great or satisfying ending. It adds intensity and completion, often through an element of the unexpected.

In *Blade Runner*, Deckard's Reversal is that he changes substantially from the person we meet at the beginning of the film who is emotionally dead, disconnected, passionless and trapped. (You get this even more in the original release with the voice over, in which he ruminates about how his ex-wife called him Sushi, cold fish.) At the end he has been awakened by Roy and he runs with it, breaking out of the system that had drafted him into service and trapped him in lifeless drudgery. He drops out of the game and makes his own rules, running off with Rachael. In *Tootsie*, Michael Dorsey undergoes such a complete Reversal in the end that he's a totally different man from the one he was in the beginning. Instead of a hustling, neurotic guy who lies to women and is a pain in the ass to work with, he is solid, realistic, straightforward, honest and clear. In *The Godfather*, Michael Corleone has also changed completely, but in the opposite direction. He starts out as an innocent and ends up a soulless, cold-blooded character who doesn't really recognize his wife anymore. At the end of *Training Day*, Jake is very different from the easily intimidated little guy he was at the beginning of the film.

Aristotle also talks about a moment of fundamental Discovery or Recognition. The example which occurs repeatedly in antiquated plays is when the prince who has been mistreating the maid for much of the play discovers that she is really his long-lost cousin and they go off happily together. Along with the advent of psychology, the internal struggles of modern/postmodern life have come to the fore and drama reflects this. Recognition or Discovery today therefore is often internal, appearing as a revelation, an awakening or an epiphany. The protagonist may discover that she has had a major blind spot that has been causing her troubles, or may find that she has been part of the problem and, seeing this, can now become part of the solution. This kind of inner Recognition can set the protagonist free to decisively resolve things.

Rick Deckard has a substantial Recognition when Roy, as he dies, shows him what living life to the fullest means. It electrifies Deckard, galvanizing him into his Resolution. Michael Dorsey's moment of Discovery is when he tells Julie: "I was a better man with you as a woman than I ever was with a woman as a man, you know what I mean? I just gotta learn to do it without the dress." He gets what it means to be in a real relationship and that helps him pull it all together in the end and make it work with Julie. Michael Corleone doesn't really have an internal

Recognition because he doesn't seem to notice how cold and hard he's become. He's a tragic figure, in spite of his total victory. Michael does have an external Recognition when he gets Carlo to verify that it was in fact Barzini who was behind setting up Sonny's execution at the toll booth. Jake Hoyt has a substantial Discovery when he learns that Alonzo has left him to be killed at the gang members' house—and this is quite a wake up call.

Aristotle maintains that Recognition and Reversal can occur anywhere, but if you cluster them around the Resolution, you will get the most impact. The Recognition will open the protagonist's eyes and enable him to conclusively resolve his dilemma and, if there's a substantial Reversal, you will enhance the overall dramatic impact even more.

GETTING STARTED USING RESOLUTION ON YOUR OWN SCRIPT

1. Does your protagonist actively resolve the dilemma? Even if it's a tragedy the protagonist should be actively taking the final step that finishes him- or-herself off.

2. What is the resolution? How does it end? What does your protagonist do to wrap it up? Can you articulate it clearly?

3. Are you clearly distinguishing between Decision & Action and Resolution?

4. Is the Resolution fixed in finality, so it isn't going to backslide or become undone?

5. Is it an ending worthy of a great movie? Is it substantial (even in a comedy)? The ending should be the biggest moment in the movie. Does it complete the magic spell that the movie has been weaving and gratify the audience?

6. What are some other possible endings? Are you missing a huge obvious possibility? Have you tried other endings?

7. Have you explored the extremes for your resolution?

8. How does the resolution gratify the audience? If it's a tragedy, does it knock the audience down and give them a powerful emotional experience that they will never forget? If it's a creative upbeat resolution, what's the audience's final mood?

9. Write about what your intention for the resolution is and then later check to see how well you fulfilled it.

RESOLUTION

6
THEME

The best way to articulate the Theme of a movie is this: *The way in which the protagonist resolves the dilemma expresses the Theme of the piece.* It's what the movie is about—it's the movie's soul, its heart, its animating spirit. It's the glue, the essence that governs the dramatic material and binds it together into one coherent action. A clear statement of Theme provides a focal point, a unifying thread around which to weave the dramatic action. Theme is the underlying idea which steers the action, and to have a unified plot you should adhere to Theme. Playwriting teacher William Thompson Price in *The Analysis of Play Construction and Dramatic Principle* (W.T. Price Pub., New York, 1908) wrote:

> All great or good plays are based upon Theme. You have only to refer to Shakespeare and Moliere to determine the truth for yourself. The ordinary commercial play is one of situations for the sake of situations and not for the sake of Theme. Until we regard Theme of first importance, we shall have few good plays. (p. 19)

The theme of a script is its central or governing idea, that which shapes the complete action of the protagonist. It works from the inside out, permeating the plot and the characters with a certain focus. The writer is often not aware of the thematic depth in the plot at first because her total focus is on telling the best story possible. But once the Theme is recognized, it lends a sense of vision to the piece, gathering the material into one main action and infusing it with a sense of meaning or intention. This is not to say that you bombard the audience with it, but that the whole script communicates it at an organic level to the soul of the audience.

Again, the way to articulate the Theme is to look at the way in which the protagonist resolves the dilemma because that expresses the Theme. You look at the Resolution and look at the *way* in which the protagonist resolves the dilemma. This enables you to put your finger on the Theme, and the more you are in touch with it the more you can work with and reinforce this fundamental life force in your story.

Price in *The Philosophy of Dramatic Principle and Method* says:

> The highest form of plays involves the philosophy of life, so that if the Theme is not worth considering, there is usually little substance in a play. With a Theme your play will be about something… Theme does not stand alone. No principle does. Mere Theme will never make a play. But it is a definite something; it furnishes a spiritual atmosphere and the philosophy of the play; it gives the clue to the actual shaping of the play… the tone depends on it. It is the largest unit of the play. (p. 2)

For example, in *Tootsie*, Michael resolves his dilemma when he finally earns Julie's trust and wins her heart. The *way* in which he does it is to become whole, to be honest and solid. Sydney Pollack, the director, said the theme of *Tootsie* is: "Becoming a woman made a man out of Michael." That's a very clean and clear understanding of the soul of the story. Sydney Pollack discusses it in Jon Stevens' *Actors Turned Directors* (Silman-James Press, Los Angeles, 1997):

> I concentrate very hard on understanding and articulating for myself and everyone else involved what I think the picture's about. By 'what it's about' I do not mean story. What a film is about, in my opinion, has nothing to do with story. Quite the opposite. It's everything except the story. It's trying to arrive at a sort of spine, if you will, of the picture—a way of viewing it that directorially instructs you on a way to view each scene.
>
> *Tootsie* was about a man who became a better man for having been a woman. If you start to look at every scene and say, "In what way does this scene illustrate the idea of a man becoming a better man for having been a woman?" you see that, in the beginning, *Tootsie* works very hard to show you that part of him which needs redeeming, because if he's going to be better at something, he has to be worse at it first. The minute I define that as an idea, I can begin to measure every scene

against it in some way. That doesn't mean it's going to be a good movie. It just means that I know what it's about, and can communicate that to the actors. (p. 12)

Many writers can only clutch abstractly at what they think is the Theme of their script. The inability to come to terms with it can weaken the material because you miss the clarifying and strengthening effect which having a grasp on the Theme brings to the process. Additionally, the word Theme is misused extensively because people will say that the Theme of the movie is teen suicide, for instance, when that is really just a story element which is part of the plot. Focusing on the way in which the protagonist resolves the dilemma keeps you right on the Theme, in the truest sense of the word.

Let's look at a working example. Say that you're writing a tragedy (a rare type of film these days) and the protagonist does something very destructive and stupid to resolve his dilemma (mistakenly thinking he's being brilliant, for example) and it gets him killed. If we look at the *way* in which he resolves his dilemma, we are, in essence, looking at the mechanics of failure. Note, we're not looking at *what* he does, which might be to betray a friend at a critical moment, but *the way in which he does it.* The way in which he betrays his friend is through this messed up thought process, perhaps telling himself he can outsmart the situation, that he's sharper, faster and more deserving. We are looking into the mind of a self-destructive character who is skilled at self-deception and whose thinking is flawed. This can give us a powerful look at aspects of ourselves—maybe a brutally unflattering look at ourselves—and that can be a wake up call. This then is the governing idea, this is what this movie is about thematically—the thought process that lures one into destruction—something we see around us in daily life. It informs the entire plot and helps tie it together, sustaining the story, shaping it, animating it and driving it. It infuses the world of the story, imbuing it with the flavor of loss and failure, even though we might not recognize it until the trap springs shut on us, along with our lead character.

This is what Sydney Pollack meant when he said that he concentrates hard to understand what the picture's about. The story in the above paragraph is about how this guy ruins his life and about his tendency to ruin it—about the mechanics of *how* he ruins it. There should be a substantial character arc, a downhill transformation, culminating in his death. If he's not telegraphing overtly the impending failure, then we can get to really care about this person and his failure will shock us profoundly. That is the power of a great tragedy.

Your sense of theme will give a focus to your story material. As you examine this particular theme above, think about your own life experience in relation to it. Think of those you've known with this type of destructive, deceptive and flawed thinking. Should you be lucky enough to know a psychiatrist or psychologist, talk to him or her about these types of behavior patterns. Perhaps your own thought process or behavior has at times been similar to that of the protagonist in the above example (hopefully on a lesser scale). Think about your own destructive behavior and how you were utterly compelled to do or say something catastrophic, and nobody could talk you out of it. Delve to the bottom of it and really try to understand it at its deepest level. This profound comprehension of this particular theme will inform your writing, your plotting, your character development, the character's dilemma, the resolution—everything connected with the script. It will inhabit the soul of this script and will give it substantial power and depth.

A theme certainly doesn't have to be profound, but some level of thematic depth can help a movie. *The Godfather* and *Blade Runner* have it, and *Tootsie*, a delightful comedy, has thematic depth. That's part of why I chose them to analyze—they have the kind of meat on their bones that lends itself to in-depth analysis.

In *Blade Runner*, the way in which Deckard resolves his dilemma is to wake up, come alive and take control of his own life. He grabs Rachael and runs, dropping out of the system he was trapped in, not only changing the rules, but transcending the whole game. It's a film about human liberation, about freedom and about living your life to the fullest. A person on their deathbed will tell you: "Live *now* with everything you've got. Don't be getting ready to live. Do it now!" Deckard learns that from Roy and his intense desire to live, and it electrifies Deckard into action and into life. This is what the movie is about: Living fully.

Conversely, in *The Godfather*, the way in which Michael resolves his dilemma is to become totally hardened, killing every single possible enemy around him and then cutting himself off from his wife and what he might have been. It's about the cost of power and about the loss of soul. Yes, he does achieve total power, but it costs him his innocence, his family, his freedom and his happiness. It brings up the question for us: "How much power do you really need and what is it worth?" This relates to normal people in their everyday lives. It's easy to overreach, maybe taking on two jobs to get your family extra things, but in the process you can lose contact with the very family you're sacrificing for. "What profits a man if he gains the whole world but loses his soul?"

In *Training Day*, the way in which Jake resolves his dilemma is to stick to his principles, to refuse to be part of the corrupt system Alonzo is dragging him into. Jake's moral compass will not allow this and he fights to keep his integrity and his life. The way in which he resolves his dilemma is to *know* what's right and to fight for that with every ounce of strength. Thematically, this is what the movie is about: Doing the right thing. That's what Jake is blazing with at the end, and we are infused with it too. David Ayer, the writer, said that the *Training Day* is about "What if one man says no?"

David Mamet says in his book, *On Directing Film*, that a script properly written will communicate the theme clearly and powerfully *once at the end*. He tells the writer to trust in that, saying that many dramatists are insecure about the ability of their plot to communicate its theme, clearly and powerfully, once at the end. A writer can panic and resort to reiterating it constantly, afraid that the audience will not get it. They restate the theme in every other scene and put it in every tenth line of dialog—to the *detriment* of the drama. His advice is to make each part of the plot do its job, and the drama as a whole will work fine. The scene is just a scene that helps make the plot work, not an opportunity to recapitulate the theme.

> The nail doesn't have to look like a house; it is not a house. It is a *nail*. If the house is going to stand, the nail must do the work of a nail. To do the work of a nail, it has to *look* like a nail. (Ibid, p. 68)

Jimi Hendrix said something interesting about music we can relate to. (It appeared on the liner notes of the *Woodstock* album.) "We plan for our sound to go inside the soul of the person actually, and see if they can awaken some kind of thing in their own mind because there are so many sleeping people." Theme then is also about art being a catalyst, triggering something in a person, awakening something in someone. If the film helps the audience awaken something within themselves, then it can become part of them, rather than merely impacting them temporarily, then fading away.

You may start out with a theme that you feel compelled to communicate and that you want to build a script around, or you may just start out with a killer story idea and gradually discover the thematic depth in it. Many people get into the film business because they have something to say. Both approaches are valid. The main thing to be aware of is that you as the dramatist want to be in touch with the theme.

As you develop the material, the theme can gradually morph into something deeper, stronger or entirely different. It is said that the theme often selects the dramatist, so you may find yourself in territory you hadn't intended. Here's Price again: "…the dramatist begins gathering his material from the moment he selects his Theme—or his Theme selects him, which, perhaps, is the better way." (*Analysis of Play Construction and Dramatic Principle*, p. 29) Many times it will be more profound, more powerful than what you set out to do. Sometimes a script will drag you into something deeper—insist on a new tack. This is part of the beauty of the writing process—the experience of changing dimensions as you develop the material. If you are too stuck on your original intention thematically, you might not be aware of how the theme gradually morphs into what might even be the *opposite* of what you intended. The audience will be getting the deeper theme osmotically, but you, the dramatist, unaware of how the theme has morphed will be the one missing the boat. You are missing one of the fundamental strengths of your script, and so cannot work with it, reinforce it or build on it.

The cure for this, once again, is to look at the Resolution and look at the way in which the protagonist resolves the dilemma, and thereby keeping in touch with the theme that is actively emerging in the material. It's the difference between seeing what you want to see and seeing what's really there. You may well be surprised by the dynamic new universe you've stumbled into. Conversely you may say, "No, I see where it has ended up, but I really *do* want it to be in line with my original intention." In that case, adjust the way in which the protagonist resolves the dilemma and steer it back to the theme you wanted it to be. This give and take is at the core of the writing process—you either let it take you or you steer it. And steering your material may mean hitting it hard with a hammer or feathering it gently—it's part directing things and part being responsive to what comes along.

The theme shouldn't come across as a platitude, as a Sunday School preaching, or as a bumper sticker. Bernard Grebanier, in his book *Playwriting* (Thomas Y. Crowell Co, New York, 1961) says:

> Starting one's thinking with a theme is intelligent enough but can be somewhat precarious too. It too easily may lead the writer into contriving heavily moralistic or propagandistic demonstrations of an idea, into merely manufacturing situation and character for purposes of *illustrating* the theme, in which case neither situation nor characters will be dramatically convincing—so that the play ends by being a kind of sermon, which a good play should never be… a good theme should be an interpretation of life, not a lecture upon it… When you have read a story or seen a play, you may not be conscious of the theme, but you may 'feel' it… the theme should, rather, be deeply embedded in the action and in the nature of the leading characters. (p. 23)

When you start to come to grips with the theme in your script, you may only have a sense of what it is. You may not be able to articulate it clearly, and that's fine. When the audience comes out of the theatre they may not be able give a clear statement of the theme of the movie, but they've got it at a gut level. As the dramatist, you shouldn't be afraid to start at a gut level. Many people panic when they only have a partial understanding of something. They try to explain it before they understand it fully and deeply. Allow yourself to relax in this partially formed understanding. Chew on it, think about it, explore, dig and develop it. Look at the example of the tragedy we just worked on. The protagonist's self-destructive thinking and behavior destroyed him in the end and that's what the story is about thematically. But can you articulate it clearly at first? It takes some time. You can feel it. You *know* what the theme is, but you have to spend some time contemplating it, digesting it and wrapping your brain and your instincts and your intuition around it before you can find the words to articulate it clearly. Don't insist on conceptualizing it at first. Otherwise it's like trying to have a baby when you're one month pregnant. You *know* what it is, so free yourself from the compulsion to put words to it prematurely.

Gradually your understanding will gel, and you'll have it more fully and completely, not so much as conscious thought, but embedded in you. You'll carry it around and work on it at a more subconscious level. As it gels, you'll find that you grow antennae in relationship to your material. You'll pick up things in the air that relate to what you're writing about, both plot-wise and thematically, and it all goes into your subconscious. At a certain point in the process your understanding will crystallize. All of a sudden you've got it— clearly, cleanly and completely—and you can express it clearly and completely.

It's important to be able to state the theme clearly and simply, but I also urge my students to beware of that cute one-liner about theme at the beginning of the process because it can oversimplify the situation. It can halt the digging process. Experts in creativity say there are often ten right answers to a problem, but many people think there is only one right answer, so they stop looking when they find one of the right answers. If you're satisfied with a shallow understanding of theme, then you won't keep exploring the idea, tunneling down deeper to get a more substantial and complete comprehension. As I said, don't be afraid of a half-formed understanding. Once you're done, it may seem perfectly obvious, but it can take a great deal of work to get to that clarity. Price said in *The Philosophy of Dramatic Principle and Method*: "We keep narrowing down from the most general Theme to a specific one; and when it becomes specific it determines the nature of the play." (p. 3)

You are really distilling your understanding of theme down to its quintessence, and when you arrive at that point the true identity of the story emerges. What was unclear at first coalesces into one entity with a recognizable 'personality,' rather than a coalition of ideas and elements, and this informs the tone, flavor, shape, color and texture of the script. If you've ever seen the formation of a hurricane on TV, the eye forms and the storm forms around it. The eye is the core of the storm—the clear point at its center around which everything swirls. In screenwriting terms, it is the living core of your story.

One of the things that I do when I'm exploring theme is to go to an encyclopedia of quotations. There are many—Bartlett's being the best known—especially on the Internet. Here are some of the quotes I found that connect with the theme of *The Godfather*, *Tootsie* and *Blade Runner*:

THE GODFATHER

Power gradually extirpates from the mind every humane and gentle virtue. Burke

is a strange desire, to seek power, and to lose liberty. Bacon

You shall have joy, or you shall have power, said God; you shall not have both. Emerson

For politicians neither love nor hate. Dryden

In the struggle for power, there is no middle ground between the highest elevation and destruction. Tacitus

A partnership with the powerful is never safe. Phaedrus

Power, like a desolating pestilence, pollutes whatever it touches. Shelley

Whose game was empires, and whose stakes were thrones; whose table earth, whose dice were human bones. Byron

TOOTSIE

Character is the governing element of life, and is above genius. Saunders

I have lost all and found myself. Clarke

Our experience is composed rather of illusions lost than wisdom gained. Roux

The wise learn many things from their foes. Aristophanes

God offers every mind its choice between truth and repose. Emerson

When first we met we did not guess that Love would prove so hard a master. Bridges

Lay me on an anvil, O God. Beat me and hammer me into a crowbar. Let me pry loose old walls; let me lift and loosen old foundations. Sandburg

Fortune is not on the side of the faint-hearted. Sophocles

BLADE RUNNER

What is life where living is extinct? Heywood

Life is a mystery as deep as ever death can be. Dodge

The fool, with all his other faults, has this also; he is always getting ready to live. Epicurus

Live all you can; it's a mistake not to. It doesn't much matter what you do in particular so long as you have your life. James

Study as if you were to live forever. Live as if you were to die tomorrow. Isidore of Seville

Dare to be wise: begin! He who postpones the hour of living rightly is like the rustic who waits for the river to run out before he crosses. Horace
Catch, then, oh! catch the transient hour; improve each moment as it flies; life's a short summer - man a flower; he dies - alas! how soon he dies! Johnson

For what is your life? It is even a vapour, that appeareth for a little time, and then vanisheth away. New Testament

Trust flattering life no more, redeem time past, and live each day as if it were thy last. Drummond

There is an eternity behind and an eternity before, and this little speck in the center, however long, is comparatively but a minute. John Brown

You'll find that quotations can be useful not only for exploring theme, but for examining story elements, characterization and possible titles. They can also suggest great dialog. You may have been mulling over a theme for several weeks, but you can find those who spent seventy years thinking about it. Be willing to spend the time reflecting. Be open to unexpected sources. Think about what you're trying to communicate to the audience with the complete action of your script. Remember what Jimi Hendrix said: "We plan for our sound to go inside the soul of the person actually, and see if they can awaken some kind of thing in their own mind." Equally important, listen to your material as it takes on a life of its own, because the unexpected can yield surprising freshness, as well as great depth and insight.

GETTING STARTED USING THEME ON YOUR OWN SCRIPT

1. Can you put your finger on the theme of your script? Even if you have trouble articulating it at first, you should be able to sense it.

2. Look at the *way* in which the protagonist resolves his or her dilemma and this will take you right to it.

3. Don't be afraid to dwell in a place of partial understanding. If you have a sense of your theme, explore that and don't feel like you have to put it into words. Let your understanding grow. Let it sit in you. Mull it over. Meditate on it. Trust your feelings and instincts.

4. What have other people said about the idea you're contemplating? Explore the encyclopedias of quotations. What are some of the most pertinent quotes that you've found? Why and how are they pertinent?

5. How has your understanding of the theme of your piece grown and changed and deepened as you spend time contemplating it?

6. Do you have a theme of substance or are you just recycling tired old clichés? Certainly not every film has to have a 'profound' theme by any means, but some people slap some worn out ideas into a script just to have something to say.

7. Has the theme taken on a life of its own as you develop the script? How has it morphed? Are you happy with where it is now? Do you want to steer it more in a certain direction? Tinker with how the protagonist resolves the dilemma to do this.

8. Could the theme be deeper, more fully developed?

9. Beware of a cute, simple one-line statement of the theme at first. Write an essay exploring the theme.

10. Look for how your understanding of the theme of your piece gives it a soul and a voice. See how it fills the script with a vision or direction.

11. Don't beat the audience to death with the theme. Don't overstate it. It will be there clearly and powerfully once at the end if you do your job right. Trust that.

7

THE 36 DRAMATIC SITUATIONS

The 36 Dramatic Situations is a key plot development tool that is extremely useful for brainstorming. It was created in the 1700's by the Italian playwright Carlo Gozzi and was endorsed by Goethe and Schiller. On the strength of those endorsements it was passed around for over a century until Georges Polti turned it into a book in 1916. Though now out of print, I will present enough of the material here for you to work with it fully. By the way, Gozzi just recently had two plays running on Broadway, *The Green Bird* and *The King Stag*.

The 36 Dramatic Situations can be compared to the Periodic Table of Elements. Every material substance can be described completely with the 118 elements; the chair you're sitting in consists of some combination of carbon, hydrogen, oxygen, and so on. Similarly, a plot can be described quite completely with the 36 Dramatic Situations. The script might contain elements of *Madness, Disaster, Ambition, The Necessity of Sacrificing Loved Ones*, and *Rivalry of Superior and Inferior*, etc.

This tool is a resource for writers and can be truly useful as a plot invention device. It's meant to jog the imagination and can trigger intriguing story possibilities for you, even if the connection doesn't necessarily make sense consciously. Don't be afraid to play with the 36 Dramatic Situations because you will get more use out of it if you're flexible with it. It can help expose you to dynamic new horizons for your plot that might never have occurred to you otherwise.

Let's first look at the list of all 36:

1. Supplication
2. Deliverance
3. Crime Pursued by Vengeance
4. Vengeance Taken for Kindred upon Kindred
5. Pursuit
6. Disaster
7. Falling Prey to Cruelty or Misfortune
8. Revolt
9. Daring Enterprise
10. Abduction
11. The Enigma
12. Obtaining
13. Enmity of Kinsmen
14. Rivalry of Kinsmen
15. Murderous Adultery
16. Madness
17. Fatal Imprudence
18. Involuntary Crimes of Love
19. Slaying of a Kinsman Unrecognized
20. Self-sacrifice for an Ideal
21. Self-sacrifice for Kindred
22. All Sacrificed for a Passion
23. Necessity of Sacrificing Loved Ones
24. Rivalry of Superior and Inferior
25. Adultery
26. Crimes of Love
27. Discovery of the Dishonor of a Loved One
28. Obstacles to Love
29. An Enemy Loved
30. Ambition
31. Conflict with a God
32. Mistaken Jealousy
33. Erroneous Judgment
34. Remorse
35. Recovery of a Lost One
36. Loss of Loved Ones

This represents one complete spectrum of ideas for a script. It is by no means the be-all and end-all in storytelling, but it is a highly useful resource for writers. Its primary function is to provoke ideas and stimulate possibilities during the development of a plot. Think of it as a free-association tool. An important thing to pay attention to with the 36 Dramatic Situations is that the less literally you take these situations, the more actual use you can get out of them. For example, *Conflict with a God* can certainly be a literal fight with a deity, but it can also refer to any conflict with a mighty power. This flexibility in interpretation can be very useful as you utilize this tool to trigger ideas for your script. Before we get into a fuller explanation of this tool, let's define each of the situations because some of their meanings can be obscure.

1. SUPPLICATION – Asking or begging for help. There are the obvious forms of this—seeking help, prayer, imploring—but there is also a situation in which someone's negative behavior represents a silent or implied cry for help.

2. **DELIVERANCE** – Rescuing or being rescued. Any time someone is saved from something, physically or emotionally—or perhaps even the *attempt* to save someone.

3. **CRIME PURSUED BY VENGEANCE** – This is pretty straightforward. A crime has been done and vengeance is sought. What constitutes a crime certainly varies among different people, so itcan be quite subjective. Vengeance, however, is universal.

4. **VENGEANCE TAKEN FOR KINDRED UPON KINDRED** – Family infighting. Getting even with your father because he beat your mother would be vengeance taken for your mom upon your dad. Bear in mind that it doesn't have to be literally kindred. You can have a 'kinship' with your neighbors, your friends and your coworkers.

5. PURSUIT – In pursuit of something or being pursued by something or someone. You can be in pursuit of something tangible, for example, a wife, or an intangible, like respect.

6. DISASTER – Disaster can be different things to different people. Obviously, it can be your house burning down, but it can also be something as seemingly trite as a bad hair day. It is context-sensitive in this respect. If you live in Beverly Hills and somebody dyes your poodle the wrong shade

of pink, this may be the end of the universe! If the situation is a disaster within your character's world, then it's a disaster.

7. **FALLING PREY TO CRUELTY OR MISFORTUNE** – Clearly this is when someone gets in trouble, is hurt or destroyed by someone else—or by fate.

8. **REVOLT** – Any kind of revolt, from a palace coup to a struggle in a marriage, friendship or family. Mental, physical, spiritual—anything that relates to revolt, either literal or metaphoric.

9. **DARING ENTERPRISE** – Doing something bold, adventurous, dynamic, or energetic. It can be an action or a state of mind.

10. **ABDUCTION** – Literally kidnapping somebody, or someone being dragged into something against their will. It can be a psychic abduction, somebody drawn into someone else's world view, as in a cult.

11. **THE ENIGMA** – The mystery, the riddle. Trying to figure out what to do, how to find something, how to get to the bottom of something, the whodunit, the quest. These can be external riddles or internal riddles, i.e. a character trying to figure out what's wrong with his psyche, his emotions, his pattern of behavior. "How did I get into this? Why do I keep making the same mistake?"

12. **OBTAINING** – Trying to obtain something in any arena, physical or psychological, whether real or imaginary.

13. **ENMITY OF KINSMEN** – Animosity between kin (again, not necessarily literal kin), hatred between kin. You hating your brother, your co-worker, your neighbors, or them bearing a grudge or hating you.

14. **RIVALRY OF KINSMEN** – Pretty much what it says, a contest, struggle or jealousy between brothers (or any form of kin).

15. **MURDEROUS ADULTERY** – Not only adultery with murder involved, but a character can be in a murderous frame of mind because of adultery. The other thing is that adultery doesn't necessarily have to do with a sexual relationship. If you're in the Mafia and start talking to the police, then you're going outside the Mafia's 'contract' and this can get you whacked.

16. MADNESS – There are many types of madness, everything from someone in a straight jacket in a padded cell to Harpo Marx chasing blondes around a hotel. The movie *Animal House* comes to mind. Madness can be madcap and crazy in a delightful way. You can also have fear of madness, partial madness or a crazy situation. It can be the descent into the darkness of insanity or the escape from it.

17. FATAL IMPRUDENCE – Doing something so unwise that it can have fatal consequences. It doesn't necessarily have to be literally fatal; in *Tootsie*, when Dorothy tries to kiss Julie, that's Fatal Imprudence. No one literally died, but their friendship was dealt a lethal blow.

18. INVOLUNTARY CRIMES OF LOVE – Both this situation and number 26, *Crimes of Love*, relate to incest. A crime of love would be having sex with your daughter, whereas an involuntary crime of love is not knowing it was your daughter, perhaps finding out later. But also, think about how crimes of love can be understood metaphorically. For example, it could be parental behavior intended to be positive which turns out to be an extremely bad example.

19. SLAYING OF A KINSMAN UNRECOGNIZED – This means in the literal sense that you kill someone and it turns out to be your brother— you didn't recognize him in the dark. Again, think about it metaphorically. It can be a drunk father coming home and treating his daughter badly. She feels 'slain' and unrecognized. "Doesn't he know that I'm his darling little daughter?" Maybe your boss puts you down, but you're the most loyal employee and you're taking the heat for others. You feel 'slain' and unrecognized.

20. SELF-SACRIFICE FOR AN IDEAL – Putting oneself on the line for an ideal. It can be literally sacrificing one's life, or being willing to sacrifice one's life, or giving up something you love for an ideal.

21. SELF-SACRIFICE FOR KINDRED – Being willing to sacrifice oneself for one's kindred (literal or metaphorical), or having sacrificed oneself for one's kindred.

22. ALL SACRIFICED FOR A PASSION – A situation where everything one is or has is at risk or is on the line for one's passion. Think of the people you know who will sacrifice themselves for their passion, or sacrifice others for it, or even sacrifice *you* for it.

23. **NECESSITY OF SACRIFICING LOVED ONES** – Not only facing the necessity of sacrificing someone you care about, but possibly betraying someone you care about. Throwing someone to the wolves, leaving them behind, selling them out.

24. **RIVALRY OF SUPERIOR AND INFERIOR** – This is always an interesting situation because it can be entirely subjective as to who's the superior and who's the inferior. From moment to moment, the perception of who's got the upper hand, who's morally superior, who's got control, who's got a higher status can flicker back and forth. Someone who sees himself as infinitely superior on a financial scale to another may feel genuinely inferior on an emotional scale a minute later.

25. **ADULTERY** – This is straightforward, unless you're dealing with the metaphoric use of it in terms of violating a contract. It can be used to play 'What if?' in a script that might need an extra complication. What if one of my characters were committing adultery? Cultural responses and consequences will vary as well.

26. **CRIMES OF LOVE** – Primarily thought of as sexual in nature, but many types of violations or perceived violations in a love relationship can be viewed as a 'crime.'

27. **DISCOVERY OF THE DISHONOR OF A LOVED ONE** – Finding out that you have been betrayed (in any number of ways); finding out that someone you love is evil, or a criminal, or untrustworthy.

28. **OBSTACLES TO LOVE** – Obviously anything that stands in the way of a relationship, be it a disapproving parent, circumstances, a jealous husband, a difference in finances, the loved one not feeling love in return; or imagined obstacles to love.

29. **AN ENEMY LOVED** – This is always an interesting one and can suggest intriguing possibilities for a plot. Falling in love with your enemy, respect for an enemy or fascination with an enemy. You can see it in *Silence of the Lambs* where Clarice—as well as the audience—is drawn to Hannibal and fascinated with him. Or in *Blade Runner*, in the way Deckard is drawn to the replicants and feels for them.

30. **AMBITION** – Not only the various strivings that any character might have, but also the permutations these may undergo as the character and

situation change. The whys and wherefores of these ambitions open up possibilities as well. Also the lack of ambition is telling and suggestive.

31. **CONFLICT WITH A GOD** – This is one situation you will almost always use metaphorically or poetically. There are films in which one is in conflict with a deity, but more often it means a situation in which one is up against the powers that be, say a weakling versus the neighborhood bully, or any weak entity up against a vastly more powerful force. It doesn't need have to have a religious connotation at all.

32. **MISTAKEN JEALOUSY** – This is not just jealousy, but mistaken jealousy. You might think your husband is having an affair, but he's really working a second job in secret to buy you an awesome anniversary gift. A great example of this is in *Tootsie* when Michael is three hours late for his dinner with Sandy. She waits outside his apartment, sees Dorothy go up and thinks Dorothy's having an affair with Michael; hence mistaken jealousy.

33. **ERRONEOUS JUDGMENT** – Any situation in which a bad assessment is made. It can be huge or microscopic. It can be a poor choice, a dangerous conclusion, muddled thinking or even just plain stupidity. Notice as well how the *fear* of making a bad choice can paralyze someone.

34. **REMORSE** – This can be someone feeling sorry for an action, a harsh word, or even a thought—all in varying degrees. There can also be the total *lack* of remorse in a character.

35. **RECOVERY OF A LOST ONE** – Finding someone that you've lost, or a loved object that was lost—even one's self-esteem or respect. Getting your real self back. Also recovering one's marriage, job, or sense of adventure.

36. **LOSS OF LOVED ONES** – Losing someone you love, either through death, or moving away, or all the ways you can lose someone. Again, it can be gigantic, like losing your entire family, or it can be your dad missing your softball game. It doesn't have to be a person that is lost; it can be a career, an object, your sanity, your self-respect.

The 36 Dramatic Situations are primarily a brainstorming tool that will help you explore the possibilities in a raw idea, break a stale plot out of cliché, develop characters, complicate storylines and provide an unexpected twist in a script. You use it as a 'What If?' tool. For instance, look at the situation, *Madness*. Ask yourself, "What if my character was crazy? What if she was totally and utterly off the deep end? Where does that take the story? Does it open up new plot possibilities or complicate things in an interesting way?" Then examine the ramifications of such a possibility. "OK, if my character is *totally* nuts, then things would veer off in *this* direction. It would entirely change this whole part of the plot. It would complicate everything having to do with this part of the story, and completely screw up my ending, but maybe that's just what it needed."

Follow these possibilities out as far as you can take them, *just to see where they go*. This is part of the creative process, part of your attack as a storyteller. Having gone out and tried that path, you may then decide either, "Wow, that's perfect! I'm going to use it," or "I see where that goes, but it's not where I want to take this plot. Or, I want to use *part* of it." It's very much like trying on shoes. You can try on 200 pairs of shoes, but you're not obligated to buy anything.

Using the 36 Dramatic Situations as a free-association tool works like this: one of the situations might trigger ten ideas, each of which can then trigger ten more ideas so that you just start exploding with possibilities. For instance, you're thinking about your plot and look at the situation, *Disaster*, and it may remind you of when a tornado hit your house when you were a kid. You remember seeing your car fly through your attic and smash thousands of family photos onto the front lawn. That might remind you of when you worked on the high school yearbook and lost the photos of all the seniors, and the captain of the football team pummeled you in the parking lot. And so on. The thing is that remembering how it felt when the captain of the football team broke your tooth may trigger an idea for an ending that's been stumping you on your script. One of the dramatic situations might just be a catalyst to trigger an idea or a flood of ideas, some of which may prove useful in developing your plot. Part of the function of the 36 Dramatic Situations is that they can break you out of your storytelling rut or help you work against any clichés you might be stuck in. If one of the situations takes you on a strange little voyage, then it's done its job.

The 36 Dramatic Situations are especially useful when you are just starting out with an idea and scrambling to get a solid plot up and running. Say you've got a raw idea for a spy story in which a curious child of a spy gets into his dad's stuff and, playing around, triggers an international emergency. It could be something like *War Games*. You don't have any plot or characters or setting or time period or ending—just a dynamic raw idea. In taking a quick cruise down the list of the 36, I see that *Supplication* suggests that the kid could be in over his head and begging for help. In addition, governments could be panicking, thinking there's a real emergency, and looking for help. The father could be pleading for help, the mother (who might not know what's really going on) certainly would be. *Deliverance* then suggests the possibility that because the kid was screwing around with his father's spy stuff, he could end up rescuing his father from a catastrophic situation in which he was trapped. Maybe this kid even saves the world. Maybe this whole adventure saves the family.

Crime Pursued by Vengeance suggests other directions for this story: has there been a great crime in the world of espionage or international politics that this kid stumbles onto? Does he learn about it just as things go off the deep end? Are there people after him for what they perceive to be a crime? Does the father flip out at the son? Does the CIA come down on the father, or on the son? *Vengeance Taken for Kindred upon Kindred* suggests some possibilities of infighting among the family. Also this may be happening inside the CIA, with turf wars going on. *Pursuit* suggests more possibilities. People after the kid, people after the father, the kid in pursuit of things he needs to solve what he's set in motion, one country in pursuit of the other because of what the kid touched off. It could be the son seeks respect or attention from his dad.

Disaster would certainly be very active in a story like this. Personal disaster, international disaster, family disaster, possible nuclear disaster, psychological disaster, people getting killed, people *almost* getting killed, the wrong people getting arrested, the wrong people getting out of jail, the end of the world, new enemies coming into power. Without going too far with this particular example, you can see that *Falling Prey to Cruelty or Misfortune, Revolt, Daring Enterprise, Abduction, The Enigma, Obtaining, Enmity of Kinsmen, Rivalry of Kinsmen, Madness, Fatal Imprudence, Slaying of a Kinsman Unrecognized, Self-sacrifice for an Ideal, Self-sacrifice for Kindred, All Sacrificed for a Passion, The Necessity of Sacrificing Loved Ones, Rivalry of Superior and Inferior, Discovery of the Dishonor of a Loved One, Obstacles to Love, An Enemy Loved, Ambition, Conflict with a God, Erroneous Judgment, Remorse, Recovery of a Lost one, Loss of Loved Ones* could all be active in this script idea. They are either already inherent in the material or could be tried on as possibilities to tweak the plot into new directions and dimensions. At first you may not see how all of these might work in this story idea, but as you spend more time with this tool you will become more versatile with it.

An important thing to bear in mind is that you could conceivably come up with these possibilities anyway without recourse to the 36 Dramatic Situations, but it helps you quickly and efficiently go over a complete spectrum of possibilities. And you may stumble over things that might *never* have occurred to you. The important thing is that these 36 basic situations stimulate your mind and trigger your imagination. Harvest all of them in your notebook. As the flow of free-association ideas cascade, get them down on paper. In the nature of true brainstorming, don't be afraid to be overwhelmed with possibilities. The 36 Dramatic Situations is often compared to a Pandora's box, in that it lets out manifold possibilities. You can get totally swamped, but it's really an embarrassment of riches since you've now got a full spectrum of ideas to play with. Just take your time and work through the possibilities.

Bear in mind that each of the situations can be utilized in various strengths or degrees of intensity. Polti describes this in the book, *The Thirty-Six Dramatic Situations* (The Editor Co., 1916).

> Murder, for instance, may be reduced to a wound, a blow, an attempt, an outrage, an intimidation, a threat, a too-hasty word, an intention not carried out, a temptation, a thought, a wish, an injustice, a destruction of a cherished object, a refusal, a want of pity, an abandonment, a falsehood. (p. 119)

Another important thing to be aware of in using this tool is that there is no one correct way to use it, and no rules—you can't make a mistake. If it triggers ideas, it's done its job. And don't be thrown by the language, you'll get used to it. If the subheadings get confusing, just ignore them at first and stick with the main headings. They'll take you as far as you want to go. You can venture into the subheadings after you get more comfortable with the process.

You'll find that this tool helps you overcome blind spots in your material. It's easy to leave out a major plot possibility or line of thought and not realize it. If you have the feeling that you are forgetting something important but can't put your finger on it, this can help ameliorate that disquieting sense. You may stumble into a new dimension with your story in such a way that you're no longer in the same 'universe.' You can fall down the rabbit hole in amazing ways because of what the 36 Dramatic Situations can suggest for your plot. It's important here to remember that you are working with the raw elements of plot—the proto-matter of your story. The potential is immense for each plot possibility you explore. Play with these, try them on for fun, be a mad scientist with them, dynamite your ideas into new realms, magnify parts of the plot, twist them, violate them, bust them out, turn them inside out, shake it all up. Think of wildly imaginative movies that you've seen and try to write with that level of abandon and adventurous spirit. The 36 Dramatic Situations will take you on many fascinating, crazy and fruitful journeys when you know how to use them fully and fearlessly.

Below are the 36 main headings with their subheadings as you would find them in Polti's book. We'll be working with the subheadings in our script analysis of *Tootsie* below, so I want to introduce them here. Again, they're a bit antiquated, but once you get the hang of the turn-of-the-century language, it's easy.

THE 36 DRAMATIC SITUATIONS WITH THEIR SUBHEADINGS

1. SUPPLICATION
(The dynamic elements technically necessary are: a Persecutor; a Suppliant; and a Power in authority, whose decision is doubtful)
A.   (1) Fugitives imploring the powerful for help against their enemies
        (2) Assistance implored for the performance of a pious duty, which has been forbidden
        (3) Appeals for a refuge in which to die
B.   (1) Hospitality besought by the shipwrecked
        (2) Charity entreated by those cast off by their own people, whom they have disgraced
        (3) Expiation: The seeking of pardon, healing or deliverance
        (4) The surrender of a corpse, or of a relic, solicited
C.   (1) Supplication of the powerful for those dear to the suppliant
        (2) Supplication to a relative in behalf of another relative
        (3) Supplication to a mother's lover, in her behalf

2. DELIVERANCE
(Elements: an Unfortunate, a Threatener, a Rescuer)
A.   (1) Appearance of a rescuer to the condemned
B.   (1) A parent replaced upon a throne by his children
        (2) Rescue by friends, or by strangers grateful for benefits or hospitality

3. CRIME PURSUED BY VENGEANCE
(Elements: an Avenger and a Criminal)
A.   (1) The Avenging of a Slain Parent or Ancestor
        (2) The Avenging of a Slain Child or Descendant
        (3) Vengeance for a Child Dishonored
        (4) The Avenging of a Slain Wife or Husband
        (5) Vengeance for the Dishonor, or Attempted Dishonoring, of a Wife
        (6) Vengeance for a Mistress Slain
        (7) Vengeance for a Slain or Injured Friend
        (8) Vengeance for a Sister Seduced
B.   (1) Vengeance for Intentional Injury or Spoliation
        (2) Vengeance for Having Been Despoiled During Absence
        (3) Revenge for an Attempted Slaying
        (4) Revenge for a False Accusation
        (5) Vengeance for Violation
        (6) Vengeance for Having Been Robbed of One's Own

(7) Revenge Upon a Whole Sex for a Deception by One

C.   (1) Professional Pursuit of Criminals

4. VENGEANCE TAKEN FOR KINDRED UPON KINDRED

(Elements: Avenging Kinsman; Guilty Kinsman; Remembrance of the Victim, a Relative of Both)

A.   (1) A Father's Death Avenged Upon a Mother

        (2) A Mother's Death Avenged Upon a Father

B.   (1) A Brother's Death Avenged Upon a Son

C.   (1) A Father's Death Avenged Upon a Husband

D.   (1) A Husband's Death Avenged Upon a Father

5. PURSUIT

(Elements: Punishment and Fugitive)

A.   (1) Fugitives from Justice Pursued for Brigandage, Political Offenses, Etc.

B.   (1) Pursued for a Fault of Love

C.   (1) A Hero Struggling Against a Power

D.   (1) A Pseudo-Madman Struggling Against an Iago-Like Alienist

6. DISASTER

(Elements: a Vanquished Power; a Victorious Enemy or a Messenger)

A.   (1) Defeat Suffered

        (2) A Fatherland Destroyed

        (3) The Fall of Humanity

        (4) A Natural Catastrophe

B.   (1) A Monarch Overthrown

C.   (1) Ingratitude Suffered

        (2) The Suffering of Unjust Punishment or Enmity

        (3) An Outrage Suffered

D.   (1) Abandonment by a Lover or a Husband

        (2) Children Lost by Their Parents

7. FALLING PREY TO CRUELTY OR MISFORTUNE

(Elements: an Unfortunate; a Master or a Misfortune)

A.   (1) The Innocent Made the Victim of Ambitious Intrigue

B.   (1) The Innocent Despoiled by Those Who Should Protect

C.   (1) The Powerful Dispossessed and Wretched

        (2) A Favorite or an Intimate Finds Himself Forgotten

D.   (1) The Unfortunate Robbed of Their Only Hope

8. REVOLT

(Elements: Tyrant and Conspirator)

A.   (1) A Conspiracy Chiefly of One Individual

         (2) A Conspiracy of Several

B.   (1) Revolt of One Individual, Who Influences and Involves Others

         (2) A Revolt of Many

9. DARING ENTERPRISE

(Elements: a Bold Leader; an Object; an Adversary)

A.   (1) Preparations For War

B.   (1) War

         (2) A Combat

C.   (1) Carrying Off a Desired Person or Object

         (2) Recapture of a Desired Object

D.   (1) Adventurous Expeditions

         (2) Adventure Undertaken for the Purpose of Obtaining a Beloved Woman

10. ABDUCTION

(Elements: the Abductor; the Abducted; the Guardian)

A.   (1) Abduction of an Unwilling Woman

B.   (1) Abduction of a Consenting Woman

C.   (1) Recapture of the Woman Without the Slaying of the Abductor

         (2) The Same Case, with the Slaying of the Ravisher

D.   (1) Rescue of a Captive Friend

         (2) Of a Child

         (3) Of a Soul in Captivity to Error

11. THE ENIGMA

(Elements: Interrogator, Seeker and Problem)

A.   (1) Search for a Person Who Must Be Found on Pain of Death

B.   (1) A Riddle To Be Solved on Pain of Death

         (2) The Same Case, in Which the Riddle is Proposed by the Coveted Woman

C.   (1) Temptations Offered With the Object of Discovering His Name

         (2) Temptations Offered With the Object of Ascertaining the Sex

         (3) Tests for the Purpose of Ascertaining the Mental Condition

12. OBTAINING

(Elements: a Solicitor and an Adversary Who is Refusing, or an Arbitrator and Opposing Parties)

A.   (1) Efforts to Obtain an Object by Ruse or Force

B.   (1) Endeavor by Means of Persuasive Eloquence Alone

C.   (1) Eloquence With an Arbitrator

13. ENMITY OF KINSMEN

(Elements: a Malevolent Kinsman; a Hatred or Reciprocally Hating Kinsman)

A.   (1) Hatred of Brothers — One Brother Hated by Several

        (2) Reciprocal Hatred

        (3) Hatred Between Relatives for Reasons of Self-Interest

B.   (1) Hatred of Father and Son — Of the Son for the Father

        (2) Mutual Hatred

        (3) Hatred of Daughter for Father

C.   (1) Hatred of Grandfather for Grandson

D.   (1) Hatred of Father-in-law for Son-in-law

E.   (1) Hatred of Mother-in-law for Daughter-in-law

F.   (1) Infanticide

14. RIVALRY OF KINSMEN

(Elements: the Preferred Kinsman; the Rejected Kinsman; the Object)

A.   (1) Malicious Rivalry of a Brother

        (2) Malicious Rivalry of Two Brothers

        (3) Rivalry of Two Brothers, With Adultery on the Part of One

        (4) Rivalry of Sisters

B.   (1) Rivalry of Father and Son, for an Unmarried Woman

        (2) Rivalry of Father and Son, for a Married Woman

        (3) Case Similar to the Two Foregoing, But in Which the Object is Already the Wife of the Father

        (4) Rivalry of Mother and Daughter

C.   (1) Rivalry of Cousins

D.   (1) Rivalry of Friends

15. MURDEROUS ADULTERY

(Elements: Two Adulterers; a Betrayed Husband or Wife)

A.   (1) The Slaying of a Husband by, or for, a Paramour

        (2) The Slaying of a Trusting Lover

B.   (1) Slaying of a Wife for a Paramour, and in Self-Interest

16. MADNESS

(Elements: Madman and Victim)

A.   (1) Kinsmen Slain in Madness

        (2) Lover Slain in Madness

        (3) Slaying or Injuring of a Person not Hated

B.   (1) Disgrace Brought Upon Oneself Through Madness
C.   (1) Loss of Loved Ones Brought About by Madness
D.   (1) Madness Brought on by Fear of Hereditary Insanity

17. FATAL IMPRUDENCE
(Elements: The Imprudent; the Victim or the Object Lost)
A.   (1) Imprudence the Cause of One's Own Misfortune
        (2) Imprudence the Cause of One's Own Dishonor
B.   (1) Curiosity the Cause of One's Own Misfortune
        (2) Loss of the Possession of a Loved One, Through Curiosity
C.   (1) Curiosity the Cause of Death or Misfortune to Others
        (2) Imprudence the Cause of a Relative's Death
        (3) Imprudence the Cause of a Lover's Death
        (4) Credulity the Cause of Kinsmen's Deaths

18. INVOLUNTARY CRIMES OF LOVE
(Elements: the Lover, the Beloved; the Revealer)
A.   (1) Discovery that One Has Married One's Mother
        (2) Discovery that One Has Had a Sister as Mistress
B.   (1) Discovery that One Has Married One's Sister
        (2) The Same Case, in Which the Crime Has Been Villainously Planned by a Third Person
        (3) Being Upon the Point of Taking a Sister, Unknowingly, as Mistress
C.   (1) Being Upon the Point of Violating, Unknowingly, a Daughter
D.   (1) Being Upon the Point of Committing an Adultery Unknowingly
        (2) Adultery Committed Unknowingly

19. SLAYING OF A KINSMAN UNRECOGNIZED
(Elements: the Slayer, the Unrecognized Victim)
A.   (1) Being Upon the Point of Slaying a Daughter Unknowingly, by Command of a Divinity or an Oracle
        (2) Through Political Necessity
        (3) Through a Rivalry in Love
        (4) Through Hatred of the Lover of the Unrecognized Daughter
B.   (1) Being Upon the Point of Killing a Son Unknowingly
        (2) The Same Case, Strengthened by Machiavellian Instigations
C.   (1) Being Upon the Point of Slaying a Brother Unknowingly
D.   (1) Slaying of a Mother Unrecognized
E.   (1) A Father Slain Unknowingly, Through Machiavellian Advice
F.   (1) A Grandfather Slain Unknowingly, in Vengeance and Through Instigation

G.   (1) Involuntary Killing of a Loved Woman

(2) Being Upon the Point of Killing a Lover Unrecognized

(3) Failure to Rescue an Unrecognized Son

20. SELF-SACRIFICING FOR AN IDEAL

(Elements: the Hero; the Ideal; the 'Creditor' or the Person or Thing Sacrificed)

A.   (1) Sacrifice of Life for the Sake of One's Word

(2) Life Sacrificed for the Success of One's People

(3) Life Sacrificed in Filial Piety

(4) Life Sacrificed for the Sake of One's Faith

B.   (1) Both Love and Life Sacrificed for One's Faith, or a Cause

(2) Love Sacrificed to the Interests of State

C.   (1) Sacrifice of Well-Being to Duty

D.   (1) The Ideal of 'Honor' Sacrificed to the Ideal of 'Faith'

21. SELF-SACRIFICE FOR KINDRED

(Elements: the Hero; the Kinsman; the 'Creditor' or the Person or Thing Sacrificed)

A.   (1) Life Sacrificed for that of a Relative or a Loved One

(2) Life Sacrificed for the Happiness of a Relative or a Loved One

B.   (1) Ambition Sacrificed for the Happiness of a Parent

(2) Ambition Sacrificed for the Life of a Parent

C.   (1) Love Sacrificed for the Sake of a Parent's Life

(2) For the Happiness of One's Child

(3) The Same Sacrifice as 2, But Caused by Unjust Laws

D.   (1) Life and Honor Sacrificed for the Life of a Parent or Loved One

(2) Modesty Sacrificed for the Life of a Relative or a Loved One

22. ALL SACRIFICED FOR A PASSION

(Elements: the Lover, the Object of the Fatal Passion; the Person or Thing Sacrificed)

A.   (1) Religious Vows of Chastity Broken for a Passion

(2) Respect for a Priest Destroyed

(3) A Future Ruined by Passion

(4) Power Ruined by Passion

(5) Ruin of Mind, Health, and Life

(6) Ruin of Fortunes, Lives, and Honors

B.   (1) Temptations Destroying the Sense of Duty, of Pity, etc.

C.   (1) Destruction of Honor, Fortune, and Life by Erotic Vice

(2) The Same Effect Produced by Any Other Vice

23. NECESSITY OF SACRIFICING LOVED ONES

(Elements: the Hero; the Beloved Victim; the Necessity for the Sacrifice)

A. (1) Necessity for Sacrificing a Daughter in the Public Interest

(2) Duty of Sacrificing Her in Fulfillment of a Vow to God

(3) Duty of Sacrificing Benefactors or Loved Ones to One's Faith

B. (1) Duty of Sacrificing One's Child, Unknown to Others, Under the Pressure of Necessity

(2) Duty of Sacrificing, Under the Same Circumstances, One's Father or Husband

(3) Duty of Sacrificing a Son-in-law for the Public Good

(4) Duty of Contending with a Brother-in-Law for the Public Good

(5) Duty of Contending with a Friend

24. RIVALRY OF SUPERIOR AND INFERIOR

(Elements: the Superior Rival; the Inferior Rival; the Object)

A. (1) Masculine Rivalries; of a Mortal and an Immortal

(2) Of a Magician and an Ordinary Man

(3) Of Conqueror and Conquered

(4) Of a King and a Noble

(5) Of a Powerful Person and an Upstart

(6) Of Rich and Poor

(7) Of an Honored Man and a Suspected One

(8) Rivalry of Two Who are Almost Equal

(9) Of the Two Successive Husbands of a Divorcee

B. (1) Feminine Rivalries; Of a Sorceress and an Ordinary Woman

(2) Of Victor and Prisoner

(3) Of Queen and Subject

(4) Of Lady and Servant

(5) Rivalry Between Memory or an Ideal (That of a Superior Woman) and a Vassal of Her Own

C. (1) Double Rivalry (A loves B, who loves C, who loves D)

25. ADULTERY

(Elements: a Deceived Husband or Wife; Two Adulterers)

A. (1) A Mistress Betrayed, For a Young Woman

(2) For a Young Wife

B. (1) A Wife Betrayed, For a Slave Who Does Not Love in Return

(2) For Debauchery

(3) For a Married Woman

(4) With the Intention of Bigamy

(5) For a Young Girl, Who Does Not Love in Return

(6) A Wife Envied by a Young Girl Who is in Love With Her Husband

(7) By a Courtesan

C.   (1) An Antagonistic Husband Sacrificed for a Congenial Lover

(2) A Husband, Believed to be Lost, Forgotten for a Rival

(3) A Commonplace Husband Sacrificed for a Sympathetic Lover

(4) A Good Husband Betrayed for an Inferior Rival

(5) For a Grotesque Rival

(6) For a Commonplace Rival, By a Perverse Wife

(7) For a Rival Less Handsome, But Useful

D.   (1) Vengeance of a Deceived Husband

(2) Jealousy Sacrificed for the Sake of a Cause

(3) Husband Persecuted by a Rejected Rival

26. CRIMES OF LOVE

(Elements: The Lover, the Beloved)

A.   (1) A Mother in Love with Her Son

(2) A Daughter in Love with her Father

(3) Violation of a Daughter by a Father

B.   (1) A Woman Enamored of Her Stepson

(2) A Woman and Her Stepson Enamored of Each Other

(3) A Woman Being the Mistress, at the Same Time, of a Father and Son, Both of Whom Accept the Situation

C.   (1) A Man Becomes the Lover of his Sister-in-Law

(2) A Brother and Sister in Love with Each Other

D.   (1) A Man Enamored of Another Man, Who Yields

E.   (1) A Woman Enamored of a Bull

27. DISCOVERY OF THE DISHONOR OF A LOVED ONE

(Elements: the Discoverer; the Guilty One)

A.   (1) Discovery of a Mother's Shame

(2) Discovery of a Father's Shame

(3) Discovery of a Daughter's Dishonor

B.   (1) Discovery of Dishonor in the Family of One's Fiancée

(2) Discovery than One's Wife Has Been Violated Before Marriage, Or Since the Marriage

(3) That She Has Previously Committed a Fault

(4) Discovery that One's Wife Has Formerly Been a Prostitute

(5) Discovery that One's Mistress, Formerly a Prostitute, Has Returned to Her Old Life

(6) Discovery that One's Lover is a Scoundrel, or that One's Mistress is a Woman of Bad Character

(7) The Same Discovery Concerning One's Wife

C.   (1) Duty of Punishing a Son Who is a Traitor to Country

       (2) Duty of Punishing a Son Condemned Under a Law Which the Father Has Made

       (3) Duty of Punishing One's Mother to Avenge One's Father

28. OBSTACLES TO LOVE

(Elements: Two Lovers, an Obstacle)

A.   (1) Marriage Prevented by Inequality of Rank

       (2) Inequality of Fortune an Impediment to Marriage

B.   (1) Marriage Prevented by Enemies and Contingent Obstacles

C.   (1) Marriage Forbidden on Account of the Young Woman's Previous Betrothal to Another

D.   (1) A Free Union Impeded by the Opposition of Relatives

E.   (1) By the Incompatibility of Temper of the Lovers

29. AN ENEMY LOVED

(Elements: The Beloved Enemy; the Lover; the Hater)

A.   (1) The Loved One Hated by Kinsmen of the Lover

       (2) The Lover Pursued by the Brothers of His Beloved

       (3) The Lover Hated by the Family of His Beloved

       (4) The Beloved is an Enemy of the Party of the Woman Who Loves Him

B.   (1) The Beloved is the Slayer of a Kinsman of the Woman Who Loves Him

30. AMBITION

(Elements: an Ambitious Person; a Thing Coveted; an Adversary)

A.   (1) Ambition Watched and Guarded Against by a Kinsman, or By a Person Under Obligation

B.   (1) Rebellious Ambition

C.   (1) Ambition and Covetousness Heaping Crime Upon Crime

31. CONFLICT WITH A GOD

(Elements: a Mortal, an Immortal)

A.   (1) Struggle Against a Deity

       (2) Strife with the Believers in a God

B.   (1) Controversy with a Deity

       (2) Punishment for Contempt of a God

       (3) Punishment for Pride Before a God

32. MISTAKEN JEALOUSY

(Elements: the Jealous One; the Object of Whose Possession He is Jealous; the Supposed Accomplice; the Cause or the Author of the Mistake)

A.   (1) The Mistake Originates in the Suspicious Mind of the Jealous One

       (2) Mistaken Jealousy Aroused by Fatal Chance

       (3) Mistaken Jealousy of a Love Which is Purely Platonic

       (4) Baseless Jealousy Aroused by Malicious Rumors

B.   (1) Jealousy Suggested by a Traitor Who is Moved by Hatred, or Self-Interest

C.   (1) Reciprocal Jealousy Suggested to Husband and Wife by a Rival

33. ERRONEOUS JUDGMENT

(Elements: The Mistaken One; the Victim of the Mistake; the Cause or Author of the Mistake; the Guilty Person)

A.   (1) False Suspicion Where Faith is Necessary

       (2) False Suspicion of a Mistress

       (3) False Suspicion Aroused by a Misunderstood Attitude of a Loved One

B.   (1) False Suspicions Drawn Upon Oneself to Save a Friend

       (2) They Fall Upon the Innocent

       (3) The Same Case as 2, but in Which the Innocent had a Guilty Intention, or Believes Himself Guilty

       (4) A Witness to the Crime, in the Interest of a Loved One, Lets Accusation Fall Upon the Innocent

C.   (1) The Accusation is Allowed to Fall Upon an Enemy

       (2) The Error is Provoked by an Enemy

D.   (1) False Suspicion Thrown by the Real Culprit Upon One of His Enemies

       (2) Thrown by the Real Culprit Upon the Second Victim Against Whom He Has Plotted From the Beginning

34. REMORSE

(Elements: the Culprit; the Victim or the Sin; the Interrogator)

A.   (1) Remorse for an Unknown Crime

       (2) Remorse for a Parricide

       (3) Remorse for an Assassination

B.   (1) Remorse for a Fault of Love

       (2) Remorse for an Adultery

35. RECOVERY OF A LOST ONE

(The Seeker; the One Found)

           No subheadings in this situation.

36. LOSS OF LOVED ONES
(A Kinsman Slain; a Kinsman Spectator; an Executioner)
A.   (1) Witnessing the Slaying of Kinsmen While Powerless to Prevent It
      (2) Helping to Bring Misfortune Upon One's People Through Professional Secrecy
B.   (1) Divining the Death of a Loved One
C.   (1) Learning of the Death of a Kinsman or Ally
D.   (1) Relapse into Primitive Baseness, through Despair on Learning of the Death of a Loved One.

THE 36 DRAMATIC SITUATIONS AS THEY APPLY TO *TOOTSIE*

MAIN HEADINGS THAT DESCRIBE THE SCRIPT AS A WHOLE:

AMBITION – Michael is intensely ambitious, seeking work. "I'll do dog commercials, I'll do anything." He is hungry with a capital 'H.' Then when he becomes Dorothy, he is even more ambitious, going after control of the show and pursuing Julie.

REVOLT – Michael is in revolt against his life, trying to force his career into action, walking off a Broadway set when the director gives him a stupid direction. As Dorothy, he leads a revolt on the show, turns the tables on John Van Horn, leads the other women in a revolt against Ron, the director, and encourages Julie's revolt in relation to Ron.

DARING ENTERPRISE – Michael embarks on a very daring enterprise by becoming Dorothy, and Dorothy has Daring Enterprise coming out of every pore. She's going after Julie, inciting revolt, changing her lines, representing strength of character, action and attack.

CONFLICT WITH A GOD – Michael is initially up against the casting directors, trying to get work. Dorothy takes on Ron, who is the ruling deity in this arena. She's also taking on male dominance in general.

RIVALRY OF SUPERIOR AND INFERIOR – The quest here is for who has the upper hand on the show. Dorothy is clearly superior in so many ways, but Ron runs things, and control flickers back and forth between them, with Dorothy winning out.

DELIVERANCE – Michael's becoming Dorothy rescues him from unemployment. Dorothy is rescuing Julie and the other women on the show from male dominance. Michael emerges at the end as a whole person and wins Julie.

OBSTACLES TO LOVE – There are many obstacles to Michael getting together with Julie. Sandy can't get Michael and is very frustrated. Les pines for Dorothy. Dorothy erects obstacles between Ron and Julie.

CRIME PURSUED BY VENGEANCE – Michael feels that the film and theatre industry has treated him badly and he seeks vengeance. Dorothy sees how Ron treats Julie, and how the male dominated structure of the show treats women poorly. Dorothy is a crusader, a masked avenger. Sandy feels the way Michael treats her is a crime.

ALL SACRIFICED FOR A PASSION – Michael sacrifices his manhood and his identity to get this job. Dorothy risks everything to take on Ron. Sandy gets sacrificed to his hunger for Julie. Michael sacrifices his role as Dorothy to escape the show. He even sacrifices his personality defects to win Julie in the end.

OBTAINING – Michael is desperate to get work and will do anything to get it. Dorothy struggles to change the power structure on the show and to land Julie. Sandy's trying to get together with Michael. Michael gets what he wants in the end, with a hot career and Julie as a girlfriend.

DISASTER – Michael's life is a disaster, both as an actor and romantically. When he uses Dorothy to escape that, it blows up in his face, becoming a full-fledged disaster when he tries to kiss Julie, Les proposes, John tries to rape Dorothy and Sandy freaks out at him. Sandy's relationship with Michael is a disaster because he's running away from her. Dorothy's appearance on the set is a disaster for Ron because she takes over and creates so much havoc and rebellion.

MADNESS – Michael is a mess. Not getting hired is making him crazy. Crazy things happen when he gets hired on the soap, like John Van Horn tongue kissing him. Things are out of control for Sandy because of how Michael's acting. Things get insane for Ron and for the show. Then the whole thing blows up in Dorothy's face at the end.

THE ENIGMA – Michael tries to figure out how to get work, wondering what's wrong with the casting agents. He runs up against many riddles once he becomes Dorothy—how to win Julie, how to deal with Sandy, how to handle John Van

Horn, how to deal with Les, how to get out of being Dorothy, etc. He doesn't try to solve the riddle of his personality defects until the end, when his survival hinges on it.

PURSUIT – Michael is in pursuit of work, willing to do anything for a job. Once he becomes Dorothy he is in pursuit of Julie. Sandy is in pursuit of Michael and Michael feels pursued by her. Dorothy is in pursuit of overthrowing Ron. Once Michael unveils and gets Julie really mad at him, he struggles to win her back.

NECESSITY OF SACRIFICING LOVED ONES – Michael has to sacrifice Sandy in his quest for Julie. The fact that Les is throwing himself at Dorothy puts Michael in a sticky situation. Michael has to sacrifice Dorothy in the end because the show is destroying him, and he has to let go of Julie in the process.

FATAL IMPRUDENCE – Walking off the Broadway set as Tolstoy because he won't walk when he's dying is 'fatal' because no one will hire him after that. Becoming Dorothy has substantial drawbacks as he finds out on his first day when John Van Horn tongue-kisses him. When Dorothy tries to kiss Julie, their friendship ends. The whole thing of becoming Dorothy is fatal imprudence for Michael because the choice leads to disaster.

DISCOVERY OF THE DISHONOR OF A LOVED ONE – This is when Julie discovers that Dorothy is really a man. Sandy realizes that Michael is avoiding her and then, much worse, he admits he's in love with another woman. Les discovers that Dorothy is a man.

RECOVERY OF A LOST ONE – Michael recovers his acting career and his dignity when he becomes Dorothy. In the end he wins Julie over. Plus he gets his real self back. Sandy recovers her sanity in the end.

INVOLUNTARY CRIMES OF LOVE – Michael doesn't mean to hurt Sandy or Julie or Les in doing what he must as Dorothy.

ENMITY OF KINSMEN – The conflict between Michael and Sandy. The breeding of animosity among the workers on the show. Julie is furious at Michael after he reveals that Dorothy is a man. Les is mad at Michael for deceiving him.

LOSS OF LOVED ONES – Sandy is losing Michael. Michael loses his friendship with Julie after he unveils and Julie loses Dorothy. Dorothy pries Julie away from Ron. Les can't have Dorothy. John Van Horn can't get Dorothy.

REMORSE – In the end Michael feels remorse for all the things he's done as Dorothy, and that's part of what helps turn him into a new man.

SUPPLICATION – Michael is begging for work. Michael is hoping for a way to get Julie as a girlfriend. Julie confides in Dorothy, asking for help. Sandy begs for Michael to carry on their relationship, or at least give her a straight answer.

SLAYING OF A KINSMAN UNRECOGNIZED – Michael is 'slaying' Sandy in the way he treats her. Julie feels 'slain' without being recognized when Dorothy unveils.

MISTAKEN JEALOUSY – Sandy believes that Michael is having an affair with Dorothy when Michael is three hours late for their dinner and she sees Dorothy go into Michael's apartment.

WORKING WITH SPECIFIC ASPECTS OF THE PLOT OF TOOTSIE

I have further broken *Tootsie* down into various aspects of the story and examined them through the lens of the 36 Dramatic Situations, using the sub-headings as well. I am addressing facets of the script that would need to be developed if you were building this screenplay from scratch. For example, 'Michael's Relationship with Julie' is a big part of the script and has to be thought out and dimensionalized. You can isolate it and look at all the subtle aspects of their relationship, leaving no stone unturned as you explore possibilities with the 36 Dramatic Situations. You can do this with different relationships, internal processes of characters, conflicts, the ending, etc. Note that I am doing script analysis here, but it is primarily intended to show you how to use this tool for plot construction. Note: the main headings are upper case and the subheadings are lower case.

MICHAEL'S DESPERATION TO GET ACTING JOBS
(Michael's struggle to get work. It's central to the story
and I examine it from many different points of view.)

PURSUIT – Michael is in pursuit of acting jobs, chasing down anything and everything.

AMBITION – He's truly desperate and is going after every job he can. Plus, he has lofty ambitions as an actor. You can see that in his teaching.
SUPPLICATION – He's practically begging for work.

OBTAINING – He *must* get work.

Rivalry of a powerful person and an upstart – He's the upstart and is in conflict with the all-powerful casting directors.

A hero struggling against a power – This is the way Michael sees himself; it's a heroic struggle.

Hospitality besought by the shipwrecked – He is shipwrecked metaphorically. Nobody will hire him and he's seeking hospitality. "I'll do dog commercials. I'll do *anything*!"

CONFLICT WITH A GOD – He's up against the powers that be in this universe—the casting agents.

War – For him, this is war. He is storming the gates.

The powerful dispossessed and wretched – He's a great actor who cannot get arrested.

A riddle to be solved on pain of death – He's got to get work or he'll die, and he's trying to figure out what's wrong with these casting agents. At this point in the story he's not taking any responsibility for his failure.

Imprudence the cause of one's own misfortune – He had the lead as Tolstoy on Broadway and he walked off weeks before the opening. It's largely his fault that he'll never work in this town again.

MADNESS – The whole situation is maddening. Plus he has personality problems.

A favorite or intimate finds himself forgotten – He used to be hot and now he's forgotten.

An outrage suffered – Nobody will hire him.

DISASTER – His career is in ruins.

FALLING PREY TO CRUELTY OR MISFORTUNE – A horrible fate has befallen him. Somehow the gods have conspired to unseat him and he's fallen to the bottom.

MICHAEL'S DETERMINATION TO SUCCEED
(Going in disguised as Dorothy—and he's angry)

DARING ENTERPRISE – This is a daring move by Michael. He's in full disguise and is on the warpath.

War – This is war and Dorothy is taking no prisoners.

AMBITION – Michael's ambition has really caught fire. His agent has inadvertently set a force of nature in motion.

REVOLT – Michael is in serious revolt mode when he goes in as Dorothy. He is going to get work, no matter what.

CRIME PURSUED BY VENGEANCE – Michael sees the way life has treated him as a crime and he's seeking vengeance. Plus he's going after it *with* a vengeance.

Efforts to obtain an object by ruse or force – He's using both trickery and force.

A hero struggling against a power – Dorothy is a masked avenger—like Batman or Zorro.

Vengeance for having been robbed of one's own – From his point of view, he has been robbed and he's seeking vengeance.

Rivalry of an ordinary man and a magician – Ron is the ordinary man and Dorothy, a shape shifter, is the magician.

Vengeance for a violation – Michael has been violated and he's seeking vengeance. A slightly different take on the one above, but a subtle distinction that might spark something specific in the writer.

Rivalry of a powerful person and an upstart – Ron is the powerful person and Dorothy is the upstart who is making trouble.

Vengeance for intentional injury or spoliation – Again, a slightly different take on the above two, but it offers another insight into Michael and how he perceives the world has been treating him: he has been intentionally injured.

OBTAINING – Look at all the things that Michael is trying to obtain—work, respect, revenge (perhaps unconsciously), being proven right, self-respect, money, artistic expression, happiness, to win a bet, justice.

Recapture of a desired object – This would be his career, his pride, and so on.

The appearance of a rescuer to the condemned – Dorothy rescues Michael, who is condemned to remain stuck.

ALL SACRIFICED FOR A PASSION – He gives up his manhood for the passion to succeed.

DOROTHY'S RELATIONSHIP WITH JULIE
(Notice that their relationship is akin to war buddies because they are trying to overthrow the male-dominated structure of the show.)

DARING ENTERPRISE – It's daring of Michael to go after Julie.

Adventure undertaken for the purpose of obtaining a beloved woman – This is very central to the whole movie because he has unexpectedly found this relationship. Actually it's a potential relationship if he can win Julie over. It complicates his dilemma and injects new life into his existence, making it that much more of an adventure.

PURSUIT – Not only is Michael pursuing Julie as Dorothy and falling in love with her, but together they're in pursuit of changing the power structure of the show.

Fugitives imploring the powerful for help against their enemies – Julie is a fugitive, trapped in her subservient role to Ron, imploring Dorothy, a mighty warrior, for help.

Hospitality besought by the shipwrecked – Julie is noticing that she's 'shipwrecked' in her relationship with Ron and she's seeking assistance and guidance from Dorothy.
CONFLICT WITH A GOD – The two of them are up against Ron the director.

Preparations for war – Changing the power structure on the show becomes a real battle for them.

Revolt of one individual who influences and involves others – Dorothy draws Julie and the other women on the show into her revolt, and it works.

Appearance of a rescuer to the condemned – Dorothy is saving Julie, who is condemned to stay stuck in her emotional and relationship patterns.

Rescue of a soul in captivity to error – Same as above, but with more of an emphasis on Julie's emotions, on her soul, on her awakening.

A fatherland destroyed – This is entirely metaphorical in that the male-dominated structure of the show gets overturned.

DELIVERANCE – Dorothy is rescuing Julie. Julie also helps Dorothy, even if Julie doesn't realize how much. In the end they get together and this creates a solid loving relationship, a deliverance for both of them.

OBSTACLES TO LOVE – There are obviously gigantic obstacles to Michael's love for Julie—physical, emotional, being trapped in the Dorothy disguise.

THE ENIGMA – How is Michael ever going to land Julie? This is a huge question because it becomes Michael's prime focus. He knows he has a real chance as Dorothy, but how to really pull it off?

A riddle to be solved on pain of death – He feels like he'll die if he doesn't win her.

MADNESS – The whole situation is increasingly crazy. Michael is going nuts because, dressed as a woman, he can only get so close to Julie.

Witnessing the slaying of kinsmen, while powerless to prevent it – Michael 'slays' Julie by revealing himself to be a man, but he is so desperate to get out of being Dorothy that there is no stopping it.

DISCOVERY OF THE DISHONOR OF A LOVED ONE – Julie discovers that Dorothy is really a man. Dorothy has seriously betrayed Julie.
Learning of the death of a kinsman or ally – Julie sees Dorothy 'die.'

Relapse into primitive baseness through despair on learning of the death of a loved one – Here the language is a bit archaic, but witness Julie slugging Michael in the stomach after he takes off the wig.

The unfortunate robbed of their only hope – Both Julie and Michael are each stripped of their best friend after Dorothy disappears.

ALL SACRIFICED FOR A PASSION – Michael gives up his role of Dorothy because he's desperate to get out of the trap he's in. Plus, his passion for Julie burns away all the negative aspects of his personality.

RECOVERY OF A LOST ONE – Michael gets Julie back in the end and Julie gets Dorothy. Plus Michael gets his real self back.

MICHAEL VERSUS SANDY

(We're not looking at their relationship, but their struggle)

ALL SACRIFICED FOR A PASSION – Michael is continually sacrificing Sandy for his passion for Julie.

Kinsmen slain in madness – There is a kinship between them and Michael is 'slaying' her through his deception, his avoidance and his unintentional cruelty.

The slaying or injuring of a person not hated – Michael certainly doesn't hate Sandy, but he's definitely busy 'hurting' her.

DISASTER – This is disaster for both of them, each in their own way. Sandy feels abandoned, mistreated and lied to, and Michael feels trapped in a stupid snare of his own making.

Helping to bring misfortune upon one's people through professional secrecy – On the day that Michael gets hired as Dorothy, he tells his roommate that they can begin rehearsal on the play. They realize they can't tell Sandy that a man got the role she got turned down for—she gets suicidal at a birthday party. They decide to say that Michael's aunt died and he inherited the money. They make a pact of professional secrecy and it brings misfortune on Sandy.

The duty of sacrificing one's child, unknown to others, under pressure of necessity – Michael has to sacrifice Sandy because he has fallen in love with Julie.

The innocent made the victim of ambitious intrigue – Sandy is the victim of Michael's love for Julie.

Abandonment by a lover or husband – Sandy gets essentially dumped, even though he's going through the motions of pretending to something that never existed anyway.

A mistress betrayed – She has definitely been betrayed, and is feeling it more and more.

Ambition and covetousness heaping crime upon crime – Michael's ambition and covetousness for Julie heaps crime upon crime on Sandy.

PURSUIT – Sandy's in pursuit of Michael and he's in pursuit of Julie.

An outrage suffered – Sandy is suffering at the hands of Michael.

Temptations destroying the sense of duty, of pity, etc – Michael's temptations for Julie destroy his sense of duty to and pity for Sandy.

MADNESS – The situation is insane for both of them.

THE NECESSITY OF SACRIFICING LOVED ONES – Michael has to sacrifice Sandy in order to pursue Julie.

A riddle to be solved on pain of death – Sandy is wondering, "What's wrong with Michael?" and Michael is wondering, "How do I deal with Sandy?"

FALLING PREY TO CRUELTY OR MISFORTUNE – Sandy falls prey to a strange mixture of Michael's personality defects and his pursuit of Julie.

False suspicions (in which jealousy is not without reason) of a mistress – When Michael is three hours late to dinner with Sandy, she waits outside his apartment, sees Dorothy go in and thinks he's having an affair with Dorothy. And she has good reason to think so.

OBSTACLES TO LOVE – Julie is the obvious obstacle to the any romance between Michael and Sandy. Michael's behavior is an obstacle to their friendship. **The innocent despoiled by those who should protect** – Michael should be protecting Sandy, but he's stabbing her in the back.

Disgrace brought upon oneself through madness – Michael is disgracing himself in how he treats Sandy.

Respect for a priest destroyed – A subtle point is to remember that Michael is Sandy's acting teacher.

DOROTHY VERSUS RON
(Two guys fighting over a girl)

Falling prey to cruelty or misfortune – Ron treats Dorothy harshly when she arrives to audition.

The suffering of unjust punishment or enmity – Another take on the same thing.

Rivalry of conqueror and conquered – At first Ron is the conqueror, but Dorothy very quickly turns the tables and becomes the conqueror.

DARING ENTERPRISE – Dorothy goes on the attack against Ron, assaulting him directly, as well as leading the other women in a revolt against his power and working to steal Julie away from him.

CONFLICT WITH A GOD – Both Dorothy and Ron are all-powerful deities and they are going at each other with a vengeance.

War – They're at war.

REVOLT – Dorothy leads the women on the show in a revolt against Ron.

A hero struggling against a power – Dorothy is obviously the hero because she sees the wrongdoing of Ron toward Julie and the other women, and becomes a crusader against it.

Rivalry of a powerful person and an upstart – Dorothy is the upstart.

Mutual hatred – It's not hard to see that they hate each other. In reality, it's two guys fighting over a girl.

Ambition and covetousness heaping crime upon crime – Dorothy discovers Ron cheating on Julie and treating her badly.

Vengeance for a violation – Dorothy sees herself as the rescuer of the women on the show, and of women everywhere. She is a masked avenger.

Efforts to obtain an object by ruse or force – She uses both trickery and force to accomplish her mission against Ron.

Rivalry of a magician and an ordinary man – Dorothy is the magician, the shape shifter and Ron is a mortal—a powerful one, but still a mortal.

Professional pursuit of criminals – This is an interesting one. You might think only of Sherlock Holmes, but Dorothy goes after Ron with the dedication and intensity of a detective on the hunt.

Fugitives from justice pursued for brigandage, political offenses – Ron is on the run from Dorothy for 'acts of piracy' and political offenses, against Julie and the other women.

Rebellious ambition – Not only is Dorothy rebellious, but she's essentially taking over the show.

Revolt of one individual who influences and involves others – Her revolt against Ron draws the other women into her struggle against him and the patriarchial structure of the show.

The powerful dispossessed and wretched – Ron is deposed by Dorothy.

A monarch overthrown – This is a way to view Dorothy's successful 'coup' against Ron.

DOROTHY VERSUS MICHAEL
(Dorothy crusades against men like Michael)

MADNESS – Hey, they're the same person, which is guaranteed craziness. This type of identity switch is often used in comedy because it creates such zany complications.

RIVALRY OF KINSMEN – There is a deep inner struggle here because Dorothy is crusading against exactly the type of male that Michael is.

REVOLT – Dorothy is a revolutionary against Michael's world and his belief systems.

NECESSITY OF SACRIFICING LOVED ONES – Michael is being left out in the cold. Dorothy is crusading for women's rights while Michael is still treating Sandy badly.

War – There is a war going on because of their conflicting beliefs.

DARING ENTERPRISE – Dorothy is on the attack against Michael's whole value system.

Rivalry of a master and a banished man – Dorothy is the master and Michael is being left behind.

Presumptuous rivalry with a god – It's presumptuous of Michael to go up against Dorothy because she is so much wiser and more powerful.

Rivalry of two who are almost equal – Dorothy *is* smarter than Michael.

Adventure undertaken for the purpose of obtaining a beloved woman – Dorothy has a shot at landing Julie, but Michael will ruin it for sure.

Duty of punishing a son who is a traitor to the country – Michael is a traitor to women because he represents everything that Dorothy is up in arms against.

The slaying or injuring of a person not hated – Dorothy doesn't hate Michael, but his old personality is being left behind. It's like the blood supply being cut off to a tumor.

DOROTHY SEEING THE PROBLEMS OF WOMEN

Rivalry of a conqueror and conquered – Dorothy sees how badly men treat women, especially Ron's treatment of Julie. For instance, when he sends out for food he doesn't check to see if Julie is hungry, when she obviously is.

The innocent made the victim of ambitious intrigue – Dorothy sees women as innocents who are being taken advantage of. Ron is cheating on Julie with April.

An outrage suffered – Dorothy has a political awakening because of all this.

CONFLICT WITH A GOD – Dorothy has a real fight on her hands in her attempt to change the status quo.

Suffering of unjust punishment or enmity – Another take on how women are treated. Dorothy sees how Ron ignores Julie and puts down the other women on the show without even realizing he's doing it.

MADNESS – What some women deal with is awful and Dorothy must solve it. She's experiencing it first hand in the form of unwanted attention from John Van Horn.

The fall of humanity – Dorothy is shocked at how women are treated with such a low level of humanity.

Fugitives imploring the powerful for help against their enemies – Julie is asking for help. Later the other women on the show rally around Dorothy.

The innocent despoiled by those who should protect – Women being mistreated by the very men who should be helping them.

DOROTHY'S RELATIONSHIP WITH LES

DISASTER – The father of the woman Michael's in love has the hots for Dorothy. There's no easy way out and it spells disaster.

MADNESS – This situation is completely insane and can only get worse.

Helping to bring misfortune on one's people through professional secrecy – Michael's keeping his secret from Julie and Les is bringing misfortune on them.

OBSTACLES TO LOVE – There are obviously gigantic obstacles to Les' love for Dorothy. This is not going to happen.

Imprudence the cause of one's own misfortune – Michael has gotten himself into this situation through his own anger and twisted determination.
The lover is the slayer of the father of the beloved – Michael is 'slaying' the father of the woman that he's madly in love with.

The innocent despoiled by those who should protect – Michael is creating problems with Les. He knows it's the worst thing he could be doing, especially if he's going to ever have a chance with Julie.

The suffering of unjust punishment or enmity – Les and Julie are suffering, or will be because of Michael.

Temptations destroying the sense of duty, of pity, etc – Michael's temptations for Julie destroy his sense of duty and pity for Les.

THE NECESSITY OF SACRIFICING LOVED ONES – Les is getting sacrificed because Michael's hunger for Julie outweighs his compassion for Les.

The slaying or injuring of a person not hated – Michael is 'slaying' Les by leading him on, but he certainly doesn't hate him.

AMBITION – Both Michael and Les have powerful ambitions for the woman they love.

War – Michael is in a battle to get Julie, and Les may end up as collateral damage.

Hospitality besought by the shipwrecked – Les is desperate for any contact with Dorothy he can get.

Remorse for a fault of love – Michael feels guilt for deceiving Les.

ERRONEOUS JUDGMENT – Michael is wondering what the hell he's gotten into. Here he is with yet another disaster because he became Dorothy.

Disgrace brought upon oneself through madness – Michael disgraces himself by deceiving Les.

The innocent made the victim of ambitious intrigue – Les is the innocent caught in the middle of Michael's ambition to win Julie.

PURSUIT – Les is seriously courting Dorothy.

MICHAEL'S NEED TO ESCAPE
(The show is trapping him and he's desperate to get out)

DISASTER – This whole charade is collapsing on Michael: he's lost Julie; all his lies have come crashing down on his head at once; he's trapped as Dorothy and is drowning in complications with Julie, Les and Sandy.

MADNESS – It all turns to insanity and is so claustrophobic that Michael has to get out or die.

OBSTACLES TO LOVE – He's totally blown it with Julie now that he has tried to kiss her, so he's dying to get out.

The ruin of fortunes, lives and honors – He's looking at the possibility of being destroyed by all this. There's no getting out of the show, Julie is mad at him, he has dragged her father into a bad situation, Sandy has been treated badly, and his agent's career is on the line if he quits.

Appeals for a refuge in which to die – He'll take any way out now. He's panicking and would rather die because it's all getting too horrible.

The powerful dispossessed and wretched – He had it made and now it's all a wreck. Dorothy's high-flying career is crashing down, so he needs to get out.

The unfortunate robbed of their only hope – His only connection with Julie is gone, and everything else is getting crazy on the show.

Hospitality besought by the shipwrecked – He'll take any rope thrown to him, do anything, or take any chance to escape.

War – This is war. It's getting messy and will get worse.

ALL SACRIFICED FOR A PASSION – He's willing to give up anything to escape. Everything is up for grabs.

MICHAEL'S TRANSFORMATION

Rescue of a soul in captivity to error – He breaks out of his old lying, hustling, neurotic pattern and ends up a new man, happy and free, with a great girlfriend.
Adventure undertaken for the purpose of obtaining a beloved woman – He goes through hell and out the other side to win Julie.

A fatherland destroyed – His old screwed up male self-image is gone.

A riddle proposed by the coveted woman – He has finally solved the riddle that allows him to get Julie. The riddle had to do with being so close to Julie, but so far away, unable to do anything about it.

OBTAINING – He finally wins Julie and gets his real self back in the process.

AMBITION – He has fulfilled his ambition.

Adventurous expeditions – This is a really brave thing that he does to land Julie in the end.

ALL SACRIFICED FOR A PASSION – He sacrificed everything, including a major role on a hit show, and it's turned out well, since he now has Julie.

A monarch overthrown – The old Michael is gone.

GETTING STARTED USING THE 36 DRAMATIC SITUATIONS ON YOUR OWN SCRIPT

1. If you're starting from scratch with a raw idea, then which of the 36 main situations trigger possible directions for a story? How many different possible stories do you see in this raw idea? If you're not seeing many possibilities for a raw idea, then it may not be all that strong, or you're not letting the 36 dramatic situations help you explode with ideas.

2. Which of the 36 situations really grab you in terms of your idea? Do any of them jump out and shout at you?

3. Which situations are the most 'radioactive' for your story? By that I mean, they're extremely suggestive and will not leave you alone. They force you to dig into the possibilities and suggest deep, dynamic story options that you cannot put your finger on right away.

4. Are you using the situations metaphorically and poetically? If you take them too literally you will miss fully half their value.

5. Are you finding active elements that can help you build a story?

6. Are the situations leading you deeper into the heart and soul of the story—what it's really about?

7. Are you playing 'free association' with the 36 situations, allowing them to take you on a journey—one that might not be logical or even sensible—but that takes you to unexpected realms?

8. Are you being exposed to ideas that might never have occurred to you through the process of exploring the 36 dramatic situations?

9. Do the situations take you inside your characters, their desires, flaws, changes and motivations?

10. Can you use these situations to shatter the cliché in your plot as you develop it?

11. Keep coming back to the 36 dramatic situations at different stages of developing your script. You will see new things in them as your story evolves and your problems as a storyteller change.

12. Try working with the 36 Dramatic Situations for *Training Day*. Which ones are central to that movie? There's a lot going on in it. One that jumps out at me for starters is *An Enemy Loved*. You should be able to find dozens of active situations in that story. Write about each one that you find—how the situation is active, how it plays out in the film, how it goes to the core of what the story is *really* about, how it defines character. Go deep and work them hard. It will enhance you skills with the tool.

13. Look at your favorite movies and see what situations leap to the front for them. Are there any in common? Do you seem to be attracted to certain elements in a film? Does this shed any light on which dramatic situations are particularly fertile ground for you as a writer?

8
THE ENNEAGRAM

The Enneagram is a deeply insightful tool for character development. Mysterious in origin, it contains ancient wisdom about human nature combined with cutting edge modern psychology. Enneagram is the name of a nine-sided star that is used as a symbol and as a working map of interconnection in this science. It purports that there are nine basic personality types, each with its own attributes. There are several 'schools' of the Enneagram, including Riso and Hudson's Enneagram Institute, Helen Palmer, Eli Jaxon-Bear, and Oscar Ichazo to name just a few. I am a relative newcomer to the Enneagram, so I am only introducing you to it rather than instructing you in it. A deep science, it has been incredibly useful to me as a screenwriter, as a teacher of dramatic writing and as a script consultant.

Each of the nine types has three different aspects: Healthy, Average, and Unhealthy. If you're moving toward integration (your life is coming together), then you will tend to exhibit Average to Healthy traits, and if you're moving toward disintegration (your life is falling apart), then you'll tend to exhibit Average to Unhealthy traits. As a dramatist, I find that the Unhealthy traits are a fascinating and rich source of character material, which are great for flawing, darkening, and deepening my characters. It's easy to like your protagonist, for instance, so you tend to not necessarily see the negative personality aspects, or if you do, you let them off too easy and end up with a shallower and more predictable character.

A person will tend to be one of these nine types, but will often have characteristics from the other types as well. If you're creating a character then you can totally mix and match if you find personality traits that you want to incorporate. The science of the Enneagram is quite sophisticated, and it will provide a wealth of highly organized and deeply insightful material, but as a writer you can also just use it as a resource to play with in creating indelible personalities for your screenplays.

The real power of this system is that it presents a deep, complex and complete understanding of how people work and what they're made of, including their very best and very worst. The Enneagram is like having a professional psychiatrist on staff who can provide personality profiles for your characters. It's a full science, and while I present a one-page synopsis of each type in this chapter, you can find great books that will take you much deeper into a highly comprehensive knowledge of the intricacies of each the nine personality types.

These descriptions are concise and from one point of view (from one particular school). To investigate other approaches check out the many books on the Enneagram which have extensive chapters on each type. These explore childhood patterns, the self-preservation instinct, the social and sexual instinct and so much more for each type. It's a gold mine of in-depth character study material and will take you deeply into human nature. For further reference, check out *The Wisdom of the Enneagram* and *Discovering Your Personality Type* by Don Riso and Russ Hudson; Helen Palmer's *The Enneagram: Understanding Yourself and the Others In Your Life*; or Eli Jaxon-Bear's *The Enneagram of Liberation: From Fixation to Freedom*. The one-sheets on the following pages come from the website of Riso and Hudson's Enneagram Institute, www.enneagraminstitute.com Their website is a rich source of information and will take you further into it all. Below is the nine-pointed Enneagram symbol on which are represented the different personality types.

1

THE REFORMER

Enneagram Type One

The Rational, Idealistic Type:
Principled, Purposeful, Self-Controlled, and Perfectionistic

Basic Fear: Of being corrupt/evil, defective
Basic Desire: To be good, to have integrity, to be balanced
Enneagram One with a Nine-Wing: "The Idealist"
Enneagram One with a Two-Wing: "The Advocate"

Profile Summary for the Enneagram Type One

Healthy: Conscientious with strong personal convictions: they have an intense sense of right and wrong, personal religious and moral values. Wish to be rational, reasonable, self-disciplined, mature, moderate in all things. / Extremely principled, always want to be fair, objective, and ethical: truth and justice primary values. Sense of responsibility, personal integrity, and of having a higher purpose often make them teachers and witnesses to the truth. **At Their Best:** Become extraordinarily wise and discerning. By accepting what is, they become transcendentally realistic, knowing the best action to take in each moment. Humane, inspiring, and hopeful: the truth will be heard.

Average: Dissatisfied with reality, they become high-minded idealists, feeling that it is up to them to improve everything: crusaders, advocates, critics. Into "causes" and explaining to others how things "ought" to be. / Afraid of making a mistake: everything must be consistent with their ideals. Become orderly and well-organized, but impersonal, puritanical, emotionally constricted, rigidly keeping their feelings and impulses in check. Often workaholics — "anal-compulsive," punctual, pedantic, and fastidious. / Highly critical both of self and others: picky, judgmental, perfectionistic. Very opinionated about everything: correcting people and badgering them to "do the right thing"—as they see it. Impatient, never satisfied with anything unless it is done according to their prescriptions. Moralizing, scolding, abrasive, and indignantly angry.

Unhealthy: Can be highly dogmatic, self-righteous, intolerant, and inflexible. Begin dealing in absolutes: they alone know "The Truth." Everyone else is wrong: very severe in judgments, while rationalizing own actions. / Become obsessive about imperfection and the wrong-doing of others, although they may fall into contradictory actions, hypocritically doing the opposite of what they preach. / Become condemnatory toward others, punitive and cruel to rid themselves of "wrongdoers." Severe depressions, nervous breakdowns, and suicide attempts are likely. Generally corresponds to the Obsessive-Compulsive and Depressive personality disorders.

Key Motivations: Want to be right, to strive higher and improve everything, to be consistent with their ideals, to justify themselves, to be beyond criticism so as not to be condemned by anyone.

Examples: Mahatma Gandhi, Hilary Clinton, Al Gore, John Paul II, Sandra Day O'Connor, John Bradshaw, Bill Moyers, Martha Stewart, Ralph Nader, Katherine Hepburn, Harrison Ford, Vanessa Redgrave, Jane Fonda, Meryl Streep, George Harrison, Celene Dion, Joan Baez, George Bernard Shaw, Noam Chomsky, Michael Dukakis, Margaret Thatcher, Rudolph Guliani, Jerry Brown, Jane Curtin, Gene Siskel, William F. Buckley, Kenneth Starr, The "Church Lady" (Saturday Night Live), and "Mr. Spock" (Star Trek).

2

THE HELPER

Enneagram Type Two
The Caring, Interpersonal Type:
Generous, Demonstrative, People-Pleasing, and Possessive

Basic Fear: Of being unwanted, unworthy of being loved
Basic Desire: To feel loved
Enneagram Two with a One-Wing: "Servant"
Enneagram Two with a Three-Wing: "The Host/Hostess"

Healthy: Empathetic, compassionate, feeling for others. Caring and concerned about their needs. Thoughtful, warm-hearted, forgiving and sincere. / Encouraging and appreciative, able to see the good in others. Service is important, but takes care of self too: they are nurturing, generous, and giving — a truly loving person. **At Their Best:** Become deeply unselfish, humble, and altruistic: giving unconditional love to self and others. Feel it is a privilege to be in their lives of others.

Average: Want to be closer to others, so start "people pleasing," becoming overly friendly, emotionally demonstrative, and full of "good intentions" about everything. Give seductive attention: approval, "strokes," flattery. Love their supreme value, and they talk about it constantly. / Become overly intimate and intrusive: they need to be needed, so they hover, meddle, and control in the name of love. Want others to depend on them: give, but expect a return: send double messages. Enveloping and possessive: the codependent, self-sacrificial person who cannot do enough for others — wearing themselves out for everyone, creating needs for themselves to fulfill. / Increasingly self-important and self-satisfied, feel they are indispensable, although they overrate their efforts in others' behalf. Hypochondria, becoming a "martyr" for others. Overbearing, patronizing, presumptuous.

Unhealthy: Can be manipulative and self-serving, instilling guilt by telling others how much they owe them and make them suffer. Abuse food and medication to "stuff feelings" and get sympathy. Undermine people, making belittling, disparaging remarks. Extremely self-deceptive about their motives and how aggressive and/or selfish their behavior is. / Domineering and coercive: feel entitled to get anything they want from others: the repayment of old debts, money, sexual favors. / Able to excuse and rationalize what they do since they feel abused and victimized by others and are bitterly resentful and angry. Somatization of their aggressions result in chronic health problems as they vindicate themselves by "falling apart" and burdening others. Generally corresponds to the Histrionic Personality Disorder and Factitious Disorder.

Key Motivations: Want to be loved, to express their feelings for others, to be needed and appreciated, to get others to respond to them, to vindicate their claims about themselves.

Examples: Mother Teresa, Barbara Bush, Eleanor Roosevelt, Leo Buscaglia, Monica Lewinsky, Bill Cosby, Barry Manilow, Lionel Richie, Kenny G., Luciano Pavarotti, Lillian Carter, Sammy Davis, Jr., Martin Sheen, Robert Fulghum, Alan Alda, Richard Thomas, Jack Paar, Sally Jessy Raphael, Bishop Desmond Tutu, Ann Landers, "Melanie Hamilton" (Gone With the Wind). and "Dr. McCoy" (Star Trek).

3

THE ACHIEVER

Enneagram Type Three

The Success-Oriented, Pragmatic Type:
Adaptable, Excelling, Driven, and Image-Conscious

Basic Fear: Of being worthless
Basic Desire: To feel valuable and worthwhile
Enneagram Three with a Two-Wing: "The Charmer"
Enneagram Three with a Four-Wing: "The Professional"

Profile Summary for the Enneagram Type Three

Healthy: Self-assured, energetic, and competent with high self-esteem: they believe in themselves and their own value. Adaptable, desirable, charming, and gracious. / Ambitious to improve themselves, to be "the best they can be" — often become outstanding, a human ideal, embodying widely admired cultural qualities. Highly effective: others are motivated to be like them in some positive way.
At Their Best: Self-accepting, inner-directed, and authentic, everything they seem to be. Modest and charitable, self-deprecatory humor and a fullness of heart emerge. Gentle and benevolent.

Average: Highly concerned with their performance, doing their job well, constantly driving self to achieve goals as if self-worth depends on it. Terrified of failure. Compare self with others in search for status and success. Become careerists, social climbers, invested in exclusivity and being the "best." / Become image-conscious, highly concerned with how they are perceived. Begin to package themselves according to the expectations of others and what they need to do to be successful. Pragmatic and efficient, but also premeditated, losing touch with their own feelings beneath a smooth facade. Problems with intimacy, credibility, and "phoniness" emerge. / Want to impress others with their superiority: constantly promoting themselves, making themselves sound better than they really are. Narcissistic, with grandiose, inflated notions about themselves and their talents. Exhibitionistic and seductive, as if saying "Look at me!" Arrogance and contempt for others is a defense against feeling jealous of others and their success.

Unhealthy: Fearing failure and humiliation, they can be exploitative and opportunistic, covetous of the success of others, and willing to do "whatever it takes" to preserve the illusion of their superiority. / Devious and deceptive so that their mistakes and wrongdoings will not be exposed. Untrustworthy, maliciously betraying or sabotaging people to triumph over them. Delusionally jealous of others / Become vindictive, attempting to ruin others' happiness. Relentless, obsessive about destroying whatever reminds them of their own shortcomings and failures. Psychopathic, murder. Generally corresponds to the Narcissistic Personality Disorder.

Key Motivations: Want to be affirmed, to distinguish themselves from others, to have attention, to be admired, and to impress others.

Examples: Bill Clinton, Oprah Winfrey, Jane Pauley, Michael Landon, Tony Robbins, Tom Cruise, Barbra Streisand, Sharon Stone, Madonna, Shirley MacLaine, Sting, Paul McCartney, Dick Clark, Whitney Houston, Ted Danson, Michael Jordan, Shania Twain, Sylvester Stallone, Arnold Schwarzenegger, Billy Dee Williams, Kathy Lee Gifford, Truman Capote, and O.J. Simpson.

4

THE INDIVIDUALIST

Enneagram Type Four

The Sensitive, Withdrawn Type:
Expressive, Dramatic, Self-Absorbed, and Temperamental

Basic Fear: That they have no identity or personal significance
Basic Desire: To find themselves and their significance (to create an identity)
Enneagram Four with a Three-Wing: "The Aristocrat"
Enneagram Four with a Five-Wing: "The Bohemian"

Profile Summary for the Enneagram Type Four

Healthy: Self-aware, introspective, on the "search for self," aware of feelings and inner impulses. Sensitive and intuitive both to self and others: gentle, tactful, compassionate. / Highly personal, individualistic, "true to self." Self-revealing, emotionally honest, humane. Ironic view of self and life: can be serious and funny, vulnerable and emotionally strong. **At Their Best:** Profoundly creative, expressing the personal and the universal, possibly in a work of art. Inspired, self-renewing and regenerating: able to transform all their experiences into something valuable: self-creative.

Average: Take an artistic, romantic orientation to life, creating a beautiful, aesthetic environment to cultivate and prolong personal feelings. Heighten reality through fantasy, passionate feelings, and the imagination. / To stay in touch with feelings, they interiorize everything, taking everything personally, but become self-absorbed and introverted, moody and hypersensitive, shy and self-conscious, unable to be spontaneous or to "get out of themselves." Stay withdrawn to protect their self-image and to buy time to sort out feelings. / Gradually think that they are different from others, and feel that they are exempt from living as everyone else does. They become melancholy dreamers, disdainful, decadent, and sensual, living in a fantasy world. Self-pity and envy of others leads to self-indulgence, and to becoming increasingly impractical, unproductive, effete, and precious.

Unhealthy: When dreams fail, become self-inhibiting and angry at self, depressed and alienated from self and others, blocked and emotionally paralyzed. Ashamed of self, fatigued and unable to function. / Tormented by delusional self-contempt, self-reproaches, self-hatred, and morbid thoughts: everything is a source of torment. Blaming others, they drive away anyone who tries to help them. / Despairing, feel hopeless and become self-destructive, possibly abusing alcohol or drugs to escape. In the extreme: emotional breakdown or suicide is likely. Generally corresponds to the Avoidant, Depressive, and Narcissistic personality disorders.

Key Motivations: Want to express themselves and their individuality, to create and surround themselves with beauty, to maintain certain moods and feelings, to withdraw to protect their self-image, to take care of emotional needs before attending to anything else, to attract a "rescuer."

Examples: Ingmar Bergman, Alan Watts, Sarah McLachlan, Alanis Morrisette, Paul Simon, Jeremy Irons, Patrick Stewart, Joseph Fiennes, Martha Graham, Bob Dylan, Miles Davis, Johnny Depp, Anne Rice, Rudolph Nureyev, J.D. Salinger, Anaïs Nin, Marcel Proust, Maria Callas, Tennessee Williams, Edgar Allan Poe, Annie Lennox, Prince, Michael Jackson, Virginia Woolf, Judy Garland, "Blanche DuBois" (Streetcar Named Desire).

5

THE INVESTIGATOR

Enneagram Type Five

The Intense, Cerebral Type:
Perceptive, Innovative, Secretive, and Isolated

Basic Fear: Being useless, helpless, or incapable
Basic Desire: To be capable and competent
Enneagram Five with a Four-Wing: "The Iconoclast"
Enneagram Five with a Six-Wing: "The Problem Solver"

Profile Summary for the Enneagram Type Five

Healthy: Observe everything with extraordinary perceptiveness and insight. Most mentally alert, curious, searching intelligence: nothing escapes their notice. Foresight and prediction. Able to concentrate: become engrossed in what has caught their attention. / Attain skillful mastery of whatever interests them. Excited by knowledge: often become expert in some field. Innovative and inventive, producing extremely valuable, original works. Highly independent, idiosyncratic, and whimsical. **At Their Best:** Become visionaries, broadly comprehending the world while penetrating it profoundly. Open-minded, take things in whole, in their true context. Make pioneering discoveries and find entirely new ways of doing and perceiving things.

Average: Begin conceptualizing and fine-tuning everything before acting — working things out in their minds: model building, preparing, practicing, and gathering more resources. Studious, acquiring technique. Become specialized, and often "intellectual," often challenging accepted ways of doing things. / Increasingly detached as they become involved with complicated ideas or imaginary worlds. Become preoccupied with their visions and interpretations rather than reality. Are fascinated by off-beat, esoteric subjects, even those involving dark and disturbing elements. Detached from the practical world, a "disembodied mind," although high-strung and intense. / Begin to take an antagonistic stance toward anything which would interfere with their inner world and personal vision. Become provocative and abrasive, with intentionally extreme and radical views. Cynical and argumentative.

Unhealthy: Become reclusive and isolated from reality, eccentric and nihilistic. Highly unstable and fearful of aggressions: they reject and repulse others and all social attachments. / Get obsessed yet frightened by their threatening ideas, becoming horrified, delirious, and prey to gross distortions and phobias. / Seeking oblivion, they may commit suicide or have a psychotic break with reality. Deranged, explosively self-destructive, with schizophrenic overtones. Generally corresponds to the Schizoid Avoidant and Schizotypal personality disorders.

Key Motivations: Want to possess knowledge, to understand the environment, to have everything figured out as a way of defending the self from threats from the environment.

Examples: Albert Einstein, Stephen Hawking, Bill Gates, Georgia O'Keefe, Stanley Kubrick, John Lennon, Lily Tomlin, Gary Larson, Laurie Anderson, Merce Cunningham, Meredith Monk, James Joyce, Bjork, Susan Sontag, Emily Dickenson, Agatha Christie, Ursula K. LeGuin, Jane Goodall, Glenn Gould, John Cage, Bobby Fischer, Tim Burton, David Lynch, Stephen King, Clive Barker, Trent Reznor, Friedrich Nietzsche, Vincent Van Gogh, Kurt Cobain, and "Fox Mulder" (X Files).

6

THE LOYALIST

Enneagram Type Six

The Committed, Security-Oriented Type:
Engaging, Responsible, Anxious, and Suspicious

Basic Fear: Of being without support and guidance
Basic Desire: To have security and support
Enneagram Six with a Five-Wing: "The Defender"
Enneagram Six with a Seven-Wing: "The Buddy"

Profile Summary for the Enneagram Type Six

Healthy: Able to elicit strong emotional responses from others: very appealing, endearing, lovable, affectionate. Trust important: bonding with others, forming permanent relationships and alliances. / Dedicated to individuals and movements in which they deeply believe. Community builders: responsible, reliable, trustworthy. Hard-working and persevering, sacrificing for others, they create stability and security in their world, bringing a cooperative spirit. **At Their Best:** Become self-affirming, trusting of self and others, independent yet symbiotically interdependent and cooperative as an equal. Belief in self leads to true courage, positive thinking, leadership, and rich self-expression.

Average: Start investing their time and energy into whatever they believe will be safe and stable. Organizing and structuring, they look to alliances and authorities for security and continuity. Constantly vigilant, anticipating problems. / To resist having more demands made on them, they react against others passive-aggressively. Become evasive, indecisive, cautious, procrastinating, and ambivalent. Are highly reactive, anxious, and negative, giving contradictory, "mixed signals." Internal confusion makes them react unpredictably. / To compensate for insecurities, they become sarcastic and belligerent, blaming others for their problems, taking a tough stance toward "outsiders." Highly reactive and defensive, dividing people into friends and enemies, while looking for threats to their own security. Authoritarian while fearful of authority, highly suspicious, yet conspiratorial, and fear-instilling to silence their own fears.

Unhealthy: Fearing that they have ruined their security, they become panicky, volatile, and self-disparaging with acute inferiority feelings. Seeing themselves as defenseless, they seek out a stronger authority or belief to resolve all problems. Highly divisive, disparaging and berating others / Feeling persecuted, that others are "out to get them," they lash-out and act irrationally, bringing about what they fear. Fanaticism, violence. / Hysterical, and seeking to escape punishment, they become self-destructive and suicidal. Alcoholism, drug overdoses, "skid row," self-abasing behavior. Generally corresponds to the Passive-Aggressive and Paranoid personality disorders.

Key Motivations: Want to have security, to feel supported by others, to have certitude and reassurance, to test the attitudes of others toward them, to fight against anxiety and insecurity.

Examples: Robert F. Kennedy, Malcolm X, Princess Diana, George H. W. Bush, Tom Hanks, Bruce Springsteen, Candice Bergen, Gilda Radner, Meg Ryan, Helen Hunt, Mel Gibson, Patrick Swayze, Julia Roberts, Phil Donahue, Jay Leno, John Goodman, Diane Keaton, Woody Allen, David Letterman, Andy Rooney, Jessica Lange, Tom Clancy, J. Edgar Hoover, Richard Nixon, and "George Costanza" (Seinfeld).

7

THE ENTHUSIAST

Enneagram Type Seven

The Busy, Fun-Loving Type:
Spontaneous, Versatile, Acquisitive, and Scattered

Basic Fear: Of being deprived and in pain
Basic Desire: To be satisfied and content — to have their needs fulfilled
Enneagram Seven with a Six-Wing: "The Entertainer"
Enneagram Seven with an Eight-Wing: "The Realist"

Profile Summary for the Enneagram Type Seven

Healthy: Highly responsive, excitable, enthusiastic about sensation and experience. Most extroverted type: stimuli bring immediate responses — they find everything invigorating. Lively, vivacious, eager, spontaneous, resilient, cheerful. / Easily become accomplished achievers, generalists who do many different things well: multi-talented. Practical, productive, usually prolific, cross-fertilizing areas of interest. **At Their Best:** Assimilate experiences in depth, making them deeply grateful and appreciative for what they have. Become awed by the simple wonders of life: joyous and ecstatic. Intimations of spiritual reality, of the boundless goodness of life.

Average: As restlessness increases, want to have more options and choices available to them. Become adventurous and "worldly wise," but less focused, constantly seeking new things and experiences: the sophisticate, connoisseur, and consumer. Money, variety, keeping up with the latest trends important. / Unable to discriminate what they really need, become hyperactive, unable to say "no" to themselves, throwing self into constant activity. Uninhibited, doing and saying whatever comes to mind: storytelling, flamboyant exaggerations, witty wise-cracking, performing. Fear being bored: in perpetual motion, but do too many things — many ideas but little follow through. / Get into conspicuous consumption and all forms of excess. Self-centered, materialistic, and greedy, never feeling that they have enough. Demanding and pushy, yet unsatisfied and jaded. Addictive, hardened, and insensitive.

Unhealthy: Desperate to quell their anxieties, can be impulsive and infantile: do not know when to stop. Addictions and excess take their toll: debauched, depraved, dissipated escapists, offensive and abusive. / In flight from self, acting out impulses rather than dealing with anxiety or frustrations: go out of control, into erratic mood swings, and compulsive actions (manias). / Finally, their energy and health is completely spent: become claustrophobic and panic-stricken. Often give up on themselves and life: deep depression and despair, self-destructive over-doses, impulsive suicide. Generally corresponds to the Manic-Depressive and Histrionic personality disorders.

Key Motivations: Want to maintain their freedom and happiness, to avoid missing out on worthwhile experiences, to keep themselves excited and occupied, to avoid and discharge pain.

Examples: John F. Kennedy, Benjamin Franklin, Leonard Bernstein, Leonardo DiCaprio, Kate Winslet, Elizabeth Taylor, Wolfgang Amadeus Mozart, Steven Spielberg, Federico Fellini, Richard Feynman, Timothy Leary, Robin Williams, Jim Carrey, Mike Myers, Cameron Diaz, Bette Midler, Chuck Berry, Elton John, Mick Jagger, Gianni Versace, Liza Minelli, Joan Collins, Malcolm Forbes, Noel Coward, Sarah Ferguson, Larry King, Joan Rivers, Regis Philbin, Howard Stern, John Belushi, and "Auntie Mame" (Mame).

8

THE CHALLENGER

Enneagram Type Eight

The Powerful, Dominating Type:
Self-Confident, Decisive, Willful, and Confrontational

Basic Fear: Of being harmed or controlled by others
Basic Desire: To protect themselves
(to be in control of their own life and destiny)
Enneagram Eight with a Seven-Wing: "The Maverick"
Enneagram Eight with a Nine-Wing: "The Bear"

Profile Summary for the Enneagram Type Eight

Healthy: Self-assertive, self-confident, and strong: have learned to stand up for what they need and want. A resourceful, "can do" attitude and passionate inner drive. / Decisive, authoritative, and commanding: the natural leader others look up to. Take initiative, make things happen: champion people, provider, protective, and honorable, carrying others with their strength. **At Their Best:** Become self-restrained and magnanimous, merciful and forbearing, mastering self through their self-surrender to a higher authority. Courageous, willing to put self in serious jeopardy to achieve their vision and have a lasting influence. May achieve true heroism and historical greatness.

Average: Self-sufficiency, financial independence, and having enough resources are important concerns: become enterprising, pragmatic, "rugged individualists," wheeler-dealers. Risk-taking, hardworking, denying own emotional needs. / Begin to dominate their environment, including others: want to feel that others are behind them, supporting their efforts. Swaggering, boastful, forceful, and expansive: the "boss" whose word is law. Proud, egocentric, want to impose their will and vision on everything, not seeing others as equals or treating them with respect. / Become highly combative and intimidating to get their way: confrontational, belligerent, creating adversarial relationships. Everything a test of wills, and they will not back down. Use threats and reprisals to get obedience from others, to keep others off balance and insecure. However, unjust treatment makes others fear and resent them, possibly also band together against them.

Unhealthy: Defying any attempt to control them, become completely ruthless, dictatorial, "might makes right." The criminal and outlaw, renegade, and con-artist. Hard-hearted, immoral and potentially violent. / Develop delusional ideas about their power, invincibility, and ability to prevail: megalomania, feeling omnipotent, invulnerable. Recklessly over-extending self. / If they get in danger, they may brutally destroy everything that has not conformed to their will rather than surrender to anyone else. Vengeful, barbaric, murderous. Sociopathic tendencies. Generally corresponds to the Antisocial Personality Disorder.

Key Motivations: Want to be self-reliant, to prove their strength and resist weakness, to be important in their world, to dominate the environment, and to stay in control of their situation.

Examples: Martin Luther King, Jr., Franklin Roosevelt, Lyndon Johnson, Mikhail Gorbachev, G.I. Gurdjieff, Pablo Picasso, Richard Wagner, Sean Connery, Susan Sarandon, Glenn Close, John Wayne, Charlton Heston, Norman Mailer, Mike Wallace, Barbara Walters, Ann Richards, Toni Morrison, Lee Iococca, Donald Trump, Frank Sinatra, Bette Davis, Roseanne Barr, James Brown, Chrissie Hynde, Courtney Love, Leona Helmsley, Sigourney Weaver, Fidel Castro, and Saddam Hussein.

9

THE PEACEMAKER

Enneagram Type Nine

The Easygoing, Self-Effacing Type:
Receptive, Reassuring, Agreeable, and Complacent

Basic Fear: Of loss and separation
Basic Desire: To have inner stability "peace of mind"
Enneagram Nine with an Eight-Wing: "The Referee"
Enneagram Nine with a One-Wing: "The Dreamer"

Profile Summary for the Enneagram Type Nine

Healthy: Deeply receptive, accepting, unselfconscious, emotionally stable and se-rene. Trusting of self and others, at ease with self and life, innocent and simple. Patient, unpretentious, good-natured, genuinely nice people. / Optimistic, reas-suring, supportive: have a healing and calming influence — harmonizing groups, bringing people together: a good mediator, synthesizer, and communicator. **At Their Best:** Become self-possessed, feeling autonomous and fulfilled: have great equanimity and contentment because they are present to themselves. Paradoxi-cally, at one with self, and thus able to form more profound relationships. In-tensely alive, fully connected to self and others.

Average: Fear conflicts, so become self-effacing and accommodating, idealizing others and "going along" with their wishes, saying "yes" to things they do not really want to do. Fall into conventional roles and expectations. Use philosophies and stock sayings to deflect others. / Active, but disengaged, unreflective, and inat-tentive. Do not want to be affected, so become unresponsive and complacent, walking away from problems, and "sweeping them under the rug." Thinking becomes hazy and ruminative, mostly comforting fantasies, as they begin to "tune out" reality, becoming oblivious. Emotionally indolent, unwillingness to exert self or to focus on problems: indifference. / Begin to minimize problems, to appease others and to have "peace at any price." Stubborn, fatalistic, and re-signed, as if nothing could be done to change anything. Into wishful think-ing, and magical solutions. Others frustrated and angry by their procrastina-tion and unresponsiveness.

Unhealthy: Can be highly repressed, undeveloped, and ineffectual. Feel inca-pable of facing problems: become obstinate, dissociating self from all conflicts. Neglectful and dangerous to others. / Wanting to block out of awareness anything that could affect, them, they dissociate so much that they eventually cannot function: numb, depersonalized. / They finally become severely disoriented and catatonic, abandoning themselves, turning into shattered shells. Multiple personalities possible. Generally corresponds to the Schizoid and Dependent personality disorders.

Key Motivations: Want to create harmony in their environment, to avoid conflicts and tension, to preserve things as they are, to resist whatever would upset or disturb them.

Examples: Abraham Lincoln, Joseph Campbell, Carl Jung, Ronald Reagan, Gerald Ford, Queen Elizabeth II, Princess Grace, Walter Cronkite, George Lucas, Walt Disney, John Kennedy, Jr., Sophia Loren, Geena Davis, Lisa Kudrow, Kevin Costner, Keanu Reeves, Woody Harrelson, Ron Howard, Matthew Broderick, Ringo Starr, Whoopi Goldberg, Janet Jackson, Nancy Kerrigan, Jim Hensen, Marc Chagall, Norman Rockwell, "Edith Bunker" (Archie Bunker), and "Marge Simpson" (The Simpsons).

GETTING STARTED USING THE ENNEAGRAM ON YOUR OWN SCRIPT

1. Which of the nine types resonate with your characters? Don't feel like you have to pick one right away. Try them on for fit. Explore them. Play with them.

2. When you find the type for your protagonist, in what way does it open up new possibilities and insights and help you build the character?

3. Do any of the types represent personality attributes that you would like your characters to have? You can actively mold characters to an Enneagram type, rather than just identify them.

4. Do you find that you can make your characters different from each other by using the nine types? Can you give each of them a distinct voice? Can you see how to heighten conflict by building contrasting character types?

5. Do you find that the specific personality traits listed for a type give you a specific handle on portraying your character onscreen? For instance "Risk-taking, hardworking, denying own emotional needs" are specific traits that can help you dimensionalize your character.

6. Does understanding the characters in your script open up new plot ideas?

7. Get a book on the Enneagram and study your characters in more depth.

8. The website www.enneagraminstitute.com has a test that you can take for $10.00 to determine your type. Take it pretending to be your protagonist, answering all the questions in character.

9. Examine several different 'schools' of the Enneagram and see how they give slightly different takes on the nine types.

9

RESEARCH, BRAINSTORMING AND INCUBATION

"Good material meets you halfway." As you do research and explore the material that's relevant to your story, you can stumble onto amazing plot possibilities that open up your story and can take it to a new level. Often they will present you with ready-made story elements that mesh magically with what you've been developing and tie your plot together.

A simple example is this: Say you're writing a piece about a crooked cop who is forced by circumstances to become honest. One of the first things I'd want to do is to talk to cops. That's not too hard, especially in LA where they are responsive to talking to screenwriters. But I'd want to talk to a crooked cop if I could. How do you find one? Certainly no one is going to admit to it. Perhaps you could locate one who's in prison. Now that's hard core research—and a much taller order. Prison is a scary place, but if you're really into it you can maybe talk to someone who has really lived the story you're trying to write. That's sticking your finger in the electric socket.

Say that this former detective tells you about a major turning point in his life where things went catastrophically wrong and he began to look at life differently and question his criminal ways. In your script this would correspond to the point of crisis and decision and action. His experiences could *dwarf* the ideas that you were imagining for your plot, and may open up a floodgate of possibilities that takes your script to Oscar-level. Your insight into your character's dilemma would likely be deepened and clarified, possibly radically altered. The material is meeting you halfway, almost as though you are on a long dangerous trek through the wilderness and someone meets you at the halfway point with specialized equipment for the journey ahead, maps, supplies and guidance.

Let's say that your theme has 'chosen' you. You are being drawn into writing on a deep or difficult subject; it's a daunting enterprise to tackle it and do it justice. But something tells you this is going to be a good movie—it has a dilemma of magnitude, it's a story that hasn't been told, and so on—so despite the obstacles ahead you launch into the script and into the considerable research needed. What seems to happen is quite amazing, almost as if some stories really want somehow to be told. People and events start coming towards you having to do with your theme and story in some way. And the research that you imagined would be laborious and take years instead unfolds quite quickly, pulling you forward and providing substantial story elements to help you pull the plot together in unexpected ways. It has come to meet you and draw you on.

Research is exploring anything and everything connected with your plot: books, legends, mythology, history, movies, talking to people with expertise. It can help you build your plot by providing raw ideas, factual knowledge, an understanding of a particular specialized world and its ambience, insight into character, unexpected possibilities and so on. It's the material out of which your plot is constructed, the cloth from which the suit is cut. Research is also important because truth is often stranger than fiction, and you'll find things you couldn't have imagined.

For example, I just saw an electrifying documentary on HBO called, *Unchained Memories: Readings from the Slave Narratives*. Here is its description from www.hbo.com:

> In the late 1930s, an estimated 100,000 former slaves were still alive in the United States. In the midst of the Great Depression, from 1936 to 1938, more than 2,000 interviews with one-time slaves were conducted for the Work Projects Administration (WPA) via its Federal Writers' Project, with the transcripts (written in the vernacular of the time) forming a unique firsthand record of slave life. *Unchained Memories: Readings from the Slave Narratives* presents dramatic selections from the extensive Slave Narrative Collection through on-camera readings by over a dozen actors, interspersed with archival photographs, music, film and period images.

It is an *astonishing* documentary, with top black actors of today doing in-character readings from these narratives. These first hand accounts in heartbreaking gritty detail make that world stunningly real. You couldn't even *begin* to write about that era in a realistic manner without exposure to material of this quality. These people *lived* it, some of them born in 1816 into a life of slavery, and their stories are research of the purest kind.

I find that I like to work with the 36 dramatic situations, dilemma, crisis, decision & action, resolution and theme before I get into research. I do this because then I have a real sense of what I'm up to and this will allow me to do much more targeted research rather than a scattershot approach. This is not only time-efficient, but also more focused. Price says: "The Theme points like a finger post to the Material, to the field from which you are to supplement your experience and philosophy." (Ibid, p. 2) Rather than just researching cops, which is a huge and vague job, or even crooked cops, I'd go directly to crooked cops who went straight. That is highly focused research and many hours can be saved this way. You go right to the very thing you need with laser targeting. This is not to say that you wouldn't be researching crooked cops, but if you can get directly on your specific target, then you're that much more efficient.

Let's look at another quote from Price's *The Philosophy of Dramatic Principle and Method:*

> Sound your Theme and Material to the bottom before determining upon your play. If you gain the idea for it, hold it in reserve, awaiting the possible chance for something better. The idea will inevitably be modified or improved in some manner. There may be hundreds of plays in that Material so why take the first thing that occurs to you? You may get a great drama instead of a superficial one by questioning and cross-questioning everything. At least you will get substance rather than shadow… nothing in details, or absolutely in outline can be fixed until you have taken all your bearings and sounded all the possibilities… The deeper you go, the more suggestive the facts. (p. 7, 10)

This is wise advice because it talks about holding possibilities in your head as you develop a script, trying on various combinations and configurations. You're not married to any one thing until you've tried them all and found what truly works for your plot. One of the habits of mind of the trained dramatist is to be plastic and flexible, always on the lookout for something that might enhance, complete or crystallize your story.

Price in *The Analysis of Play Construction and Dramatic Principle* gives the following advice on gathering together your research material:

The real dramatist goes to real life. He will find everything there waiting for him; he does not create everything, he adapts it…Go back, then, to nature for your Material, and trust to your art to make use of it. The minerals in the mines have to be delved for. No miner can manufacture gold, and no dramatist can create human nature. Your play must have substance… What a trivial vanity it is that some authors have that they must 'create' everything, spin it out of their brains without recourse to the facts of the world… Cease mere dreaming and empty imaginings and reach out your hand for the Material that lies about you in abundance… The trained dramatic mind is occupied much longer in gathering the Material and in constructing the play, shaping his material, than in the actual writing. How long or short it requires to 'write' a play is immaterial, but if we assume that a year is given to it, three fourths of that time had best be applied to the preliminary research and thought. (p. 26-32)

He is not saying that you ought to spend nine months out of a year researching, but that you can spend that much time figuring out a script before you write it. Part of that time includes research, but it's also developing and structuring it. Price emphasizes that you can take all the time that normally goes into rewrites and put it into engineering your script properly before you write it.

Research can be utterly crucial to developing a story, but it's also easy to fall into the trap of endless research which can become a means of avoiding work. You can get to love your material and won't want to stop steeping yourself in it. Sometimes you just have to jerk yourself out of it and get on with building your script. You can always go back to your reading later on. I have established many lifelong fascinations with subjects that I had utterly no interest in beforehand through researching screenplays. That's one of the exciting things about it. An important thing to remember is that the facts are not necessary in telling a story. They can be handy, but don't be a slave to them. You're the creator—do whatever you want, bend or twist anything you need. It's just a movie. There's a great old saying, "Never let the facts get in the way of a good story."

Good research also leads you away from the fallacy that you should only write what you know. Such thinking is a cruel trap because you can learn anything you want or need, especially now that information is on tap for virtually any topic. I write because I want to *create*. I don't need some writing teacher steering me back to my own closed loop for story material. I've lived a really interesting life, but I don't want to be stuck rehashing it. If I want to write about building satellites and I don't know the first thing about it, I will go out and *learn*. I will read for months if that's what it takes. I'll talk to experts. I'll go a lab where they build them if I can. All of this will be a great adventure and, as a writer, I'll be ecstatic. This is fun. This is freedom. This is not me being stuck with the same old stuff—rebreathing the same old air.

I'm very passionate about this and when I found an article on this very subject, I tore it right out of the magazine in the waiting room and took it with me. I started reading it to my students around 1991 and have read it to thousands since. One of them, a VP at a Hollywood film studio, said she thought it should be reprinted every month in *Variety* just to remind the industry of its point. I sought out the writer and got permission to reprint it here.

Doom Eager: Writing What We Need to Know

by Steven Dietz

PETEY (broken): *"Stan, don't let them tell you what to do!"*
Harold Pinter, *The Birthday Party* (1958)

"Write about what you know." The words echo down from above us with the authority of soldiers. The words sit on our laps as we stare at our typewriters. They fester inside us like a computer virus left over from a well-meaning mentor. "Write about what you know." A cunning phrase, which takes a moment to utter and can take a lifetime to overcome.

Obviously, every playwright writes out of personal experience in either a direct or oblique manner, whether consciously or unconsciously. At its most innocent, the "stick to what you know" admonition provides a sort of creative comfort. It is a way of saying, "Yes, there are interesting, important things about your life that you can relate to others. Trust that and tell your stories." I am not worried about the harmless, cheerleading use of this phrase. But I hear it used in the theatre with increasing regularity for a different purpose. I hear it used to censor playwrights.

If you've been present at discussions of new plays, or involved in the developmental process in any way, you have heard statements not unlike the following: "Who are you, a heterosexual man, to write about the love between two women?" "Who are you, a black woman, to write about the patriarchal Native American culture?" "Who are you, a well-to-do kid from Seattle, to write about the struggles of immigrants in the Rio Grande valley?" "Who are you, an aging white man, to write about the experiences of inner-city black youth?" Stick to *your own life* is the implication. Your life is the sole palette from which you may draw your material. So learn that. Learn to stay on your side of the creative yellow line. In our bohemian smugness, it never occurs to us that this is, in any way, censorship. Far from it. In fact, we've become experts at making this attitude a virtue. Instead of censorship, it is called "sensitivity." It is called "multicultural awareness." Most frighteningly, it is called "politically correct." And, as often as not, these who-are-you-to-be-writing-that comments are not coming from audience members who find something unpleasing or offensive about the given play—these words are coming from workers in the profession, from directors, dramaturgs, actors and incredibly, other playwrights. I believe that uttering these words to a playwright is tantamount to becoming the small-minded, censor-happy goons that we so vocally abhor.

We cannot have the ethics of our creativity both ways. We cannot on one hand support and pursue the long overdue call for nontraditional casting, and on the other hand tell playwrights that their sex, age, race, creed, sexual preference and physical condition determines the kind of plays they can write. We cannot, belatedly, rail against the politics of the National Endowment for the Arts, and in the same breath tell a writer that a given topic is the exclusive province of someone else. We cannot wear Rushdie on our sleeve and Helms in our heart. That is not "awareness." That is fear. What we fear is that we may be surprised by what we find buried in the unfamiliar; that our cherished and entrenched beliefs may be put in danger; or, perhaps, that we may discover, in others, similarities to ourselves. We must remember that the theatre only shines when it pries at the locked door, when in dares to look fear in the face.

What better way to begin to close the distance between our various communities (ethnic, religious, political, sexual) than by opening doors and venturing in? Where is the long overdue call for nontraditional playwriting? What value is there in taking refuge in the idea that "I'll never know how a woman/man thinks. I'll never know how a black/white/Hispanic/Asian person thinks. I'll never know how a gay/straight/lesbian/bisexual persons thinks. I'll never know what it's like to be a veteran, or a Native American, or a mother, or a white supremacist, or a brain surgeon or a spy, or an Olympic athlete, or a communist, or a dock worker, or an antiabortion activist, or Jewish/Catholic/Muslim, or a disabled person, or a southerner, or an orphan, or a high-fashion model, or an 18th century poet, or a feminist, or a foreign visitor, or the Amish, or a Republican, or a person with a terminal illness, or a father, or the homeless." No, perhaps you won't. But be advised that you have chosen a profession in which it is your *mandate* to be an explorer, not a curator, of your society. A profession which is to be questioned, as Brecht said, "not about whether it manages to interest the spectator in buying a ticket, but about whether it manages to interest him in the world."

Our integrity, not merely as artists but as citizens of the world, centers on engaging in dialogue with the "out there," probing the parts of our world that are foreign to us. Only through this sort of active engagement will we begin to approach "awareness." Only through dialogue, and not entrenchment, will we arrive at a truly "multicultural" art form. We will get nowhere by waiting for others to address our burning questions, with the cunning rationalization that the topic is better served by someone else. That doesn't wash. Never did, never will. We learn only when we lean into, not away from, our questions.

The signal we must send is this: Yes, certainly, "write about what you know," but, should the spirit move you, be brave enough to "write about *what you need to know.*" Write about cultures that mystify you, write absolutely everything you think about the opposite sex, write about strangers who intrigue you, write with gusto about the people you will never meet, write with abandon about anything outside of your experience that fascinates, frightens, inspires, angers or seduces you. "But how do I know what they're thinking?" You're a *writer.* You *guess.* You *invent* their lives and action with as much truth and passion as you can summon. You make your case and you await the verdict of the audience, of critics, of your peers. *At that point* is when they should have their say about the value of your attempt, and not before. *At that point* they should have every opportunity to question, praise, denounce, inform, trash, prize, badmouth, bless, boycott, emulate or burn your work. *At that point* you may bask in the realization that you have broadened your horizons and those of your community. Or you may find out that you were just dead wrong. And that, too, will teach you something. Attempts, not results, are the only sacred things in the theatre.

So be "doom eager." Wrestle with what is uncertain to you. Venture into those places that the world tells you belong to someone else. Did you get into theatre to think *small?* Did you become a writer so other people could *tell you what to do?* Do not let *anyone,* no matter their title or position, no matter their notoriety, no matter the cause or people they are championing, tell you what you are allowed to write. We risk the greatest loss when we allow our questions to be made smaller.

"Nothing can stop progress in the American theater except the workers themselves," Robert Edmund Jones wrote in 1941. Nearly 50 years later, those words shine like a beacon.

Steven Dietz is a director and playwright who lives in Seattle. His plays include *Fiction, Lonely Planet, Private Eyes* and *God's Country.*

BRAINSTORMING

At the end of your research you can get super-saturated, feeling like you've already covered the territory. This is a good time to get into brainstorming because you're loaded with great material. Brainstorming is the vigorous and explosive exploration of all the various possibilities in a plot. Obviously you're brainstorming at any given point in the development of a story, but once you've acquired a specialized knowledge you can draw on and build with so much more. How can you brainstorm about building a satellite if you have no concept of what's involved in it?

You really want to stretch the envelope as much as you can. Take each idea and explore it in every possible direction, no matter how crazy it may seem. Experts in creativity say that people who have solved age-old problems that plagued mankind for millennia often tried out a crazy idea. Other people may have *had* the idea before, but never went all the way with it. As a writer you want to have a healthy and vigorous imagination, and you want to give it free reign. Remember, the key word in the entertainment industry is Outrageousness.

Let your brain explode like popcorn. Does certain music make you go wild? Do certain writers inspire you? Dancing? Watching a favorite movie? Whatever it is, get it going and let it run wild. Don't edit yourself but let it flow. If you try to make it come out clean and organized, then you're editing yourself to death, slowing it down to a trickle. Just get it all down on paper and sort it out later. The emphasis is on freedom, new ideas bubbling out, raw possibilities, even if they don't make sense. It can be like surfing a giant wave. Just get on it and ride. You may have ten ideas per second pouring out of your brain for hours on end. Just ride it and scribble it down. Think about how the wildest movies have elements in their plot that are so unexpected, fresh and creative, and try to entertain your audience that way.

INCUBATE AND PERCOLATE

At a certain point in brainstorming you get burnt out. This is a good time to give your brain a rest. Let the ideas settle in your mind. It's an important part of the creative process to get away from the intensity of your work, both mentally and physically. Get away from your desk and take a walk on the beach. Turn your brain off for a while and let it sit. The conscious mind can be like an AM radio that just yammers on endlessly. Switch it off and let things incubate.

Your subconscious mind is a powerful creative entity and when it gets some computing time it can offer up amazing poetic solutions. The is called 'giving your subconscious a chance to think.' Ideas that you might never have thought of consciously can bubble up. For this to happen you have to be able to 'get out of your own way.' The poetic genius of your subconscious knows what you're trying to create because you've focused so much attention on your story and its problems and, given a chance, it can feed you ideas. You may have a dream, a wild thought percolating up from out of nowhere, an auditory hallucination, coincidental or synchronistic things appearing before you in print. This is your subconscious providing you with solutions. To become aware of how they are coming to you, learn to relax and open up because being receptive is an important part of the creative process.

REVISITING THE 36 DRAMATIC SITUATIONS

After having gone through and used these tools, your script has probably come light years from where it started. This is a good time to go back and review the 36 Dramatic Situations. Even if you just take a quick cruise through them, you may find new things jumping out at you. Your script is entirely different from what it was when you were starting out and you will no doubt see many new things by going back to it. Plus, you're wrestling with new plot problems, trying to nail down your ending, struggling to understand your characters more completely, refining various ideas. The 36 Dramatic Situations is a resource that you can keep coming back to as needed.

RESTATE DILEMMA, CRISIS, DECISION & ACTION, AND RESOLUTION

Now go back and look at the dilemma again. It may have changed as you developed the script, because as you make certain plot choices, things can morph. Articulate the dilemma as it stands now by stating it as two equally unacceptable alternatives. Are they still equal? Things can slowly alter and it may no longer really *be* a dilemma in the true sense of the word: two equally painful choices. Get down to brass tacks with it. You'll find that since you have spent so much time thinking about your character's dilemma, you will be able to state it more fully and completely. You may have started out with a rather tentative statement of dilemma—she's damned if she does and damned if she doesn't—which can truly help you get a handle on it, but it's good to come back and articulate it with all its ramifications, layers and dimensions.

Go back and revisit the crisis because it may have grown and changed, too. You may be able to add to it or simplify it or make it work better. It's good to go back and nail it down again in much the same way that you might check your roof rack on a cross-country trip to make sure it's still tied down tightly.

Decision and action is a crucial turning point in the script and it's important to check it again. Does what you came up with earlier in the development process still hold up? Can you make it better? Do you understand it more clearly now that you've spent a lot of time thinking about it?

The resolution is the ending and it completes the transformation of the audience. You can keep tinkering with it because it doesn't generally send ripples of change through the rest of the script, because this *is* the end. Think about the mood you want your audience to be in when the movie is over and see if your resolution causes that to happen.

Check in on your theme as well. The theme almost always grows as the plot does, so it may easily no longer be what it used to be. If it has morphed into something else, are you satisfied with it now? Look at the resolution and the way in which the protagonist resolves the dilemma. This enables you to put your finger on the theme.

A WORD ABOUT THE ANTAGONIST

Hitchcock said the more powerful your antagonist is, the more complex and dangerous the situation is, the more formidable your protagonist has to be to overcome it and therefore the more powerful the movie is. There is another saying "The movie is only as good as its villain." If you ratchet up the antagonist, the whole energy of the script goes up. Sometimes you'll find that you haven't paid much attention to the antagonist and you can pump him up quite a bit. But you can almost always get a little more out of your antagonist. Stack your antagonist up against the all-time greats. How do they compare against Keyser Soze? Hannibal Lecter? Darth Vader? Against any of the other all time great villains?

GETTING STARTED USING RESEARCH AND BRAINSTORMING ON YOUR OWN SCRIPT

1. What are some good sources for research on the story you're developing? What would be the best possible source? How can you get to it?

2. Do you know any experts in the field? Do any of your acquaintances know someone? Remember that there is a difference between classroom expertise and someone who has lived it. Both can be useful, but a soldier who fought in Vietnam will probably bring a lot more to the table than a professor on the subject. That said, a professor might well have insights the soldier doesn't.

3. Do you know how to use the Internet properly for research? How to use Internet book searches? Do you know how to use the library? Do you know about online library catalogs? About books on tape (free at the library)? Research experts? Information retrieval firms?

4. Dig deep into research so that you might find unexpected nuggets that meet you halfway, offering fantastic platforms on which to develop and build your story.

5. Are you wide open to your material or are you already locked down to the first conception of your plot? Does your research lead from possibility to possibility, helping you expand the plot and its potential as you go?

6. Don't get trapped in perpetual research. That's easy to do. Details are important to a convincing representation of reality, but don't get lost in a black hole.

7. Does the brainstorming process explode wildly for you? Are you afraid to let it really take off? Do you try to steer it too much? Are you too married to your earlier conception of the plot, so that you can't open up to wide-ranging free-form brainstorming?

8. Are you afraid of chaos or do you welcome it as a storyteller? Are you an adventurer as a storyteller or do you like to be in control all the time? Do you like getting yourself in trouble as a storyteller?

9. Do you end up with the same old stuff everybody else is writing? Do you go to the movies and rant about all the lousy films getting made, and then go home and work on a predictable and anemic screenplay?

10. Does the process of turning off your conscious mind and drifting scare you? Do you doubt the ability of your subconscious mind to generate creative solutions? Give it a try. Turn off the yammering brain and let go. Observe your dreams, your visions, your muse. Listen to your poetic impulses and play with them. They like to play.

10

THE CENTRAL PROPOSITION

This is tool will take you to the core of your plot and help strip the complete action down to its most basic essentials. It helps you find the central story in the material and tie it all together into a coherent whole. It also gives you an x-ray of your material and provides an invaluable degree of objectivity.

This tool was created by William Thompson Price, who founded the American School of Playwriting in New York City in 1901. As I mentioned he had twenty-eight students and twenty-four of them had hits on Broadway. Price reminds us that we can have all the things that Aristotle talked about and still not necessarily have a functional drama. To have a great race car, you need a good strong engine, a solid transmission and so on. You can *have* an engine, but it may be sitting on a workbench, and you may have a transmission, but it's on the garage floor. You've *got* all these things, but they're not yet functioning together as something you can actually drive around. What Price did was to create a tool that can help tie all the parts of a script into a coherent whole.

Price was a highly educated, world-traveled lawyer who largely gave up his legal practice to devote himself to his true passion, the theatre. He worked for some of the top producers of the day and read thousands of plays. Many of them were very poorly written and he began to despair. He wondered what was tripping these playwrights up. They weren't stupid and often had good stories to tell, but they just didn't have solid craft as dramatists. He tried to figure out if he could create a tool that would help them make their scripts work. As a lawyer, he was trained to use logic to strip a complex argument down to a clear statement of the facts, so he brought this kind of thinking to dramatic structure.

He went back to the syllogism of formal logic. A syllogism is two premises leading to a conclusion, and the most famous of them is this:

> All men are mortal.
> Socrates is a man.
> Therefore Socrates is mortal.

This argument is logically true—it's irrefutable. Price said that a plot has its own logic and you ought to be able state the complete action of the plot with this level of simplicity and clarity. A proposition is a type of syllogism. A lawyer goes through this same process in preparing a case for presentation in court. A lawyer is putting forth a proposition or a proposal to the court. You say my client stole this car, I can prove he wasn't in town that day, therefore my client is innocent. The ability to structure a solid, logical argument can be very useful in constructing a dramatic plot because argument or conflict lies at the core of a movie.

What Price did was to use the proposition of formal logic and adapt it to drama. We can use it to strip the plot down to a simple statement of the facts. One of the things this tool focuses on is the central conflict of the script. Conflict is to drama as sound is to music. This is clearly context-sensitive, in that the conflict in a romantic comedy is going to be very different from that in a spy story or an action-comedy—but there should definitely be conflict or opposition at some level. If we're stripping down a plot to its absolute core in terms of conflict, then we're talking about setting up a potential fight, touching off a fight to the finish, and bringing it to a conclusion. Price adapted this tool by changing the third step, but we'll get to that in a minute. First, let's look at what it means to set up a potential fight.

Let's say that we are developing a plot in which two gold miners are fighting over a claim. Our hero is struggling to keep a claim jumper from stealing his hard earned mine with phony paperwork and pure thievery. If, fairly early in the plot, the encroacher brings in a fake sheriff and a trumped up charge to try to force our miner off his claim, then the two combatants would go at it and our guy could drive them away. They have crossed swords and we, the audience would be saying, "These two are going to go at it big time before this movie is over." We have *set up a potential fight*. Then, later in the script, if the crooked prospector comes in with the heavy hitters and tries to take our guy out again, our miner would go on an all-out attack to try to finish him off. Now the *fight to the finish* has begun.

Below is a diagram to give a sense of proportion for this.

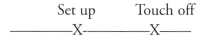

The first X is roughly where the set up of the potential fight often occurs and the second X is where the fight to the finish is touched off.

When the fight to the finish *has only just started*, an interesting thing happens to the audience. They come up on the edge of their seats, wondering how it's going to turn out. We've created substantial Dramatic Action. If, at this point, we could wave a magic wand and freeze everything—including the audience—then we can go out into the audience and get a close look at them. Let's focus on one member of this frozen audience. As the dramatist, we want to know how much on the edge of their seat is this person? Is her pulse racing? Is she white-knuckled? Are her eyes popping out of her head? Just how intensely do we *have* this audience member now that we're at this high point of suspense? These are crucial questions because if we don't have the audience at this point, then we're not doing a very good job. The plot that we've set up and touched off is not working well dramatically. And if it's not, then can we put our finger on why it's not working, and correct it?

Price said that part of our job as dramatists is to engage the audience in an unresolved situation. We set up the potential fight and touch off the fight to the finish, so the audience is on the edge of their seats. The fact that they're on the edge of their seats *is what's dramatic about the plot*. This is an important point. Think about the nature of drama. Remember, it's *all about the audience*. Think about how the best movies catch you up in an unresolved story, and the degree to which you need to know how it ends is a measure of how dramatic the plot is.

Now, at this point, when the fight to the finish has *only just begun*, a question appears in the mind of the audience as to how it's going to turn out. This is called the Central Dramatic Question. It exists *only in the mind of the audience*. It's not onscreen, it's not in dialog—it's only in the mind of the audience. In our miner's story, the Central Dramatic Question would be something like, "Will our miner defeat this claim jumper and keep his gold mine?"

The question will be highly specific because the audience is watching a highly specific set of events. It will not be generic, as in "Will the good guy win?" If this question in the mind of the audience is weak, then it indicates that the drama we're proposing is ineffective. If the question is strong, it's an indication that the plot is riveting. If the Central Dramatic Question *does* turn out to be weak, then we can experiment with strengthening it. If we alter how we set it up or how we touch it off then it will change the response of the audience and the power of the question. What we are doing is experimenting with a working model of the plot. Before engineers build a fifty million dollar bridge, they construct a wooden model and subject it to crush tests and shear tests to see how it holds up. If it crushes too easily then they might double the uprights and then see how it performs, adjusting it as needed. Once the model performs well, they build the full-scale bridge. This is a similar process. Once you set up the conflict and touch it off, then try to gauge how much you've got the audience. Do you have them or not? On a scale of 1 to 10, *how much* do you have them?

One of the necessary skills in using this tool is to be extremely objective with the Central Dramatic Question. It's very much a mind reading trick because you want to know what is *really* the question in the mind of the audience once the fight to the finish starts. Not what it *should be*, or what *you insist it must be*, or what it *would be* if the audience wasn't stupid—but what the question *actually is*. Imagine having a magic camera that enables you to take a picture of the question in their mind. It's about being in touch with what you've done to the audience— how much they're on the edge of their seat. Here's a trick that I have evolved from using this tool over the years. At the point when the fight to the finish has just started, I go out into the audience (in my mind) and sit with them. I look at this fight that just ignited and ask, "What's the question in our collective mind now?"

In *Training Day*, Jake touches off the fight to the finish with Alonzo late in the movie when he tries to arrest Alonzo and take the million dollars. The question in our mind is: Is Jake going to be able to take Alonzo down? The audience is intensely riveted. If you are writing this script and mapping out the plot, you'd be able to get a sense of its power by gauging the strength of the Central Dramatic Question. The potential fight is set up much earlier in the script when Jake challenges Alonzo about ripping off the Sandman's cash (using the fake search warrant). They square off about how undercover work is done, and Alonzo tells him he either plays street-style or he can go back to cutting parking tickets.

An important thing to bear in mind as you work with the proposition is that you're dealing with the main action only. Bernard Grebanier in his book, *Playwriting*, says it very well: "Proposition is an analysis of the *main action* only. It has reference *only to action*, not to motives, psychological states, moral issues or theme, for plot is entirely a matter of action." (p. 86) Aristotle says something quite similar in *Aristotle's Poetics* (Hill and Wang Pub., New York, 1961, translated by S. H. Butcher):

> Most important of all is the structure of the incidents. For Tragedy is an imitation, not of men but of an action and of life… it is by their actions that men are happy or the reverse. Dramatic action, therefore is not with a view to the representation of character; character comes in as a subsidiary to the actions. (p. 62-63)

With the central proposition we're cooking the entire plot down to its essence, focusing on the conflict. This process strips the plot right down to its absolute core with two main actions leading up to a question in the mind of the audience. However, since there are hundreds of actions in a script, how do you tell which of them sets up the conflict and touches it off? There is a process for this.

THE PROCESS OF CONSTRUCTING A PROPOSITION

The first step is we want to *visualize the fight to the finish*. Can you *see* it, literally seeing the fight to the finish in your mind as though it's a finished movie? In *Blade Runner* we can see Deckard and Roy on the roof in their fight. Again, the conflict is very context-sensitive to your own script. Does the level of conflict in your script build to a fight to the finish, and can you really see it?

The second step in this process is to ask: *What's the question in the mind of the audience once the fight to the finish has only just started and they don't know how it's going to turn out?* We start with the fight to the finish and the Central Dramatic Question because it's easy to find this high point of suspense in your script. It's like trying to find the tallest tent pole in a circus tent. You can look up and just see it there. Once we have that, then we'll work our way backwards, using deductive logic to find the actions that set the conflict up and touch it off. I underlined the words *has only just started* because the emphasis is on that. The fight to the finish has only just started and we truly don't know how it's going to turn out. There really is a question about the outcome. In *The Godfather* the Central Dramatic Question is: *Can Michael defeat Barzini and save the family?*

Our third step in this process is to ask: *What action by the protagonist touches off the fight to the finish, giving rise to the Central Dramatic Question?* We're focusing on the action of the protagonist because the audience is focused on the action of the protagonist. In *The Godfather* the action by Michael that touches off the fight to the finish is that he declares war on Barzini by throwing down the gauntlet at Barzini's agent, Moe Green. This is where the point of no return is crossed. It is somewhat hidden in *The Godfather* because Michael never goes directly head-to-head with Barzini since Barzini operates entirely behind the scenes. But if you look at that scene in Vegas again you'll see that Michael is white hot. This is not a casual business meeting. He tells Fredo to get rid of the girls, that he's here to do business, and then he goes right after Moe Green.

Michael says Moe has to sell the Corleones his share of the hotel and casino that they co-own. Moe explodes back at him, saying that the Corleones are washed up in New York and were chased out of town by Barzini. Moe says that he talked to Barzini and can make a deal with him to keep his hotel and casino. Francis Coppolla and Mario Puzo highlight this in the next scene when Don Corleone warns Michael that Barzini will have him assassinated at the meeting where his safety is guaranteed. Michael has truly declared war in this scene and we are left with the Central Dramatic Question: Can he defeat Barzini?

The fourth step in this process is to ask: *What action by the protagonist sets up the potential fight?* For this we're moving back a giant step in the story. In our proportion diagram for the whole script, the fight to the finish tends to start late in the script. Setting up the potential fight happens earlier.

Set up

The first X indicates roughly where the potential fight is often set up. Remember that we're trying to incorporate the full proportion of the entire script with this tool, trying to encompass the complete action. Essentially, this setting up the potential fight is a point at which the protagonist and the antagonist "cross swords" or have a run in. This is like a shoving match that will burst into a fight later. We are setting up the conflict.

In *The Godfather*, Michael executes Sollozzo, Barzini's messenger, insuring there is going to be a fight. It's as if the leader of the Crips sends a messenger to the leader of the Bloods and they kill the messenger—you know there's going to be a fight. Again, Michael's conflict with Barzini is indirect because Barzini always operates behind the scenes. But with Sollozzo dead, a significant player has been taken out, and even though a turf war breaks out among the families, there's also a much bigger conflict brewing; this turns out to be a power play by Barzini in his attempt to overthrow the Corleones.

So at this point we have worked our way backwards from the Central Dramatic Question, back through the touch off of the fight to the finish, and finally back to the set up of the potential fight. This helps construct the proposition by first isolating its parts. However, there is one more step in the development of the proposition, and for that we go back to our formal syllogism, paying attention to what's known as the *common term*.

> All *men* are mortal.
> Socrates is a *man*.
> Therefore Socrates is mortal.

In formal logic, the proposition consists of two premises leading to a conclusion and they are connected by a *common term*—in this case, the word, 'man.' The common term creates a *valid chain of logic* between the two premises and is part of the reason why the above argument is irrefutable. We're borrowing from the proposition of logic because it has power but we need to borrow *properly* so as to use that power fully in our dramatic proposition. As dramatists, we want a valid and powerful connection between the set up and the touch off of the fight. This will link them together in a way that makes the argument coherent and solid. We're really talking about a connecting rod—something that ties the two of them together. This is not always an easily definable entity and in truth, various things in a story can serve as the common term. We're not trying to be too rigorous about this part of the tool—we just want to pay attention to having the set up and the touch off be *connected in some way*. If this part of the tool is confusing, don't get too hung up on it now. Finish the book and then come back to this and you'll see it more in the complete context of the entire process.

So for the last step in creating our dramatic proposition, we ask: *Is there anything in common between the set up and the touch off of the fight that can bind them together?* In *Training Day*, a potential fight is set up when Jake challenges Alonzo about stealing money from the Sandman. And we've seen that the fight to the finish between them is touched off when Jake tries to arrest Alonzo and take his million dollars. Now, in order to look at what might be the common term in this proposition, we ask: Is there anything similar or common between when he challenges Alonzo the first time and when he declares war on him during the robbery and the attempted arrest? In both situations, Jake is shocked by Alonzo's brazen criminality and challenges Alonzo on it. Jake's intensity grows as he discovers the depth of Alonzo's corruption. So, the thing in common between the set up and the touch off of the fight is that Jake cannot allow Alonzo's blatantly corrupt activity to go unchallenged.

Now let's put the proposition together with its three parts:

Setting up the potential fight
Unable to be silent after Alonzo robs the Sandman, Jake challenges Alonzo on his conduct.

Touching off the fight to the finish
Now knowing how totally corrupt Alonzo is since Alonzo tried to have him killed, Jake tries to arrest Alonzo and seize his million dollars as evidence.

Central Dramatic Question
Will Jake be able to take Alonzo down?

This is a very stripped down version of the proposition for *Training Day*. We will come back later and state it more completely, but first let's finish our example of *The Godfather*.

What we want to know at this point is: Is there anything in common between Michael executing Barzini's agent, Sollozzo, and his declaring war on Barzini by going after Moe Green? In both instances he has been thrust into a position of power. In the first instance Sollozzo wants a meeting with him and, in the second, his father has just put him in charge of the family. He also takes control in both situations: firstly, by insisting that he will kill Sollozzo and, secondly, by telling his men that he will solve all their problems with the move to Las Vegas. What is common to the set up and the touch off of the fight is that he's thrust into a position of power and takes control of the situation. Do you see the process here? I'm looking at the point at which the conflict gets set up and when it gets touched off, and seeing if I can find anything that might be common to both. So let's look at the proposition for *The Godfather*. I'll italicize the common term.

Setting up the potential fight
Michael, *finding himself thrust into a position of power, takes control of the situation* and executes Barzini's agent, Sollozzo.

Touching off the fight to the finish
Michael, *now having been put in charge of the family by his father, takes control* and declares war on Barzini by throwing down the gauntlet at Moe Green.

Central Dramatic Question
Will Michael defeat Barzini and save the family?

THREE ADDITIONAL TERMS FOR THE CENTRAL PROPOSITION

I want to introduce three terms now:

> Condition of the Action
> Cause of the Action
> Resulting Action

These come from Price and are derived from legal terms. He called the first the Conditions of the Action, and are the conditions out of which the conflict arises. But Bernard Grebanier, a playwriting teacher who improved upon Price's application of the proposition, said that Conditions of the Action in the plural indicates a host of things that might set up the potential fight, when in fact we are only looking for one main action. He said that if you drop the 's' from conditions, then it reminds the novice to focus one thing, hence 'condition.' The Cause of the Action is more intuitive because we're touching off the action when the fight to the finish starts. Resulting Action means that you've created Dramatic Action because things are left unresolved in the form of a question.

What we've done is to strip the plot down to its most basic skeleton—

right down to its chassis and engine. This is an important process and can help you see the plot without any padding whatsoever. However, Price did emphasize that once you've got it stripped down this far, it's good to let a little bit of information back into the proposition so that a stranger to the story can make sense of it. For instance, who the heck is Michael? He could be a car mechanic in Portland for all we know. So with a few phrases here and there added into the mix, we can give a clear picture of the movie that we're proposing.

CONDITION OF THE ACTION (Setting up the potential fight)
Michael Corleone, son of a Mafia don in the 1940s, does not want to enter the family business, but when an attempt is made on his father's life, he finds himself in the driver's seat when Sollozzo asks for a meeting with him, and taking control of the situation, he assassinates Sollozzo and his bodyguard, McCluskey.

CAUSE OF THE ACTION (Touching off the fight to the finish)
Having been made head of the family operation by his father, Michael takes control and launches a surreptitious attack on Barzini, the don behind it all, by pretending to retreat and then telling Moe Green that he's going to buy out Moe's share of their hotel and casino, like it or not.

RESULTING ACTION (Central Dramatic Question)
Will Michael destroy Barzini and save the family?

Now for a look at *Blade Runner*. First, we isolate the separate parts of the proposition.

Visualize the fight to the finish.
We visualize Deckard and Roy Batty fighting it out on the roof.

What's the question in the mind of the audience once the fight to the finish has only just started and they don't know how it's going to turn out?
Will Deckard be able to defeat Roy?

What action by the protagonist touches off the fight to the finish, giving rise to the Central Dramatic Question?
Deckard goes on the attack against Pris and Roy.

What action by the protagonist sets up the potential fight?
Deckard follows clues to Zhora, the snake lady, and kills her. He's starting to take the replicants out.

Is there anything in common between the set up and the touch off of the fight that can bind them together?

The common element is that he is beginning to feel for the replicants and see things from their point of view, making him reluctant to kill them.

Assembling the full proposition, with a little more information included:

CONDITION OF THE ACTION (Setting up the potential fight)
Rick Deckard, a retired bounty hunter in a dystopian future, is drafted back into the police to destroy four dangerous genetically engineered slaves known as replicants, but when he meets their cruel creator, Tyrell, he begins to see things from the replicants' point of view, to feel for them, and so becomes reluctant to kill them, yet he finds Zhora, the snake lady, and kills her.

CAUSE OF THE ACTION (Touching off the fight to the finish)
Although Rachael has saved his life and he has now fallen in love with her, thus feeling more for the replicants and less willing to kill them, he is forced to kill Pris and face off with Roy because Roy has killed Tyrell.

RESULTING ACTION (Central Dramatic Question)
Will Deckard be able to defeat the incredibly powerful Roy?

We've already done the groundwork for the proposition for *Training Day*. Now let's incorporate more details.

CONDITION OF THE ACTION (Setting up the potential fight)
Jake Hoyt, a rookie policeman on his first day as an undercover narcotics cop, finds himself under the supervision of Alonzo Harris, a wild, unconventional veteran who shakes up Jake's entire view of police work. When Alonzo robs a drug dealer, Jake cannot allow this corruption and challenges Alonzo on his conduct.

CAUSE OF THE ACTION (Touching off the fight to the finish)
As Jake gets drawn deeper into the questionable world of Alonzo and his crazy, criminal mode of policing, things escalate when Alonzo and his crew of rogue cops rob a big-time dealer and kill him, then order Jake to claim he was the shooter. When Jake refuses to be part of it, Alonzo sets him up to be murdered but Jake escapes. Now seeing how fully and completely corrupt Alonzo is, Jake goes to Alonzo, tells him he's under arrest and tries to take the million dollars that Alonzo needs to buy his way out of a contract on his life.

RESULTING ACTION (Central Dramatic Question)
Will Jake be able to take Alonzo down?

THE CENTRAL PROPOSITION

Tootsie is very challenging to break down because it has a more complex structure. It's essentially a play within a play: you have Dorothy's drama inside Michael's drama. When I asked "What is the high point of suspense?" I found it's when Dorothy is unveiling on live TV. This seems to be the point of no return where the audience is hanging on every word and wondering how it's going to turn out. At first, I was looking at who has most of the conflict throughout the script, and it seemed to be Dorothy and Ron (two guys fighting over a girl). That holds up to a degree. Their fight comes to a head when Julie is about to break up with Ron, and Dorothy tells him that she knows him a lot better than he thinks. But that's the play within the play and it doesn't give rise to the Central Dramatic Question of the script.

I find that I'm most on the edge of my seat when Dorothy is coming down the stairs telling this gigantic lie as she tries to reveal that Dorothy is actually a man. In terms of conflict, it brings up an interesting angle—a conflict between Michael and Julie. There has been some of that brewing since Michael propositioned Julie with her own pick-up line and gets a drink thrown in his face. They're definitely in conflict until he finally wins her over at the end of the movie. In many romantic comedies, the lovers are often at odds and that seems to be the case here. Let's look at it in these terms.

Visualize the fight to the finish.
Michael is struggling to land Julie, now that he's infuriated her.

What's the question in the mind of the audience once the fight to the finish <u>has only just started</u> and they don't know how it's going to turn out?
Will Michael be able to win Julie back?

What action by the protagonist touches off the fight to the finish, giving rise to the Central Dramatic Question?
Michael unveils on live TV, revealing that Dorothy is really a man who has been substantially deceiving Julie and her father, Les.

What action by the protagonist sets up the potential fight?
Michael tries Julie's own recommended pick-up line on her, which she finds insulting.

Is there anything in common between the set up and the touch off of the fight that can bind them together?
It's that Michael is trapped as Dorothy but is utterly desperate to get Julie.

Now to assemble the proposition, with enough detail so that a stranger to the story can make sense of it.

CONDITION OF THE ACTION (Setting up the potential fight)
Michael Dorsey, a 'difficult' actor no one will hire, disguises himself as a woman and muscles his way into a role on a soap opera where he falls in love with Julie, a beautiful woman who's trapped in a powerless relationship with Ron, the director. As Dorothy inspires Julie to free herself from Ron, they become good friends and when Michael, desperate to win Julie, tries a pick-up line on her that she suggested to Dorothy, he gets a drink thrown in his face.

CAUSE OF THE ACTION (Touching off the fight to the finish)
As Michael falls more in love with Julie, he gets trapped in his role as Dorothy when her contract on the show gets extended. At Dorothy's prompting, Julie breaks up with Ron, and Michael, dressed as Dorothy, tries to kiss her but Julie freaks out and ends their friendship. Michael, now more desperate than ever to land Julie, and completely trapped as Dorothy, reveals on live TV that Dorothy is really a man.

RESULTING ACTION (Central Dramatic Question)
Will Michael somehow manage to win Julie back?

The proposition can be a tricky tool to master, but once you get the hang of it, it can be extremely useful in pulling together a plot that is under construction. It was slow going learning it for me and it was only through hard study and repeated application on all kinds of plots as a writer, teacher and consultant that I gained a mastery of it. I have found that the proposition will generally pull a mere collection of clever story elements into a coherent whole plot. It forces you to get right down to the nucleus of the plot and state it clearly, cleanly and completely as a logical argument.

One of Price's students, Arthur Edwin Krows, who wrote *Playwriting For Profit* ([the publishers made him use this title] Longmans, Green and Co., New York, 1928) sums up the Proposition:

> …Price's formulation is primarily a manner of stating succinctly: first, the circumstances out of which the action proper grows; second, the precipitating act which compels a fight to the finish; and finally, the objective of the play as a whole, expressed in alternatives—one in favor of one side at issue, the other in favor of the other. (p. 90)

It's very easy to be hypnotized by your own material because you can feel it has so much great 'stuff' in it: "How can it not be good? It's got all these great elements." This tool can objectify what you've *really got* in terms of plot and allow you to see it from a distance in order to evaluate it. You may find that stripping it down this far leads you to the question, "Is that all I've got?" Conversely, you may say, "Wow, I didn't know it was that solid." If it's not working, this is a good time to notice that. You don't want to find out that your Central Dramatic Question is weak on the opening night of your thirty million dollar movie—and it will be painfully obvious at that moment. You don't want the audience to be asleep right when you expect them to be the most spellbound. The ability to realize your plot is not kicking while it's still in your workshop is extremely valuable. That's what this tool is all about. *You're putting forth a proposition.* You're proposing a movie. It's a *pitch*—and either it works or it doesn't. You set it up and then touch it off— and the dramatic question in the mind of the audience gives you a measure of its power. If it isn't working, you can tweak it, either in a big way, or just a bit, as needed.

The proposition is the true starting point for plot construction. Prior to this, we've been collecting good 'parts' with which to build a movie. Dilemma, crisis, decision and action, and resolution are all solid components, but they don't automatically make a plot work. The 36 Dramatic Situations are good elements. Research, brainstorming, all the hard work that goes into creating a plot still doesn't pull it all together. With the proposition, we begin to have a real shape. If you're building a house, you and your spouse have discussions with the architect about how you want your kitchen to be and so on. But there comes the moment when the architect shows up with the finished blueprints so that actual construction can begin. This tool can get you to that point in the development of a script.

You can try different propositions as you experiment and shape your plot. The thing to remember is that it's a *proposal*. You can say, "OK, what if I try the plot this way? Hmmm, not bad. What if I try it *that* way? Interesting. What about *this*? Weak. How about this take? Wow! That really kicks, and if I add in this bit, then I'm really onto something." You'll see me use the proposition to experiment with and tune the plot that I develop in the second half of this book.

Once you find a proposition that works, the genetic identity of the plot is determined. You've got it down to a single-celled organism. This is the most compact rendering of the complete action of your plot. Before you were conceived, you were a sperm and an egg, but once they combined, your genetic identity was determined. All the cell division and growth thereafter carry that same identity. Here is where you get to shape your script at its nucleus, and that is a big part of the power of the proposition.

Price reflects on the proposition in *The Philosophy of Dramatic Principle and Method*:

> One main proposition is the essence of unity; it is unity, and unity can be procured in no other way. It is impossible that two main ideas exist in the same play. The house will be divided against itself. Two bodies cannot occupy the same space at the same time. The play itself, that which is developed from the one idea, is about many things; but the discerning eye of the author should penetrate to the heart of things. True dramatic instinct (which is largely the product of training) usually does this with unerring promptness, for that one idea is naturally the largest idea... A proposition involves the whole play. It must have a certain magnitude and the play must be commensurate with it. It suggests action, for the last clause requires that a problem be worked out. Doubt is expressed. The facts are given. Opposition is encountered. (p. 23-24)

When I started learning writing I spent three years reading two books, Price's *The Analysis of Play Construction and Dramatic Principle* and Krows' book, *Playwriting For Profit*. After that I decided to see what other playwriting books had to say about Price. I didn't find many references, but one book had lots of them. I took it back and read the quote below to my playwriting teacher, Irving Fiske:

> Eventually Price was able to formulate his law of plot, the proposition—which, we are quite willing to agree, is the one significant contribution to the science of playwriting since Aristotle's *Poetics*. This was the judgment of many of his students, among whom were the most successful American dramatists of their generation. It is a large remark, but as we say, we do not dispute it—even though Price's very name seems unknown to the public or to the scholars these days. If we ourselves were asked to whom we were indebted for the basis of our ideas about playwriting, we should have to answer, "Aristotle and Price." (p. 85)

After I read it to Irving he said, "Wow, he really understands Price. Who wrote that?" I turned the book over and read the name off the cover, "Bernard Grebanier" (from the book, *Playwriting*). Irving said, "He was my teacher!" It turns out that Irving had studied with Grebanier in New York in the 1930s and the textbook for that class was *Playwriting For Profit*. This is how I found out that I was the fifth generation in this school of playwriting, something I never would have known that if I hadn't stumbled over that quote and brought it to Irving.

THE CENTRAL PROPOSITION

GETTING STARTED USING THE CENTRAL PROPOSITION ON YOUR OWN SCRIPT

1. Make sure you're thinking in terms of the full scope of the entire script. A sense of proportion is important in working with this tool.

2. Have you developed conflict in your story? If you haven't, this tool will point that out very quickly. It will suggest the creation of conflict or opposition, which is always a good thing to have in a dramatic plot of any genre.

3. Can you cook your script down to two central characters who are in conflict? Remember that the oldest Greek theatre had only two characters in the whole play and try to see your plot *that* stripped down. It takes you right to the core of the action.

4. Does their conflict break out into a 'fight to the finish' near the end? Can you visualize that fight—really see it—as though you were watching the end of your movie in your head?

5. Think about the beginning of the fight to the finish. This is the beginning of a war (entirely within the context of your material—one thing for an action film and another for a romantic comedy). Now in your mind, go out and sit with the audience as one of them and get a feel for what the question is in your collective mind.

6. Is this question powerful enough? Do you have a feel for how intense the Dramatic Action you're creating is? Could it be more powerful or are you surprised by its strength?

7. What action by the protagonist starts the fight to the finish? You're looking for a powerful action by your main character to touch it off.

8. Reasoning backwards a giant step, what action by your protagonist sets up a potential fight? Is there some substantial conflict early on that gets the pressure going and the audience engaged in the opposition? Again, make sure you're looking at the full proportion of the entire story.

9. Is there anything in common between the set up and the touch off of the fight to the finish that can bind them together? You want there to be some

kind of valid logical connection between the two. This will help you tie the whole script together into a coherent whole.

10. Now stand back from the proposition and evaluate it. Does this simple clear representation of the core action of your script grab you as much as you hoped it would? Is it powerful? Is it pathetic? Somewhere in between? What are you going to do about it?

11. If it is weak, then play with either the set up or the touch off of the fight to try to invigorate the plot. You're trying to create Dramatic Action. You want the audience on the edge of their seats. Look at everything in the story that contributes to the dramatic power of the plot and work on all of it to make the proposition more powerful.

12. Try the proposition several different ways. Don't be afraid to try radically different propositions. Experiment. This is a great place to do that because it's so economical. You're working with a scale model of your plot, so it's cheap and easy to try out unusual possibilities.

11

SEQUENCE, PROPOSITION, PLOT

Sequence, Proposition, Plot is a three-step process guaranteed to make your script tighter and more dramatic. You apply it first to your whole story, then to each act, then to each sequence and then to each scene. Let's start with the first step, called *Sequence*. First, however, let's take a minute to distinguish between the process known as 'Sequence' and that part of a screenplay which happens to be called 'a sequence.'

A screenplay is divided into acts, and acts are divided into sequences. There are two to five sequences in an act. For instance, in a heist movie you would have the *planning sequence*, the *robbery sequence* and then the *getaway sequence*. These three sequences would constitute the entire act. The *planning sequence* itself would consist of several different scenes. In one scene they would case the bank, studying it in detail. In the next scene they would draw up a plan, hashing out the mechanics of the robbery, and in the third scene they would rehearse the job, working in a mocked-up model of the bank. These three scenes, taken together, would constitute the *planning sequence*.

The tool that I am presenting in this chapter is a three-step process called 'Sequence, Proposition, Plot.' It was created by Price, developed further by his student Krows, and then I took it to the next level. The first step, Sequence, *is the process of creating a tight chain of cause and effect in the story by building backwards.* I often refer to it as the 'reverse Sequence of cause and effect' and it is a highly specific method of structuring a dramatic plot. So what we will be doing in this chapter is to apply a process called 'Sequence' (reverse cause and effect) to a section of the story known as 'a sequence' (as in the above example, *the planning sequence*). I will denote the *process*, Sequence, with a capital 'S.'

REVERSE SEQUENCE OF CAUSE AND EFFECT

A dramatic plot should have good cause and effect, such that the first step causes the second, which causes the third, and so on. This keeps the story moving forward and helps create consistently compelling Dramatic Action without dead spots that can lose the audience. But how do you create tight cause and effect? You do it by working backwards from the ending, moving from an effect to its cause, thereby constructing an unbroken chain of events. What is the actual process for this on a real script?

Start by asking: *What is the Object of the script?* The Object is where you're trying to end up—the final thing on the horizon that you're moving toward. The ability to state the final object of any exercise can be very clarifying. If you go into a lawyer's office and say, "I can't get this, I've got to have this, I need this, they're doing this to me," the lawyer will stop you and ask, "Wait a minute. What's the *point*?" Then you'd say, "Oh, I need *this*," and the lawyer says, "OK, now we can talk." Or if you're trying to get rich, then your objective is to have millions in the bank. If the sheriff gets the bad guy and saves the ranchers at the end of the movie, then that's the object of your film. It's the purpose, the goal, the target.

Let me be specific. In *The Godfather*, the Object of the script is that Michael achieves total power but loses his soul in the process. This is the writer's objective—*not* Michael's objective. If you are trained as an actor then you might think in terms of your objective as a character, but this is different; this is where you, the writer, want the script to end up, and it might be diametrically opposed to what the character intends. Michael didn't set out to gain total power at the cost of his soul, but this is the object that Mario Puzo and Francis Coppolla were aiming at. The Object is a simple clear statement of where you want the story to end up.

Now we want to know: *What is the Final Effect that demonstrates this object onscreen with real actors?* The Object is *what* we want to achieve. Now we have to actually stage it with real actors. The Final Effect in *The Godfather* is that Michael is officially recognized by his top men as the new don and Kay is shut out. This shows that Michael has achieved total power but has lost his soul. The Object can be abstract, but the Final Effect which demonstrates the Object should be real and actable.

Next we want to know: *What is the Immediate Cause of the Final Effect?* The Immediate Cause of Michael being officially recognized by his top men as the new don and Kay being shut out is that he completes his ascent to power in the killing of Tessio and Carlo, the traitors in his organization, then lies to Kay about it. Now we ask: *What's the cause of him killing his traitors?* It's because he has killed all of his external enemies when he has the heads of the five families executed simultaneously. This causes him to turn his attention to killing the traitors inside his own organization. Not wanting to make waves or alert anyone, Michael didn't kill his enemies within until he got those on the outside.

What we are doing is reasoning backwards from an effect to its cause. In *The Godfather*, the church scene in which Michael stands godfather to Connie's baby and renounces the works of Satan while his men are out there killing all his enemies is considered one of the great scenes in the history of film. This scene is, in and of itself, a powerful effect and now we want to know: *What is the cause of him killing off the heads of the five families?* This one is not as straightforward as the others, but the cause is that he gets verification that Barzini is coming after him; this happens when Tessio proposes the meeting that Don Corleone has warned Michael about. He has been betrayed by his own man, and his mortal enemy, Barzini, is about to kill him, so this causes Michael to execute them all. Plus he's got his traitor. If he moved before he knew who was betraying him then he'd never know who it was. *What's the cause of Michael discovering that Tessio is the traitor?* It's that his father warns him that Barzini will set up a meeting in which someone he absolutely trusts will guarantee his safety, and that he'll be assassinated at that meeting. *What's the cause of Don Corleone warning him?* It's because Michael has essentially declared war on Barzini by throwing down the gauntlet at Moe Green in Vegas. We'll go through the entire reverse cause and effect for *The Godfather* soon, but this ought to illustrate how it works.

To further understand reverse cause and effect, notice what we have done in each instance is ask what is the *cause* of each effect, not what comes before it. This is a major distinction. This helps us do something important—to separate the necessary from the unnecessary. *The ability to separate the necessary from the unnecessary is a crucial skill for the dramatist.* The screenplay is an extremely lean literary form that demands total economy. You can really see this if you're turning a 400 page novel into a 110 page script. There's an awful lot of material that simply cannot make its way into the script and it's your job to decide what's necessary and what's not. Bernard Grebanier in his book *Playwriting* says, "Drama has a tendency to be stripped of matters unessential to the plot… In the best plays everything counts. There is no place for tangential material or merely graceful ornamentation." (pg. 16) The trick for separating the necessary from the unnecessary is to ask: What is the cause of a given effect, and not what came before it? *Any number of things can come before it, but only one thing actually caused it.* This helps you find the spine of the plot, unencumbered by unnecessary detail.

Price said that the work of the amateur is characterized by the unnecessary. Scenes tend to be overwritten, dialog is overdone, acts bloated and so on. He said that you may have whole scenes that are unnecessary, or you might have an entire act that is unnecessary; for that matter, your entire script might be unnecessary. It may sound funny or harsh, but if you've ever worked as a studio script reader, it's no joke.

Good cause and effect is important because it helps the material move forward in a solid way without getting off on tangents that slow things down. When you put a cause in motion, you create an expectation in the audience, and when you deliver on it then you've got them. If you set a cause in motion and then wander off onto something else, the audience is expecting something and not getting it, and you've got a dead spot—a section that's flat dramatically.

So the trick is to ask only, what is the cause of something and not what came before it. Suppose your sister calls you one morning and practically orders you to buy a lottery ticket because she had a dream, and when you do so you win a ton of money. Now a number of things happen before you win the money, like you lose your car keys, buy some cigarettes and get a parking ticket, but the cause of your winning the lottery is that your sister made you do it. Reasoning backwards through a story in this way helps you find the main building blocks of the plot. You won't get trapped in the profusion of detail unnecessary to a clear telling of the story.

The ability to be freed from this profusion of unnecessary detail can help you enormously as a writer because you can then see the forest for the trees. It's so easy to get caught up in your story, and hard to step back and get some objectivity. This tool allows you do that because it strips your plot down in the same way that radically pruning a tree exposes the major branches. When you radically and correctly prune a tree, it improves the tree's health because its work is simplified and clarified. In terms of constructing a plot, this process can help you get at the essentials and feed them, rather than expending your energy in details that detract from the central work. Many screenwriters will have a beautifully written scene in a script that doesn't work. It's like having an ornately furnished room in a house that's falling down. You've got oak trim, gold leaf, carved marble and so on, but the house is caving in. It's necessary to get the big picture working first, and getting caught up in the too much detail can make that hard to do.

I use another analogy to drive this home: say that you're building a skyscraper and you're doing the steelwork, the girders and beams. One of your workers comes rushing up in a panic and says, "Hey boss, what about the wallpaper in the bathroom on the tenth floor?" You'd say, "We'll deal with that when it becomes necessary. You're only gumming up the works at this point." It's necessary at first to get the girders and beams up properly. That gives you the shape of the building, the superstructure, the support. Once you've got that, then it becomes necessary to put in floors and walls. Next comes the plumbing and wiring, then the sheetrock and the painting. Finally it's time for the wallpaper in the bathroom on the tenth floor. You do it as it becomes necessary. Dealing with details before they become necessary only clogs up the works.

This is all part of the habits of mind of a trained dramatist. Here we're thinking structurally, getting the macro up and running, and then gradually working our way down to more and more detail as it becomes necessary. Price said that you can take all the energy that goes into rewrites and put it into engineering the script properly before you write it. You will see more how to do this as we get further into this tool.

Let's look at reverse cause and effect for *The Godfather*. Remember that the Object is what we want to achieve by the end of the script and the Final Effect demonstrates this object with onscreen with real actors.

OBJECT OF PLOT: Michael emerges as the new Godfather, having taken out all his opposition, but loses his soul in the process.

FINAL EFFECT: Michael is recognized officially by his top men as the new Godfather, and the door closes on Kay.

IMMEDIATE CAUSE: Michael cleans up his own organization as he has Carlo and Tessio killed, then lies to Kay about it.

CAUSE: Michael eliminates his major enemies by killing the heads of the five families, plus Moe Green.

CAUSE: He gets proof that Barzini is out to kill him when Tessio proposes the meeting with Barzini at which Michael knows he will be assassinated.

CAUSE: Don Corleone warns Michael that Barzini will set up Michael's assassination by suggesting a meeting through someone that Michael absolutely trusts, and that he'll be assassinated at that meeting.

CAUSE: Michael throws down the gauntlet to Barzini when he goes after Moe Green in Las Vegas. Green says he has talked to Barzini and can cut a deal to keep the hotel and casino.

CAUSE: Vito makes Michael the head of the family, and Michael says that they are moving their operation to Las Vegas, where he will solve all their problems.

CAUSE: Vito calls a meeting of all the family heads in the country and makes a truce in which drugs will be distributed but controlled; he arranges for Michael's return from Italy.

CAUSE: Sonny is machine-gunned at the tollbooth when he goes to avenge his sister's beating by Carlo.

CAUSE: Sonny keeps the war with Tattaglia going in spite of Tom's advice to end it.

CAUSE: Michael goes to Italy to hide and Sonny takes the heat at home as war between the families breaks out.

CAUSE: Michael shoots Sollozzo and McCluskey at their arranged meeting.

CAUSE: Michael says that he will kill Sollozzo and McCluskey, and that they can connect McCluskey with drugs to reduce the heat from killing a cop.

CAUSE: Sollozzo requests a meeting with Michael; the family discusses how Sollozzo is invulnerable with a police captain as a bodyguard.

CAUSE: Sonny kills Bruno Tattaglia. (We don't see this onscreen)

CAUSE: Michael thwarts the second murder attempt on Don Corleone at the hospital.

CAUSE: The Godfather is shot in an assassination attempt, but not killed.

CAUSE: The Godfather turns down Sollozzo's request, saying drugs are a dirty business.

CAUSE: Sollozzo says that he needs political and police protection, together with big money to finance a major narcotics distribution network.

(Note: the cause of Sollozzo asking for help is not that they put the horse head in Jack Waltz's bed. It comes before it but it doesn't cause it.)

Essentially *The Godfather* has a conventional three act structure with an extended exposition that essentially adds an act up front. The marriage and the horse head are basically all exposition, setting up the story and who's who. The footage of the marriage turned out better than they expected and they used more than they planned, so the exposition runs act-length. If we subtract the opening, we can look at the regular three act script that starts with Sollozzo sitting down to the meeting. At the end of what we can call Act I then Michael executes Sollozzo and leaves for Italy. At the end of Act II we see Don Corleone making the truce about the drugs and arranging for Michael's return from Italy.

To continue with the explanation of the tool, once you've done reverse cause and effect for the script as a whole, then you break the script down into acts and begin the process of doing reverse cause and effect for Act I. At the act level you go back through reverse cause and effect again, but now in more detail. You're moving from the general to the specific. You say: *What is the object of the Act?* Where do you need to be by the end of the act? If it's a spy story, then perhaps the object of the act is that the spy has been betrayed by his partner and is now being hunted by the police. That's a good statement of the object of an act. Next you want to know: *What's the final effect that demonstrates the object onscreen with real actors?* The spy gets ambushed by his partner and just barely makes it out of the building, and now the local police are hot on his tail for a crime his partner framed him for. Next we want to know: *What's the cause of that?* You work your way backwards through the cause and effect, developing a little more detail than you did at the script-as-a-whole level. You keep referring back to the reverse cause and effect work you already did for the whole script. That's your map for expanding the story into a little more detail.

Once you've gone through the acts, then you divide each act into sequences and begin doing reverse cause and effect for each of them. Again, a sequence is a major section of an act, consisting of two to five scenes. Remember our example, in which an act consisted of the *planning sequence*, the *robbery sequence* and the *getaway sequence*.

So now you're saying: *What's the object of this sequence?* It's that they get the gang back together. Next: *What's the final effect that demonstrates the object onscreen with real actors?* The last guy reluctantly joins in. *What's the cause of that?* They tell him they'll hurt his daughter if he doesn't. *What's the cause of that?* He refuses. *What's the cause of that?* They land the second-to-last guy and go after the last guy. You keep going backwards through the sequence until you reach its beginning, at each point asking only what is the cause of the previous effect, not what came before it. You're still separating the necessary from the unnecessary, so that the sequence doesn't get larded with unnecessary stuff. It's still lean and mean and moves forward well. The bulk of the work is doing this for all the sequences.

Next you divide your sequences down into scenes and then you do reverse cause and effect for each scene. You're developing just a little more detail, but now you're down to final detail. But you've done it gradually, systematically, only developing the detail as it became necessary, so that you are never paralyzed by too much unnecessary detail.

It's important to recall what a scene really is. A scene is not a camera set up; a scene is a *complete unit of action*. For example, imagine a comedic mugging in which the victim is not at all intimidated. The mugger may grab the victim in the subway and demand all her money, but she laughs and shoves him down the stairs. The mugger races after her and accosts her again on the street. It's a new location and a new camera set up, but it's part of the same scene. He may now pretend to have a gun in his pocket but she reaches down and breaks his finger and breaks his glasses with her purse. She may climb in a cab and the mugger leaps in after her with a knife and goes after her but she uses her karate to take the knife off him, force him to hand over his wallet and then throw him out of the moving cab. The scene may end when she finds a huge wad of loot in his wallet and has the cabbie stop at an expensive shoe store. All of that was the mugging scene, even though it took place in several locations.

PROPOSITION – THE SECOND STEP IN SEQUENCE, PROPOSITION, PLOT

The next step of this process 'Sequence, Proposition, Plot' is *Proposition*. Here, we're using a more advanced form of the proposition that we worked with in tool number three, the Central Proposition. We're still setting up a potential fight, then touching off a fight to the finish, with the Central Dramatic Question arising in the mind of the audience. Here we are working with a *two-sided proposition* in which both the protagonist and the antagonist are each putting forth their own argument.

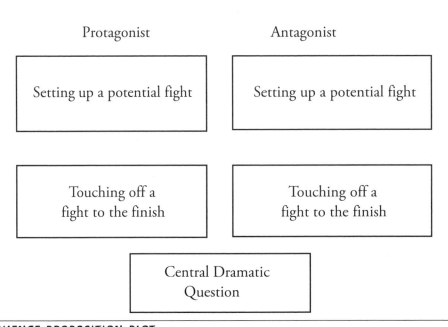

What we're doing is representing both sides of an argument, because there are actually two active arguments in it. If we're having an argument, then you have your argument and I have mine. There are literally two separate arguments. In formal logic this form is called the Double Proposition or Parallel Syllogisms. We're still setting up the fight and touching it off with a Central Dramatic Question arising, but it's now two-sided.

Before we see Proposition in its final form, there is one more thing to take into account and that is audience sympathy. Part of your job as a dramatist is to get the audience sympathy for the protagonist and to keep it. If our hero starts doing something despicable, we will usually stop rooting for him. You have to both secure and maintain the audience sympathy. If you're disinterested in the fate of a protagonist in a movie, then it isn't compelling.

One way to set up the potential fight and get the audience sympathy for the protagonist is for the antagonist to commit the *Initial Act of Aggression*. It's the evil land grabber coming in and saying, "We're taking over your ranch and there's nothing you can do about it." Once you become aware of this, you'll see it in films all the time. In *The Godfather*, the Initial Act of Aggression is the attempt on Don Corleone's life. This comes a bit late in the movie, but remember, the first part of that story is exposition. Once Sollozzo makes his pitch about drugs and gets turned down, the hit attempt on Vito comes very soon. This opens up the active conflict or opposition and allows the protagonist to retaliate with the sympathy of the audience. This is called *Justified Retaliation*. In *The Godfather*, it's when Michael executes Sollozzo in the restaurant. If you see this scene in a theatre with an audience, people will sometimes stand up and cheer because they feel Michael is so justified in putting that bullet through Sollozzo's forehead.

Next, in order to move the conflict toward the point of open warfare and *keep* the audience sympathy for the protagonist, we can have the antagonist aggravate the situation. This is called the *Aggravation of the Issue*. In *The Godfather*, it's when Barzini has Sonny killed and tries to kill Michael in Italy, but gets his bride. It is in response to this now that the protagonist can throw the first punch and literally start the fight to the finish. This response is called the *Precipitating Act*. To precipitate means to make something happen before it's ready to happen. You precipitate rain by seeding the clouds; you precipitate a psychosis by pushing somebody's buttons really hard, and you precipitate a fight by jumping in on someone, taking the fight to them. We tend to want our protagonist to be *proactive*, to be the maker of events, the one who takes the offensive, rather than the one who merely reacts. The protagonist is the doer of the Precipitating Act.

This can be a subtle distinction, because the protagonist is obviously reacting to the antagonist in various ways, but we're talking about going on the offensive—taking the conflict to a whole new level. A great example of someone precipitating a fight is in *Tootsie* when Dorothy shows up for the first time and Ron, the director, tells her she is not right for the part, not tough enough, and she then explodes on him. "How about if I knee your balls through the roof of your mouth? Is that tough enough for you?" She is not merely reacting to him—she is jumping right down his throat, escalating the fight massively. She acts precipitously.

In *The Godfather*, Michael touches off the fight to the finish when he declares war on Barzini by going after Moe Green. Now the fight to the finish has been touched off and this gives rise to the Central Dramatic Question. In *The Godfather* it is: Will Michael defeat Barzini and save the family, or will Barzini destroy the Corleones? Here's the Proposition laid out for *The Godfather*:

Protagonist	Antagonist
	Initial Act of Aggression
	Sollozzo (acting for Barzini) tries to assassinate Don Corleone.
Justified Retaliation	
Michael executes Sollozzo in the restaurant.	
	Aggravation of the Issue
	Barzini has Sonny killed and tries to kill Michael, but kills his Sicilian bride instead.
Precipitating Act	
Michael declares war on Barzini by going after Moe Green.	

Central Dramatic Question

Will Michael defeat Barzini and save the family,
or will Barzini destroy the Corleones?

Here we have set up the potential fight, then touched off the fight to the finish and given rise to the Central Dramatic Question. Plus, all of this directs the audience's sympathy. Proposition will become increasingly transparent with further examples as well as the utilization of it in the second half of this book where I develop the sample script.

THE THIRD STEP IN THIS PROCESS, KNOWN AS 'PLOT'

The third part of Sequence, Proposition, Plot—called 'Plot'—answers the Central Dramatic Question and completes the action, essentially wrapping up the plot. Here again we need to stop and clarify term 'Plot' because it has a specialized definition. So far with Sequence we reasoned backwards through the story, tying it together with cause and effect; then with Proposition we set up a two-sided conflict and touched it off, leaving it hanging in the form of a question. Now with the third section, which Price called 'Plot' we *answer the question and complete the action*, thereby wrapping up the plot of the movie.

In other words, the fight to the finish is touched off at the two-thirds or three-quarters point and now, this is the last part of the movie, continuing on from the point of unresolved conflict (the Central Dramatic Question) through to the end. And we already know the ending because we've done it with reverse cause and effect. As defined by Price, 'Plot,' within the context of Sequence, Proposition, Plot, is "the steps necessarily taken to get from the central dramatic question to the pre-established ending."

In this diagram, the first X sets up the potential fight (Initial Act of Aggression and Justified Retaliation) and the second X touches off the fight to the finish (Aggravation of the Issue and Precipitating Act). The section after the fight to the finish starts, which is indicated by + marks, is 'Plot.'

So if we're talking about your story, your script idea, then we're using the word 'plot' in its conventional sense: "Did you figure out the plot of your new screenplay?" If we're talking about Sequence, Proposition, Plot and we're referring to the steps that answer the Central Dramatic Question and complete the action, then we use the specialized term, 'Plot,' signified in this book with a capital 'P.' The other distinction is that when I refer to 'Plot' it's just Plot; when I'm referring to plot it's *the plot*.

In Plot, we could just list the steps that answer the question and complete the action, but we can continue on in this two-sided format we've been using for the proposition. This will help you map out the rest of the conflict, through the ending. It also helps give you what is known as Balanced Opposition, an even mix of the back and forth between the protagonist and the antagonist.

THE THIRD STEP, 'PLOT,' WHICH WRAPS UP *THE GODFATHER*

Let's look at the major events that happen once Michael makes his move into Vegas and goes after Moe Green. Note that at the point of the Precipitating Act, the fight to the finish *has only just started* and we don't know how it's going to turn out. Therefore the steps that come in this section called 'Plot' represent most of the fight to the finish itself, since prior to it only the 'first punch' has been thrown and the Central Dramatic Question has been raised.

CENTRAL DRAMATIC QUESTION
Will Michael destroy Barzini and save the family,
or will Barzini destroy the Corleones?

PROTAGONIST	ANTAGONIST
	Moe Green lashes out and says that Barzini chased them out of New York. He says he can make a deal with Barzini, and keep his hotel and casino.
Vito warns Michael that Barzini will send someone that Michael absolutely trusts to call a meeting, and that Michael will be assassinated at that meeting. Michael is on his guard.	
	Tessio emerges as Barzini's agent when he suggests the meeting on his territory. He's the traitor.
Michael kills all his enemies in one fell swoop and becomes the Godfather.	

Now let's put it all together.

SEQUENCE, PROPOSITION, PLOT FOR *THE GODFATHER*

OBJECT OF PLOT: Michael emerges as the new Godfather, having taken out all his opposition, but loses his soul in the process.

FINAL EFFECT: Michael is recognized officially by his top men as the new Godfather, and the door closes on Kay.

IMMEDIATE CAUSE: Michael cleans up his own organization as he has Carlo and Tessio killed, then lies to Kay about it.

CAUSE: Michael eliminates his major enemies by killing the heads of the five families, plus Moe Green.

CAUSE: He gets proof that Barzini is out to kill him when Tessio proposes the meeting with Barzini at which Michael knows he will be assassinated.

CAUSE: Don Corleone warns Michael that Barzini will set up Michael's assassination by suggesting a meeting through someone that Michael absolutely trusts, and that he'll be assassinated at that meeting.

CAUSE: Michael throws down the gauntlet to Barzini when he goes after Moe Green in Las Vegas. Green says he has talked to Barzini and can cut a deal to keep the hotel and casino.

CAUSE: Vito makes Michael the head of the family, and Michael says that they are moving their operation to Las Vegas, where he will solve all their problems.

CAUSE: Vito calls a meeting of all the family heads in the country and makes a truce in which drugs will be distributed but controlled; he arranges for Michael's return from Italy.

CAUSE: Sonny is machine-gunned at the tollbooth when he goes to avenge his sister's beating by Carlo.

CAUSE: Sonny keeps the war with Tattaglia going in spite of Tom's advice.

CAUSE: Michael goes to Italy to hide and Sonny takes the heat at home as war between the families breaks out.

CAUSE: Michael shoots Sollozzo and McCluskey at their arranged meeting.

CAUSE: Michael says that he will kill Sollozzo and McCluskey, and that they can connect McCluskey with drugs to reduce the heat from killing a cop.

CAUSE: Sollozzo requests a meeting with Michael; the family discusses how Sollozzo is invulnerable with a police captain as a bodyguard.

CAUSE: Sonny kills Bruno Tattaglia. (We don't see this onscreen)

CAUSE: Michael thwarts the second murder attempt on Don Corleone at the hospital.

CAUSE: The Godfather is shot in an assassination attempt, but not killed.

CAUSE: The Godfather turns down Sollozzo's request, saying drugs are a dirty business.

CAUSE: Sollozzo says that he needs political and police protection, together with big money to finance a major narcotics distribution network.

CAUSE: Sollozzo says that he needs political and police protection, plus big money to finance a major narcotics distribution network.

PROTAGONIST	ANTAGONIST
	INITIAL ACT OF AGGRESSSION When Sollozzo is refused by the Godfather, he has an assassination attempt made on the Don.
JUSTIFIED RETALITATION When Sollozzo sets up a meeting, Michael has a weapon snuck in and he kills Sollozzo and McCluskey.	
	AGGRAVATION OF THE ISSUE Barzini attempts to kill Michael in Sicily but kills his wife. Sonny is also assassinated.
PRECIPITATING ACT Michael throws down the gauntlet at Barzini when he tells Moe Green that he wants to take over the hotel and casino that they co-own.	

CENTRAL DRAMATIC QUESTION
Will Michael destroy Barzini and save the family,
or will Barzini destroy the Corleones?
[From here down is 'Plot']

	Moe Green lashes out and says that Barzini chased them out of New York. He says he can make a deal with Barzini that lets keep his hotel and casino.
Vito warns Michael that Barzini will send someone that Michael absolutely trusts to call a meeting, and that Michael will be assassinated at that meeting. Michael is on his guard.	
	Tessio emerges as Barzini's agent when he suggests the meeting on his territory. He's the traitor.
Michael kills all his enemies in one fell swoop and becomes the Godfather.	

What we're doing here is, first, tightening the script by doing reverse cause and effect and then dramatizing it by throwing it into the form of an unresolved conflict which gets the audience on the edge of their seat, and then wrapping it up, completing the story.

That explains Sequence, Proposition, Plot, but now let's see how you actually use it. First you apply it to the script as a whole, making the whole plot tight and dramatic. Next you divide the script into acts and apply Sequence, Proposition, Plot to each act. Now you are going from the general to the particular, developing a little more detail as it becomes necessary. As you do reverse cause and effect for Act I you lay in a little more detail. Then we do Proposition, Plot for the act, in which we set up a potential fight, touch off a fight to the finish, giving rise to a dramatic question in the mind of the audience, and then complete the action with the step called 'Plot.' So there's a point two-thirds or three-quarters of the way through the act that gets the audience on the edge of their seats. This helps render Act I itself dramatic. We're creating Dramatic Action by turning Story into Drama, incorporating conflict into the structure of the Act I.

Next we do Sequence, Proposition, Plot to Act II. Again, we work our way backwards through the cause and effect of the act, then put it into the form of the two-sided conflict, getting the audience on the edge of their seat, and then wrapping it up with 'Plot.' This makes Act II tight and dramatic, helping to cure a dead second act. After Act II, you then apply Sequence, Proposition, Plot to Act III.

After dividing the acts into sequences, you do Sequence, Proposition, Plot for each sequence. You take the opening sequence and say, "What's the Object of this sequence?" then "What's the Final Effect that demonstrates this Object onscreen with real actors?" and so on. Now it becomes necessary to develop yet a little more detail than you had at the act level. Next you do Proposition, Plot, making this particular sequence tight and dramatic in and of itself. You don't want to revert to mere Story. You don't want the sequence to be flat dramatically. You do this for all the sequences in the script, make them each solid and compelling. This is a lot of work, but so are fifteen rewrites. Remember, you can take all the energy that goes into rewrites and engineer your script properly before you write it. Remember David Mamet's quote about taking the time to design the chair properly before you glue it together.

Next divide the sequences into scenes and apply Sequence, Proposition, Plot to Scene 1. Then you write the dialog. At the scene level you're doing reverse cause and effect at yet a little more detail, but now you're down to final detail. You're really figuring out the detailed mechanics of precisely what happens in the scene. You have gradually moved from the general to the specific. All the work you've done for all the levels of the script and on the scene itself helps dramatize the scene. Conflict and tension fill the scene, rendering it gripping, actable and dramatically engaging. Then do Sequence, Proposition, Plot for the next scene, and write the dialog for it.

It's really important for each scene to work dramatically because the scenes are, in one sense, the only thing that the audience really interacts with. It's just like the Michelin Tires commercial in which they say that the little square section of tire that touches the road is the only contact your car has with the road, so you should buy the best tires available. The scene is the only part of the script that the audience actually interacts with. Movies are one scene and then the next. During the movie the audience is not sitting there asking, "Wow, did you check out the second act structure?" No, they don't see the underlying structure, anymore than you see the steel girders in a finished skyscraper. This underlying structure is absolutely crucial, but all that is seen is the final detail—the sheetrock, the paint and the trim.

Constructing your script using Sequence, Proposition, Plot creates Unity of Action. Each scene is its own coherent dramatic unit and is part of a sequence, which is in and of itself coherent and compelling. Each sequence moves the plot forward and is part of an act, which is in itself tight and dramatic. Each act is a working part of the whole script, which, itself, is coherent and dramatic. Continuous, coherent and compelling Dramatic Action is the name of the game. Price in *The Analysis of Play Construction and Dramatic Principle* puts it this way:

> You must have perceived by this time that a law of Unity runs through a play, each principle in a play and each part of a play being distinct in itself, but with relations to the other principles and parts. At the very outset the Theme demanded Unity. You considered the Proposition and saw that it must be ONE thing, one definite thing, so that when asked what your play is about you could reply briefly and would not wander off into a multitude of Details. You saw that each act was about one thing, each scene about one thing, and that each step was a development toward one given end. Following this out, you have seen that a play is a Unit made up of other Units. (p. 146)

Further examples follow to make all this more tangible. I've done Sequence, Proposition, Plot for an act in *The Godfather*, as well as for a sequence and a scene. As I said, *The Godfather* is a conventional three act structure with an act-length exposition up front, so what I'm calling Act II here starts with Sollozzo coming in asking for help. At the act level, a little more detail is let in as we move from the general to the particular. Proposition, Plot focuses on the conflict within the act, and there's plenty. It's a very dramatic act and the audience is rapt. Here's a dramaturgic x-ray that helps show why:

SEQUENCE, PROPOSITION, PLOT FOR ACT II OF *THE GODFATHER*

OBJECT OF THE ACT: Michael has killed his father's attacker and is dragged into the family business.

FINAL EFFECT: Michael flees the country and goes into hiding in Sicily.

CAUSE: He murders Sollozzo and McCluskey.

CAUSE: Sonny gets the secret location of the meeting and they plant a gun there.

CAUSE: Michael says he'll kill Sollozzo and McCluskey and that they can use their newspaper people to say McCluskey was a crooked cop.

CAUSE: Sollozzo wants a meeting with Michael.

CAUSE: Sonny assassinates Bruno Tattaglia.

CAUSE: Michael foils a second attempt on his father's life at the hospital and McCluskey breaks his jaw.

CAUSE: Michael discovers there are no guards on his father.

CAUSE: Don Corleone survives the assassination attempt.

CAUSE: He is shot on the street with Fredo guarding him.

CAUSE: He turns down Sollozzo's offer.

CAUSE: Sollozzo wants him to bankroll and protect a major narcotics distribution network.

PROTAGONIST	ANTAGONIST
	INITIAL ACT OF AGGRESSION Sollozzo has Vito shot for refusing his narcotics distribution offer.
JUSTIFIED RETALIATION Sonny has Pauly killed for selling out the Godfather when he should have been guarding him.	
	AGGRAVATION OF THE ISSUE Sollozzo, through McCluskey, is making another attempt on Vito at the hospital.
PRECIPITATING ACT Michael discovers the second attempt in the making at the hospital and acts to prevent it.	

CENTRAL DRAMATIC QUESTION
Will Michael save his father, or will Sollozzo
succeed in his attempt to have Vito killed?
[From here down is 'Plot']

	Captain McCluskey breaks Michael's jaw.
Sonny has Bruno Tattaglia assassinated.	
	Sollozzo proposes a meeting with Michael to work out the situation.
Michael has a weapon hidden at the meeting place and kills Sollozzo and McCluskey there.	

Now let's do Sequence, Proposition, Plot for a sequence within Act II. Notice that we're including yet a little more detail in reverse cause and effect as it becomes necessary.

SEQUENCE, PROPOSITION, PLOT FOR ACT II, SEQ. 3 OF *THE GODFATHER*

OBJECT OF THE SEQUENCE: Michael is drawn into the conflict and is really solid.

FINAL EFFECT: McCluskey breaks Michael's jaw.

CAUSE: Michael asks McCluskey how much the Turk is paying him to set up his father.

CAUSE: Captain McCluskey orders Michael to leave.

CAUSE: The hit squad leaves and the police show up.

CAUSE: Michael and Enzo scare the hit squad off when they guard the hospital front.

CAUSE: Enzo arrives and Mike enlists his aid.

CAUSE: Michael moves Vito into another room.

CAUSE: Michael discovers that no one is guarding Vito.

PROTAGONIST	ANTAGONIST
	INITIAL ACT OF AGGRESSION Michael discovers that the guards have been pulled off of his father at the hospital.
JUSTIFIED RETALIATION Michael calls Sonny for help and moves Vito to another room. He enlists Enzo's help in guarding his father.	
	AGGRAVATION OF THE ISSUE A car with the hit squad arrives at the hospital.
PRECIPITATING ACT Mike and Enzo face the hit squad down by pretending to have guns, trying to scare them off.	

CENTRAL DRAMATIC QUESTION
Will Michael scare the car of killers away or
will they call Michael's bluff and kill them all?
[From here down is 'Plot']

	The police arrive and McCluskey tells his men to lock Michael up.
Michael asks him how much the Turk is paying him to set up his father.	
	McCluskey breaks Michael's jaw.
Tom arrives with private detectives as guards for Vito and helps Michael.	

Now we do Sequence, Proposition, Plot for a scene within the sequence. Here we're down to final detail, and if you were writing this scene you would have a tight dramatic map from which to work. You will see this writing process in action later in this book where I utilize Sequence, Proposition, Plot on the script that I develop.

SEQUENCE, PROPOSITION, PLOT FOR ACT II, SEQ. 3, SC. 3 OF *THE GODFATHER*

OBJECT OF THE SCENE: Michael stops Captain McCluskey from killing his father.

FINAL EFFECT: McCluskey calls off his men and leaves, furious.

IMMEDIATE CAUSE: Tom tells McCluskey that he's an attorney for the Corleones and that these men are private detectives hired to protect Vito. He warns McCluskey that if he interferes he will have to appear before a judge in the morning to show cause.

CAUSE: Michael is reeling from the punch when Tom Hagen shows up with a car full of Corleone guys.

CAUSE: McCluskey slugs Michael in the jaw as hard as he can.

CAUSE: Michael demands to know what Sollozzo is paying him to kill his father.

CAUSE: McCluskey orders his man to arrest Michael.

CAUSE: Michael refuses to leave until McCluskey has some guards protect his father.

CAUSE: McCluskey orders Michael to get out of the hospital and stay out.

CAUSE: Michael demands to know where the men guarding his father went.

CAUSE: Police cars show up. McCluskey gets out of the car and accosts Michael.

PROTAGONIST	ANTAGONIST
	INITIAL ACT OF AGGRESSION McCluskey shows up and orders Michael to leave the hospital and not come back.
JUSTIFIED RETALITATION Michael says he's not leaving until McCluskey puts some guards on his father.	
	AGGRAVATION OF THE ISSUE McCluskey tells his man to arrest Michael.
PRECIPITATING ACT Michael asks McCluskey what Sollozzo is paying him to set up his father.	

CENTRAL DRAMATIC QUESTION
Will Michael stop McCluskey from killing his father
or will McCluskey manage to kill Don Corleone?
[From here down is 'Plot']

	McCluskey slugs Michael in the jaw as hard as he can.
Tom shows up with some Corleone men and takes control of Don Corleone's security, threatening McCluskey with legal action.	
	McCluskey is furious and is forced to abandon his assassination attempt.
Michael is taken away safely and the Corleone's men are protecting the don.	

GETTING STARTED
USING SEQUENCE, PROPOSITION, PLOT
ON YOUR OWN SCRIPT

1. Start by stating the Object of your script. The Object should be stated simply and clearly. It's the mark you're shooting for, the point on the horizon that you're trying to reach. If it's for an act, then it's the point in the plot that you have to get to by the end of the act. (The Object of Act II is that Michael has executed Sollozzo and fled to Italy.)

2. What's the Final Effect that demonstrates the Object onscreen with real actors? The Object is what you want to achieve, now you have to stage it, giving real actions to real actors.

3. What is Immediate Cause of the Final Effect? Not what comes before it, but what *causes* it. When you're doing it for the whole script, make sure you're not getting into too much detail. When you get to the second half of the book, you'll get more experience with Sequence, Proposition, Plot because I'll be doing it a lot.

4. Keep working backwards and *only look for the cause* of a given effect. You're working to separate the necessary from the unnecessary. You'll be surprised at the things that don't make it into your first pass. These things will be picked up on successive passes. Also, when you're done, there will be story elements that never became necessary and they can be left out of the script. This will make the script lean and mean. For instance, when you're done making a suit, there is cloth left on the floor.

5. As you do reverse cause and effect for the acts, then the sequences and then the scenes, add in *only a little more detail* as it becomes necessary. Imagine that you're gradually filling in a weave. Remember you're working from the general to the specific.

6. In doing Proposition, the Initial Act of Aggression doesn't have to be at the very beginning of the script. Remember in our proportion map that the set up of the potential fight often comes a third of the way into the script. It can certainly come earlier, but there's usually some exposition before the conflict gets rolling.

7. Does your protagonist retaliate? This helps create a proactive protagonist. If it isn't there, the tool will suggest it, and you create it, enhancing the act or sequence dramatically.

8. Remember that the Aggravation of the Issue will tend to be out at the two-thirds or three-quarter point. This is true for the whole script, for each act, and for the sequence or scene. This sense of proportion is an important habit of mind to acquire as a trained dramatist.

9. The Precipitating Act should be a strong action by the protagonist that really starts the fight to the finish, whether it's for the whole script, an act, a sequence, or a scene. It will get the audience on the edge of their seat in each, helping turn Story into Drama.

10. The Central Dramatic Question will be different for each act, for each sequence and for each scene. Be in touch with the question that's really in the mind of the audience for each of them.

11. Remember that the section labeled 'Plot' is the continuation of the action, a continuation of the fight that has just started in the Precipitating Act. Plot answers the Central Dramatic Question, completes the action and wraps up the plot.

12. In doing Proposition, write out the labels, *Initial Act of Aggression, Justified Retaliation, Aggravation of the Issue, Precipitating Act* and *Central Dramatic Question*. This will help keep you on track so you're not just filling in blocks of action, but really directing the action, the conflict and the audience sympathy.

13. Do Sequence, Proposition, Plot for *Training Day*. That will give you a great workout with this tool. It shouldn't be too hard to do, but it will take all your skills and will be excellent practice. If you are stumped, wait until you've finished the whole book and worked your way through the full development of the script that I build here. In the last section I do a full demonstration of Sequence, Proposition, Plot. Study that entire second half of the book and then come back to this exercise.

12
UTILIZING DILEMMA
IN CREATING A SCREENPLAY

Now let's actually use dilemma on a screenplay that we develop from square one. We'll start with a raw idea for a movie and create, develop and structure it, using all the tools that I've explained. This necessitates a certain amount of brainstorming so I'll be laying down a trail of notes as part of the process. Please be aware that because I am truly starting from scratch, this process will be a detailed and full exploration of story possibilities, as well as a complete use of the tools, so it will not be quick or simple. This is an original screenplay that I am *actually* writing, so I'm not cutting corners or doing it only for demonstration purposes. It may be dense going for you, the reader, but it will definitely provide a thorough look at my process. I'll be imagining you looking over my shoulder, anticipating your questions and pointing out to you detailed uses of the tools presented in the first half of this book. So I urge you to forge ahead but know you are signing on for some hard work, the real work of building a movie from scratch. I guarantee you will learn a lot and hope that the process is also a fun read.

At its most basic, I want to do a perfect crime plot with a twist, with the promise of great wealth but also the threat of significant danger. I played with some possibilities and came up with this idea: *A reformed pathological liar and kleptomaniac with two strikes against him gets blackmailed into a revenge-oriented perfect crime by his crazy former cellmate, to whom he owes his life.* I see this told in the style of Elmore Leonard (*Out of Sight*, *Get Shorty*), fun, wacky and dangerous.

This is obviously just a raw idea and needs so much in order to become a screenplay. A premise is the simple explanation of a movie idea, like "three nuns accidentally rob a bank, get stuck hiding out in the criminal underground and end up taking down a huge crime lord." All I've got now is an intriguing premise—but a bad premise will not make a good movie. You should always be on the lookout for that *rare great premise*—the one that a producer would kill for. For instance, look at the premise of *Back to the Future*: A kid accidentally goes back to 1955 in a mad scientist's time machine where his mother falls in love with him, preventing his parents' marriage and therefore his own creation, so he has to scramble to make his parents fall in love before he ceases to exist, all the while trying to get back to the future.

Here is how I would state the premise of this script if I was pitching it to a studio: *a rollicking thriller about a reformed pathological liar whose former cellmate blackmails him into one last wild bender that's a lethal cross between a perfect crime and revenge.*

So here we're looking at someone who used to be a pathological liar and a kleptomaniac. Let's call him Cutter, and let's say he's the best liar anyone can imagine, as well as a thief par excellence. He's got two strikes against him so that a third conviction will send him back to the pen for life. We are also saying that he's reformed. So let's create a wife, Margarita, to whom he has vowed that he will never lie or steal again. And he's been keeping his word. Into his nice reformed world comes his former cellmate, a colorful, dangerous rogue who saved Cutter's life in prison. Let's call him Apollo. (I came up with this name by looking through *Final Draft's* name database, which is amazing.) Apollo says he has the chance to take down a heinous villain who we'll call St. Nick. He's the guy who betrayed and murdered Cutter and Apollo's closest friend in prison, who we'll call Frenchy. Frenchy got himself off heroin, turned his life around while in jail and became a genuinely good person, loved by everyone. But when Frenchy got out, St. Nick sunk his hooks into him and completely destroyed his life by using him in the execution of a crime. Apollo has a perfect opportunity to get mega-revenge on St. Nick and make him and Cutter rich for life, but he needs Cutter's special skills in the lying and stealing department.

Can you see that this idea has a dilemma inherent in it? He's damned if he does and damned if he doesn't. Let's isolate this dilemma, articulate its components and then maximize it. So at the most basic, *it's unacceptable for Cutter to get involved in this gig because he has sworn off crime, and it's equally unacceptable to not get involved because he's being blackmailed, plus he'd miss the chance to take out the monster who betrayed and killed a great friend.* It's unacceptable to get involved because it would draw him back into his addiction to lying and stealing, threaten to destroy his marriage, and pull him into a deadly game against a man, St. Nick, who is catastrophically dangerous. But we're also talking about Cutter hating St. Nick so much—unbelievably brutally hating him— and loving Frenchy so much that he is raging for revenge and would give anything for a chance to ruin St. Nick in the worst way. If the pull is *equal* in both directions, then he will short circuit like Robbie the Robot, unable to send a command in either direction.

Remember, the more magnitude the dilemma has, the higher the dramatic tension. Clearly we need to build up the importance of his marriage, his new straight life and his profound need to stay in this world of solidity, goodness, sobriety, sanity and happiness. We need to make sure that St. Nick is a true monster and the need to take him down is absolutely critical. The more Cutter is totally justified in destroying him, then the more we will connect with that half of his dilemma—that it's unacceptable to *not* do it. And the more we see how much Cutter's promise to his new wife means to him, as well as how dangerous St. Nick is, the more we substantiate the other half of his dilemma—that it's equally unacceptable to go ahead with it. He's damned if he does and damned if he doesn't. This should be a *ferocious* tug of war, a high stakes debate that not only traps Cutter, but draws us in as well. And even if it's a comedy, it should be high stakes for our protagonist. In other words, it can be funny for us, but will usually be quite serious for our protagonist.

Let's start with some possible reasons why Cutter cannot get involved with his former cellmate's plan. If Cutter used to be a pathological liar and a kleptomaniac, then he probably had real problems. He's done serious time, has two strikes against him and cannot afford another fall—that would mean life in prison. Let's say that when he got out of prison he fell in love with a deeply religious woman who got him on the straight and narrow. He made a solemn vow to never lie or steal again and has lived up to his word. He has a nice life and is a decent, hardworking model citizen, possibly even a pillar of his community. Do we want to give him children? That can certainly give him more reasons to not get involved with Apollo.

What if Cutter has a son (let's call him Mischa) by his first marriage, but missed most of his childhood because was in prison. Cutter's ex-wife has forbidden Mischa to be around his father, but because Mischa has just turned 18, he is now spending a lot of time with Cutter. What if Mischa is a troubled youth, drifting toward criminality, and Cutter has to be a good example to steer him right? This can complicate Cutter's dilemma. If Cutter gets caught and goes to jail again, then Mischa could easily end up getting into a life of crime.

It could be that Mischa has heard rumors of some of the wild things Cutter used to do and he might idolize his cool dad and want to be just like him. But Cutter would downplay all that and tell him it was bad and crazy and destructive. Mischa would probably be swayed, but is also fascinated and inspired by the snippets of stories he has gleaned over the years. His son is clearly hanging in the balance and Cutter is determined to pull him into a solid good life and not allow him to drift into the dissolute life.

This can be complicated by the fact that Mischa has the 'gift.' He can lie like nobody's business and Cutter knows that this energy and brainpower can be channeled into something good. All this could be complicated by Apollo telling Mischa some stories about his father's legendary exploits, like the time Cutter stole the Rolling Stones' limousine—with them in it and went on a three-day, five-state bender in which they did twenty six million dollars worth of damage, got 116 people arrested, five groupies pregnant, forced two people to flee the country and it ended up with the mayor of a Midwestern city quitting his job and running off with the Stones to be Keith Richards' assistant guitar tech. The Stones still claim that it was the single wildest party they've ever been to. Apollo telling this to Mischa can be part of how he blackmails Cutter to work for him—you play ball with me or I'll tell him the *really* crazy stuff.

Cutter's finally got the life he dreamed about for years in prison. He senses that, like an alcoholic, if he gets started lying and stealing again, it will explode into full-fledged addiction. Another huge factor is that the mark, St. Nick is extremely dangerous and vengeful, and to go after him is suicidal. The word among the criminal element on St. Nick is that at one point he got caught cheating at the racetrack in a small town with a racehorse he owned and was disqualified. To get even he set up a fake chemical spill that killed the entire town on Christmas Eve, and then out of pure vindictiveness he went from house to house robbing them, even opening presents and taking things he fancied. He was never caught for it, but it's a legend in the underworld. This is how he came by the nickname St. Nick. Getting caught crossing him will get your entire family killed, probably your whole neighborhood. He's a treacherous twisted monster, but is also immensely perceptive, reads people well and has a genius IQ.

Now let's go into more depth about why Cutter cannot walk away from Apollo's job. I want him foaming at the mouth to get even with St. Nick. Why? What are some of the worst things he could have done? We said he betrayed and killed one of Cutter's best friends, but how can we make that *really* bad? After all, if Frenchy was a crook and got killed doing a crime by another crook, why is the audience going to get all bent out of shape over that? We're saying that Frenchy had turned his life around in prison and that he helped everybody in there and was universally loved. This has to be very strongly established because we need to feel the force of Cutter's drive for revenge, and the stronger we feel it, the more we connect to Cutter and his dilemma. Are there more reasons why Cutter might hate St. Nick? What are the worst things that St. Nick could have done? I'm assuming that he hasn't done anything in person to Cutter because then Apollo wouldn't be able to use him on the inside since Cutter would be recognized. At this point I'm not sure what else there could be, but I want more and I'll be on the lookout for it. Essentially I'm picturing St. Nick as a rabid dog in the neighborhood that needs to be shot.

What are some possibilities for a perfect crime against St. Nick? If what gets robbed is illegal, then he can't report it (although he may not go to the police for anything). But then he'd still come after Cutter and Apollo. What about if St. Nick thinks he sees the stolen material destroyed in an accident, and thus believes it wasn't gotten away with? Similarly, if he thinks the perpetrators are dead, or believes he sees them die, then he won't pursue it. Maybe he's got a huge deal brewing and is putting most of his assets on the line for a short period, leaving him vulnerable. Let's say St. Nick wants to go legitimate, maybe buy a bank. He'd have to put up his ill-gotten gains—converted into legitimate assets—and that exposes him to the pesky formalities of operating legally and by the book.

That would mean that there would be money coming in from off-shore accounts; drug money in the form of cash, maybe diamonds, gold, bonds and real estate. All of this could be sold or used as collateral or put in escrow, making it vulnerable. This would be a substantial transition in which St. Nick would be at genuine risk. The assets would have to come out of hiding and the protagonists could destroy him when he's in this vulnerable state. What if St. Nick's wife has a lot of his assets in her name to keep them protected? What if she could be turned against St. Nick, or manipulated, or robbed?

Presumably Apollo—Cutter's old cellmate—has found out about this opportunity, has set a plan in motion and needs Cutter for a specialized job. Maybe as a bank examiner with a complete false identity, fake history and so on. This can get him access to the funds that St. Nick has to deposit in escrow to fulfill legal obligations of buying a bank. *This gives us something specific with which to construct a plot.* It makes use of his lying abilities and puts him in an active position to be able to help take down St. Nick. He would be the inside man, working in a position that would require good lying skills and steady nerves. It also puts him face to face with St. Nick, and that will make for plenty of dramatic tension.

As you work with dilemma, you'll find that you can go very deep into it and either discover or create many plot and character possibilities. You'll find that after you've spent a great deal of time thinking about your protagonist's dilemma you will come to understand it fully. It can be highly useful to write a detailed essay about the dilemma at that point. Another way to explore Cutter's dilemma is to write about it from Cutter's point of view. You can also write about it from Apollo's point of view, since he helped created this dilemma and will be busy taking advantage of it. The antagonist doesn't always create the dilemma, but will always be there to exploit it.

GOING TO THE 36 DRAMATIC SITUATIONS FOR IDEAS

The 36 dramatic situations is a remarkable brainstorming tool and it is especially useful at this point in the development of a screenplay. I have a raw idea that I'm scrambling to build. It needs everything. I like what I've got, but it's still totally unformed in so many ways. It is absolutely wide open, which is really fun, but it's also daunting. Part of my process is to go through the 36 dramatic situations to see what it triggers. For me it's like pouring gasoline on a fire—it makes *everything* flare up. The 36 dramatic situations is a complete spectrum of dramatic elements and human emotional conflicts, and it opens up unexpected avenues and dimensions. I get like a kid in a candy store with them.

So now stop reading this chapter and skip ahead five chapters to *Utilizing the 36 Dramatic Situations* to follow what I did at this point in the development of the script. What follows in the rest of this chapter on *Utilizing the Dilemma* contains ideas from brainstorming with the 36 dramatic situations. Speaking of brainstorming, you should also read the chapter on *Utilizing Research and Brainstorming* because as soon as I got the idea for this script I was casting around for useful research and I was exploding with ideas, some of which are represented in that chapter. For clarity of presentation, I teach the four tools in a certain order, but as you gain a mastery of the tools you'll find yourself skipping around to them as needed.

CONTINUE FROM HERE WHEN YOU COME BACK

As you saw, one of the things that I hit upon in those chapters is that I want to make Apollo a really wild character—very unpredictable and dangerous, but extremely fun and crazy. It created a lot of new possibilities that can enhance Cutter's dilemma quite a bit. Because Apollo is so unpredictable and mischievous, it makes Cutter that much more damned if he gets involved with him. Because Apollo is such an adventurer and a wildly free person, it makes Cutter that much more damned if he doesn't join in (this is intended to add a new layer to the dilemma that's already there, not displace it).

But Cutter also knows that nothing is what it seems with Apollo; that there's always something going on behind the scenes; that you always get more than you bargained for; that there is *always* trouble involved. He knows things will get out of control; that crazy complications will ensue; that the unsavory characters Apollo attracts will draw more problems in as well. He knows that Apollo will stop at nothing to win and sees it all as a test, a gamble, a pissing contest with the fates. He also knows that Apollo will drag him back into lying his head off, stealing, cheating, running, hiding, lying to cover the lies, and all the craziness of The Life. And yet he also sees Apollo as an irresistible urge, a breath of fresh air into what he is beginning to feel is a stultifying existence, proscribed by the limits that Cutter has imposed on himself to keep his pledge. He shouldn't, but he does begin to think of Apollo as someone who really could pull off a perfect crime on St. Nick for revenge. He knows that it will be an adventure that he wouldn't miss for worlds. It brings him back to life, draws him out of the dormant state that he's put himself in to survive his self-imposed exile.

A good way to work with dilemma is to represent the two equally unacceptable alternatives in a two-sided chart. Why is Cutter damned if he goes along with Apollo and he's damned if he doesn't? Let's see.

CAN'T GO ALONG WITH IT	CAN'T REFUSE IT
Could lose his freedom	Could miss out on revenge
Family duties	Debt to an old friend
Loyalty	Compulsion
It's dangerous	It's a call to adventure
Fear that it will wreck his life	Afraid that he'll miss big money
Two strikes, one more is life in prison	Can't let St. Nick get away with it
Apollo will screw things up	He owes his life to Apollo
Can't break his vow to his wife	Can't resist his instincts
He can't go back to his old ways	He's suffocating in his new life
He's proud of his new life	His pride is hurt by low-end job
The danger is freakily scary	The danger is intoxicating
It won't be as simple as Apollo claims	It will be unpredictable and fun
His lying addiction will reactivate	He'll die of boredom if he stays
Apollo is crazy	Apollo is wild and free

St. Nick is catastrophically dangerous	St. Nick must be taken out
He could easily die on this job	St. Nick killed his close friend
His family needs him badly	Being rich for life would help
Common sense	Adventurous instinct
He's becoming sane in his new life	He's going crazy with boredom
He loves his wife	He took pride in being the best
He fears his lying addiction	He craves the wide-open freedom
He can accomplish a lot if he stays	He could really destroy St. Nick
He can't be a bad example to his son	Son sees him as a loser and a wimp
The community needs him	St. Nick's removal is public service
His new religion makes his life work	Going after St. Nick is a crusade
He's got enough money to get by	More money would help marriage
He can make this life work	Possibile family money crisis
Life is predictable	It's all too predictable
He's a domestic animal	He's a wild animal
This will destroy him	This will create him
The plan is too free-floating	The challenge is inspiring
Failure would be catastrophic	The revenge would be delicious
Apollo will complicate things hugely	Apollo's a genius who can do it
Failure is not an option	There's a chance of winning big

Panic and fear of death	Surging adrenaline
Must stay on track in new life	Foaming at mouth to ruin St. Nick
He hates being blackmailed	Apollo will turn him in to the cops
His wife will know he's lying	Apollo will tell her Cutter's secrets

You can see how you can keep going with this two-sided chart as a way to explore Cutter's dilemma. It allows you to polarize the two sides of the dilemma and to run with each one. What I've done here is to play one side of the chart off against the other, matching them up. You could also just make a long list on one side and then work on the other side without trying to connect each one to its opposite. Don't be afraid to let the lists ramble. You can explore different shades of meaning and allow yourself to explode on paper with all the ramifications of a dilemma. It doesn't have to be neat or exact or clear. It doesn't matter if you repeat yourself because the more angles you see your central character's dilemma from, the clearer and more completely you will understand it. This two-sided chart is a good way to explore the extremes too, because you can keep stretching the possibilities as you play with the list, twisting the dilemma, trying things on, breaking it out in different directions, experimenting wildly with it.

Now let's get more of the plot itself up and running. What we're talking about here is a revenge robbery that Apollo claims is a perfect crime. A major question is: Is this a straight theft or a con? This question occurs because Cutter is a fabulous liar, and while I'm sure this could be a fun con movie, I think I'll keep it a robbery. It's an arbitrary choice on my part. So, our crew is going to rob St. Nick, an *extremely* dangerous big-time criminal.

A WORD ABOUT TITLES

Something that I read in the chapter about titles in Krows' book, *Playwriting for Profit* has always stayed with me. A London playwright told Krows (pronounced Kraus) that the measure of a good title is if it looks good on a bus. This sounds funny, but the writer explained that plays are advertised on buses and it is actually a legitimate gauge. Anyway, I tend to not get too caught up in trying to find a title when I'm starting on a script because I stumble onto potential titles routinely as I work through the material. I'll be writing notes for the story and happen on a phrase that clicks for me, and say, "Wow, that would make a good title." I actually find titles all the time in the course of daily life and I keep them in a file. You acquire an ear for a good title.

Here is a list of potential titles that I compiled for this script.

1. Don't Get Me Started
2. Good Old St. Nick
3. Count Your Blessings
4. Believe You Me
5. You Don't Want to Know
6. Straight and True
7. Laughing All the Way to the Bank
8. The Slush Fund
9. It's Only Money
10. You Bet Your Life
11. The Whole Truth
12. The Trickle Up Effect
13. Golden Opportunity

There are a few decent ones in there, but I kept coming back to *Good Old St. Nick* because somehow it just worked for me. I could have generated many more, but I liked *Good Old St. Nick* as soon as I hit on it, and while I collected others, none had the juice that it had for me. It has a ring to it, and although it conjures up images of Christmas, I kept feeling like it had an interesting sound to it and a certain playfulness. Could it still be changed? Absolutely. But I think it would look good on a bus.

One thing to be aware of is that a film title cannot be copyrighted. There were, in fact, two films in feature release called *Black Rain* in 1989. Studios have agreements not to step on each other's titles, but legally you can put any title on a screenplay.

13
UTILIZING CRISIS

In our story, by the time Cutter's dilemma comes to a Crisis point, the dilemma has been getting tougher and more complex; finally it comes to the make-or-break moment. Remember that the crisis tends to come at about the two-thirds or three-quarters point in a script, and forces an immediate decision and action. Now in this story, what I want is for this crisis to cause Cutter to snap and go on a wild and crazy lying spree that lasts pretty much the rest of the movie. I want this to be flat out one of the most astonishing feats of lying we've ever seen in a movie. Like any writer faced with a daunting task, I don't know if I can pull it off, but I know what I want. So let's look at some possibilities for precipitating a crisis.

The most obvious possibility is that St. Nick finds out who Cutter is and what he's up to. Generally, if it's a hidden identity movie, the point of crisis includes discovery by the opposition. However, I feel that if what I want is a huge lying fest, then what is there to lie about once your secret identity has been uncovered? Why would St. Nick even begin to believe him, especially if he knows Cutter is there for revenge? It's possible that if St. Nick learns who Cutter is, but not *why* he's there, then some seriously good lying could ensue.

Certainly a *near* discovery could be part of a good crisis. What about Cutter being betrayed by Apollo? I've been talking about Apollo having something to do with counterfeit money. This would be a good time to do it. Even if

Apollo just shows up with the money and doesn't try to palm it off at this point, his hidden agenda can then be surfacing. What about Mischa showing up? He sees a chance to inject himself into his dad's world in such a way that he cannot be ignored or gotten rid of, or perhaps he feels that he can make himself valuable or even indispensable. Does Margarita find out where Cutter is, or that he's been having an affair with St. Nick's secretary?

This is certainly an appropriate time for Shallott to be murdered. This can also lead to the near discovery of Cutter. Does Shallott snap? Does he slip up? Is there something he does that brings suspicion down on Cutter? Why would St. Nick kill Shallott? How would Cutter distance himself from Shallott, since Shallott is the one who brought him in? Is the FBI investigating St. Nick? Does this screw everything up, or can Senator Hutchings quash the investigation? (Again, if you haven't read the chapter, *Utilizing the 36 Dramatic Situations*, then you will be confused by much of this, and you should skip ahead and read it now.)

Is Cutter going crazy because his medications are missing? Has Apollo swapped placebo pills for them to make this wild liar come out? Have the pills gotten lost? Does Mischa think his dad is pathetic and gets rid of his meds so he can see the old Cutter emerge? Does Cutter 'losing it' jeopardize his operation? Does he realize his meds have worn off? Are there no more to be found? Is he glad they're gone?

Is the opportunity for revenge against St. Nick vanishing? Did the situation in Africa change so that St. Nick has to move immediately? Does Hutchings find a way to speed up the final approval or actually get it finalized? Does St. Nick move his hidden accounts around just when Cutter was getting to the bottom of them? Does St. Nick suspect something? Are his instincts picking up on something? Is it just bad luck? All of this is moot if the plans have changed when St. Nick promotes Cutter higher up into his organization. Wouldn't that mean that Cutter now has an opportunity to take St. Nick down in a bigger way, and maybe stop the theft of billions from the U.S. taxpayers? Maybe the original plan to take down St. Nick is still on standby in case everything fails.

Does it come out that the CIA is involved? That can often happen when covert funds are being moved overseas. (Historically, dictators have been utilized as bulwarks against perceived greater threats, for instance, Communism.) Money earmarked for innocent purposes can be co-opted and used to provide covert military assistance and so on. If the CIA is involved, then Cutter is in even deeper water, and most importantly, it won't be easy at all to pull off the revenge against St. Nick and set up Senator Hutchings without getting in huge trouble any longer. These two will have powerful allies working behind the scenes to shut down any investigation, citing national security. This is a nice bomb to drop at this point. There can also be drugs coming in from Africa, drug money, money laundering and so on. This messes things up in a cool way and opens up unexpected possibilities for everything to erupt into pandemonium, especially for our wild liar. Cutter could be lying to spies, senators, dictators, bankers, thieves, FBI agents, drug dealers, customs officials, lawyers and so on. But we'll deal with all that in the section on Decision and Action.

What we've done is to explore possibilities for crisis. You can see that there are many different things that could happen. Remember, in general, crisis is the worst possible things happening at the most crucial time, and it's generally out toward the end of the story. Now let's move on to Decision and Action.

14

UTILIZING DECISION AND ACTION

If we've done our job well, Cutter is in a horrible situation that's now blowing up in his face. This dilemma has built-in intensity and now it has come to emergency status. He has no time to contemplate his dilemma from a distance any longer. Now is the time to make a crucial decision and take a key action: everything hangs in the balance. Plus, we've been engineering this script to have the old Cutter burst out in a fearsome onslaught of explosive lying and stealing.

Depending on exactly how he is backed into a corner at the point of crisis, he will explode in varying ways. But I do see him making a conscious choice to embrace his dark gift as a weapon of war. This is his Decision. It's the classic story of the gunslinger who has sworn off violence and is now forced to use it. He has to come out swinging as hard as he can if he's going to stand a chance of surviving. It's important to keep the entertainment value in mind, especially if we're trying to keep this funny to whatever degree feels right. It should definitely have an edge, but it shouldn't go so dark that it's a savage thriller. At this point there are enough comic possibilities that it's no longer a question of whether or not to use them: it seems to be going that way. It's fun when a script takes on a life of its own. Now it's a matter of keeping it on that track.

One of the key things I see is what I call the 'Judy Garland transformation.' I read an amazing article about this reporter who was granted backstage access to Judy Garland for a performance that she did toward the end of her career. She was running quite late and when she finally showed up the reporter thought she was the cleaning lady come to straighten up Judy's dressing room. But it was Judy. She was insecure and worn out, scared and out of it, but her handlers got her ready. Then, because of his special access, he was allowed to stand backstage right before she went on and watched as she pulled herself together. He said that this shrunken little run-down woman literally transformed before his eyes. She drew herself up and actually grew a foot taller as she seemed to suck power from out of nowhere, transfiguring into the mighty Judy Garland as he watched, thunderstruck. I want Cutter to go through that—and I want Mischa to be watching from a hidden position, maybe an air duct.

What are the possibilities for him breaking out into an onslaught? He's going to be lying to St. Nick, for one. If St. Nick had taken him into his circle, then Cutter is going to have to be fighting to stay in his trust or he'll lose his opportunity to take St. Nick down, and Cutter could easily get himself killed. If the bank certification is on shaky ground, then he'd be cooking up a whopping lie to help keep it in line. Does he tell a crazy lie to Umbotha, the African dictator, who's getting worried that he's not getting his deal? (Read *Utilizing the 36 Dramatic Situations* chapter if you're confused.) How would he lie to Senator Hutchings? Does he have to explain away who Mischa is and what he's doing here? What about Apollo? Has Apollo been around for a while in disguise, or has he showed up now? Does Cutter have to tell a whopper to Apollo? Is he trying to chill out a furious Margarita because she has found out that he in involved in his old life, in this deadly caper, that Mischa has gotten involved, and that Cutter is having an affair with the secretary?

He could be lying to the CIA about some aspects of the bank operation, or could be telling one set of lies to the CIA and another to the FBI. He might be able to set things in motion here that could come together in a phenomenal way at the end. He would be playing with bits of information that people know, and capitalizing on what they don't know. This is where studying the most world class liars in literature, mythology, history and film can help me to build on the best, or as many writers say, to "steal from the best."

Also, a great possibility is that Cutter seems to have really turned into a hard core criminal once he emerges as the wild man. He may explode into his lying persona so much that he lies to everybody all the time. The genie is out of the bottle and nobody's safe. As far as we can tell, he has joined the dark side. Cutter may be convincing St. Nick that he's betraying Shallott or Apollo or Mischa. Mischa may do something stupid in his attempt to thrust himself into his father's life and Cutter may seem to be betraying him. This path has a lot of possibilities because one of the options I've been playing with is that Margarita could talk him back onto the good side at the very end, breaking the spell and leading him to tell the whole truth, ending everything. Here then, we can imagine a real demon emerging at the crucial moment. This can kick the story into high gear where things get scarier, funnier and crazier.

It is often glibly suggested that structural technique destroys creativity, but professionals know that it actually can liberate the creative process. For instance, David Mamet, again from *On Directing Film*:

> *The purpose of technique is to free the unconscious.* If you follow the rules ploddingly, they will allow your unconscious to be free. That's true creativity. If not, you will be fettered by your conscious mind. Because the conscious mind always wants to be liked and wants to be interesting. The conscious mind is going to suggest the obvious, the cliché, because these things offer the security of having succeeded in the past. Only the mind that has been taken off itself and put on a task is allowed true creativity. (p. 6)

You can see that I am still experimenting with many possibilities. Decision and Action suggests that my character kick into action in a big way here and I am trying on many options, but everything is still entirely open-ended. I'm shaping the story into a form that can work dramatically, but I'm not a slave to technique. Knowing how to use the tools gives me great confidence as a dramatist and I'm having a blast making up this movie!

15
UTILIZING RESOLUTION

Cutter's Resolution will consist of several powerful actions. At the point of Decision and Action it seemed as though he has gone off on such a wild lying bender that he's gone over to the dark side. He may seem to have thrown in with St. Nick and Senator Hutchings, but it's hard to tell. Mischa may panic and not know who this monster is that used to be his father. Apollo may just be riding the tornado that Cutter has become, content to have it serve his purposes if he can steer it that way. Margarita might be seeing her marriage falling apart at a rapid rate. But Cutter will also be taking steps in terms of the lies he tells to the FBI, to the CIA and to Umbotha to create some bizarre opportunities to take down St. Nick and Hutchings (See *Utilizing the 36 Dramatic Situations* chapter if confused). It should be such a flurry of contradictory lies that Cutter will seem like an insane god.

If Margarita is able to get through to him and steer him back to some semblance of connection to their stable life and his vow never to lie again, he may begin to 'snap to' at the crucial moment. Then he can kick events into the right direction when it looks like all is lost. A good possibility is that a massive quantity of St. Nick's and Hutchings' money gets burned up in an accidental fire, destroying it all, with them watching. In actuality, it was Apollo's counterfeit money, but because they believe it to be destroyed, St. Nick and Hutchings won't be looking for the missing money. This is a classic part of a perfect crime in which the mark sees the money or whatever irretrievably lost before their own eyes, so that, though they freak out, they are also not going to be looking for it. This allows the thieves or con men to leave with it safely.

Another key thing I see Cutter doing is telling the whole truth about the complete plan at a live TV press conference. This would be unprecedented honesty about politics to the public and would detonate the Senator's career. It could turn out that Apollo knows Umbotha because they played as kids together when their dictator fathers visited each other to do business. The system of interlocking lies that Cutter tells could convince Umbotha that St. Nick is ripping him off and he could fly into a murderous rage. Cutter and Apollo could set up St. Nick so that he becomes a prisoner of Umbotha, and is taken back to Mambia, where he will become a highly guarded prison laborer, a fate worse than death for many years to come.

The money—and we're talking a vast amount here—could get taken to a Democratic Party mailing center and sent out in the mail. A substantial amount of this cash could get sent to every taxpayer who makes under $100,000. As Cutter speaks on live TV, this money would already be arriving in the day's mail. He could tell one last white lie, saying St. Nick felt so bad that this money was stolen from the American taxpayer that he is returning it. The interviewer would claim that he has caused immense chaos and Cutter says that St. Nick should be held accountable, except that he is nowhere to be found. He says that there will certainly be a lot of happy poor people out there today and for the wealthy taxpayers who didn't get packages not to worry because the money will trickle up. Cutter, Margarita and Mischa can start again with a new life. Mischa has been scared straight from this; the three are a tight family, with three envelopes of cash arriving in the mail to help them along.

16
UTILIZING THEME

The way in which Cutter resolves his dilemma expresses the theme of the plot. He defeats St. Nick and Hutchings, as well as his own demons. The way in which he does it is to burst out with a wildly creative positive solution, finally using his gift for good. It didn't work to bury it, he had to transform into a force for good in order to be truly liberated. He finds his core of integrity, courage and wisdom, and bursting out with an ecstatic freedom that changes his whole world.

The audience experiences his unstoppable exuberance, his indomitable transcendent new energy. It's a theme of life, freedom, energy, happiness, health, integrity and the power of creation. It's a creation myth, a shamanic self-transformation, the creation of new life in the midst of a barren desert, an oasis.

Knowing the theme—having it in my bones—helps govern the shape, tone and energy of the script, beginning with Cutter miserably trying to suppress his gift. There's an entire growth process from nothingness to exuberance. This screenplay is not a lecture on life or energy or integrity—it's a rollicking comic adventure movie about a guy figuring out how to navigate his own native energy and harnessing it for good, for health, for happiness and for family.

Do I infuse the script with this by constantly reiterating it and beating the audience over the head with it? I certainly hope not. That would be the ruin of this movie. I trust that this movie will communicate this theme once, clearly and powerfully at the end. Trusting that, I make each part of the plot do its job, telling the story itself as well as possible, using the full arsenal of my craft as a dramatist.

Notice that the theme is built into the central proposition because the set up of the potential fight is when Cutter attacks St. Nick when he accuses Cutter of lying. The touch off of the fight to the finish Cutter going on the attack to try to prove that he's not lying. In both instances he actually is lying, but he cannot allow himself to be called a liar. At that moment his own self-recognition is that, at core, he isn't. It goes back to Price's quote in *The Analysis of Play Construction and Dramatic Principle* about theme and proposition: "Thus, the Proposition is governed by the Theme." (p.22)

BELOW ARE A FEW QUOTES THAT EXPLORE THE THEME OF *GOOD OLD ST. NICK*

The charm of the best courages is that they are inventions, inspirations, flashes of genius.
Halifax

There are pioneer souls that blaze paths where highways never ran.
Foss

Fortune is not on the side of the faint-hearted.
Sophocles

Not even hell can lay a hand on the invincible.
Parmenion

In great straits and when hope is small, the boldest counsels are the safest.
Livy

The depth and strength of a human character are defined by its moral reserves. People reveal themselves completely only when they are thrown out of the customary conditions of their life, for only then do they have to fall back on their reserves.
Leon Trotsky

God offers every mind its choice between truth and repose.
Ralph Waldo Emerson

Wisdom is to the soul what health is to the body.
La Rochefoucauld

Character is the governing element of life, and is above genius.
Saunders

Lay me on an anvil, O God. Beat me and hammer me into a crowbar. Let me pry loose old walls; let me lift and loosen old foundations.
Sandburg

Truth is the cry of all, but the game of few.
George Berkeley

Truth to tell, we are all criminals if we remain silent.
Stefan Zweig

Truth is a clumsy servant that breaks the dishes while washing them.
Karl Kraus

The truth is a snare: you cannot have it, without being caught. You cannot have the truth in such a way that you catch it, but only in such a way that it catches you.
Soren Kierkegaard

Character consists of what you do on the third and fourth tries.
James A Michener

My name was Isabella; but when I left the house of bondage, I left everything behind. I wa'n't goin' to keep nothin' of Egypt on me, an' so I went to the Lord an' asked him to give me a new name. And the Lord gave me Sojourner, be-cause I was to travel up an' down the land, showin' the people their sins, an' bein' a sign unto them. Afterward I told the Lord I wanted another name, 'cause everybody else had two names; and the Lord gave me Truth, because I was to declare Truth to the people.
Sojourner Truth

Truth is the beginning of every good to the gods, and of every good to man.
Plato

Truth-telling frightens me. Lying confuses me.
Mason Cooley

17

UTILIZING THE 36 DRAMATIC SITUATIONS

The 36 Dramatic Situations are so useful in developing this story because they help open the floodgates of possibility. It may sound chaotic, which it certainly can be (and which is one of its greatest strengths), but I am also going through it very methodically, trying everything on for fit. I go into great depth on each of these situations and making a special effort to try and explore *all* the possibilities, permutations and ramifications for this rapidly expanding plot.

1. SUPPLICATION: (Asking or begging for help)

Cutter is clearly asking and begging for help, both in dealing with Apollo as well as St. Nick. He's literally praying for guidance from God since he's now a churchgoer, and if he can talk to his wife, Margarita, about what's going on, he will also be appealing to her for guidance. She will definitely be pleading with him not to get involved because she knows where it can lead: all his old addictions kicking back in and ruining their life. If she doesn't know what's happening, then she'll beg Cutter to tell her, because she knows it's no good. She will also be praying for him.

Cutter will beg Apollo to let him off the hook. He's begging for his life, for his marriage, his wife, his son, his happiness, his sanity. He knows that crossing St. Nick could get them all killed, possibly even a fate worse than death. Apollo is begging Cutter for help. He's in over his head and needs Cutter's skills in this once-in-a-lifetime opportunity to take down St. Nick. What if Apollo is in trouble with St. Nick? Cutter's son, Mischa, begs for a glimpse of Cutter's old life, which Cutter implores him to let go of. He wants his son to embrace a normal life and not get dragged into criminality. He's working hard to influence Mischa and to show him by example how to live a good life. Cutter also perceives that much of his son's behavior is a cry for help.

Also, isn't his old addiction to lying pleading to be let out of its cage? The proposed caper obviously demands that he lie (that's part of the fun of the story), but he may be keeping it under control. He's begging his addiction to stay dormant. But part of Cutter's dilemma is that he's also going to be hungry to take St. Nick down. Monster that St. Nick is, Cutter will be begging for an opportunity to find the chinks in his formidable armor and an opportunity to strip him financially, get him in trouble with his superiors, get him in trouble with the law, destroy him, betray him or ruin his life. Cutter is begging the gods for a handle on this guy.

On the other hand, St. Nick is asking or begging for help to get into this incredibly lucrative world of legitimate banking in high level shadow government circles. Having gotten a glimpse of the phenomenal amount of legal thievery that he can be a part of, he is desperate to jettison his stone age criminal ways for the space age, the street-legal way of robbing that the government not only doesn't prosecute, but covertly can be party to. Had he only known this all along, he would have started out this way years ago, saving himself trouble with the police and the lowlife that now populate his world. The Promised Land reveals itself when one of the senators with whom he did business as a crook clues him into the variety of legal ways to fleece, rob, plunder, thieve and pillage that yields dividends rather than grand jury investigations. St. Nick is foaming at the mouth to get into this club, and that makes him vulnerable at this particular moment. His desire for legal larceny is causing him to lower his defenses, a genuine first for him.

Cutter is frustrated and bored with his straight, normal life and is begging to get back his old ways, feeling the hunger for high-intensity, high-risk action. A ravenous beast circles his campfire at night, calling to Cutter to drop this domesticated charade and return to the life of the wild. The part of him that is frustrated, feeling trapped, dead ended, semi-broke and claustrophobic secretly desires to break out and be free.

Let's get a look at the subheadings of *Supplication*.

A.   (1) Fugitives Imploring the Powerful for Help Against Their Enemies
      (2) Assistance Implored for the Performance of a Pious Duty, Which has Been Forbidden
      (3) Appeals for a Refuge in Which to Die
B.   (1) Hospitality Besought by the Shipwrecked
      (2) Charity Entreated by Those Cast Off by their Own People, Whom They Have Disgraced
      (3) Expiation: The Seeking of Pardon, Healing or Deliverance

(4) The Surrender of a Corpse, or of a Relic, Solicited

C.   (1) Supplication of the Powerful for Those Dear to the Suppliant

     (2) Supplication to a Relative in Behalf of Another Relative

     (3) Supplication to a Mother's Lover, in Her Behalf

Clearly we've got *Fugitives imploring the powerful for help against their enemies.* Apollo is asking Cutter for help against St. Nick. Is Apollo a fugitive? It's an intriguing possibility. If he's on the run from St. Nick, then he is asking Cutter to pay him back for saving his life. That could complicate things in an interesting way. The fact that Cutter is a stand up guy (which we tend to want our hero to be) means he cannot refuse to pay Apollo back. Maybe Apollo is lying, but Cutter might not know that until later.

Hospitality besought by the shipwrecked is an interesting subheading. Apollo could be coming from this point of view—he could be in big trouble, with no hope left of surviving. Being shipwrecked is a vivid poetic image and suggests loss, pain, isolation and desperation. My first thought was that Cutter would get in a bad situation once he infiltrates St. Nick's inner circle and be seeking any kind of help. In thinking about absolute desperation, certainly his wife could be experiencing this because she feels lost and abandoned. Cutter's son would be feeling the same way at some point.

Next there is *Supplication of the powerful for those dear to the suppliant* which would be active if Cutter and Apollo's scheme falls apart and St. Nick is on to them. He may take Mischa hostage and Cutter would be begging for his life. In this instance or similar ones Cutter would clearly be would be seeking *Expiation: The seeking of pardon, healing or deliverance.*

2. DELIVERANCE: (Rescuing or being rescued)

Cutter is trying to rescue himself from his former criminal lifestyle (his destructive lying and stealing habits) which are now straining to overwhelm him. When the story starts he has, in fact, delivered himself and been delivered by his wife. He is trying to rescue his son, Mischa, from a potential life of crime. He's also trying to solidify his family life by getting more money, having a child, helping the church and community, being a good husband and a responsible citizen. His focus is on Deliverance in the same way an alcoholic goes to AA several times a week to stay sober.

If Cutter can pull this caper off and get out of the trap Apollo has gotten him into, then it will be Deliverance. If he rescues himself by destroying St. Nick (and/or Apollo), or gets away from their sphere of influence then it's also Deliverance. Note that at this point in developing this script there is genuinely no ending—it is truly unexplored territory. In the back of my mind there's an ending in which the old Cutter, in a full-blown explosive frenzy of phenomenal lying, manages to save the day and destroy the monster(s). But any ending will obviously be an outgrowth of how the story complicates itself and grows and gets crazy and dangerous and screwed up. I don't know what's around the bend. I don't know what the Crisis might be or the Decision & Action or the Resolution. It's all *wide open*. I'm exploring the 36 Dramatic Situations to try to find some great possibilities.

St. Nick is seeking Deliverance into this lofty world of legal thievery, into his kind of heaven where the streets are not only paved with gold, but the CIA helps you fleece the marks. He's on the edge of having it made. His immediate problem is to be admitted into this rarified club, and he's jumping through all the flaming hoops to pass the test.

One possibility for Apollo is that he's stolen a huge amount of counterfeit money, or has made a bunch of it, and is seeking a way to pass it or foist it onto someone. His Deliverance will depend on how much pressure he's under to get rid of it, which in turn will determine how hard he pushes. Does his life depend on it or is he just greedy?

Let's look at the subheadings:

A. (1) Appearance of a Rescuer to the Condemned
B. (1) A Parent Replaced upon a Throne by his Children
    (2) Rescue by Friends, or by Strangers Grateful for Benefits or
    Hospitality

Appearance of a rescuer to the condemned may be how Cutter looks to both Apollo and St. Nick when he starts his job, each for different reasons. Apollo knows that Cutter has the skills to take down St. Nick, and nobody else does. St. Nick sees Cutter as the key to gaining entrance to his heaven. This subheading suggests that St. Nick is 'condemned,' maybe not being able to get in unless Cutter certifies him. Maybe he's struck a serious roadblock in terms of getting money into the reserve fund so that he can operate a bank. Though this part of the plot is unformed at this point, let's speculate on the possibilities. Could the unfortunate St. Nick be having difficulties getting money from offshore havens into legitimate accounts in the U.S.? Maybe the IRS wants to know why this money was never declared before. Maybe it opens up St. Nick's treasure chest to snooping eyes. Without making the deposit, he cannot complete the certification of his new bank. Maybe there's an unforeseen complication with law enforcement or another criminal stepping on his action. It's open at this point.

Is Cutter knowledgeable and bribable enough to provide the solution to St. Nick's problem? (Do you see how I'm using the questions raised by this situation to ponder and dig deeper into the mysteries of how to make this plot work, letting it suggest possibilities as a free-association tool?)

Rescue by friends, or by strangers grateful for benefits or hospitality suggests that since Cutter owes his life to Apollo, he is willing to rescue him. What about Cutter's relationship with St. Nick? Is it possible that Cutter does something that saves St. Nick, either by fast thinking, quick action or skillful lying? This could win St. Nick's undying gratitude (at least until Cutter's real identity and intention are discovered). This could be a fascinating possibility: if St. Nick finds himself in a sticky situation, Cutter could come up with a fabulous lie on the spur of the moment that gets St. Nick off. I might have stumbled on a way to get him into St. Nick's good graces and also reveal to St. Nick and his crooked associates that Cutter is not entirely honest. This is exactly what Cutter needs to get St. Nick to start to trust him.

This brings up questions about the kind of problems St. Nick might be having in of acquiring his bank. It may be hard to get information on how to buy a bank, but I'll start working on it. I have read that one of the legal requirements to buy a bank involved proving that you were not currently in jail. I've decided that St. Nick has gone through all the application process and is now down to just getting the reserve set up. He could be experiencing problems and Cutter could be there and maybe help him circumvent those. It's also possible that the certification process is not over, so I'm still playing with that.

3. CRIME PURSUED BY VENGEANCE:

The most obvious aspect of this is that St. Nick has betrayed and murdered their friend from prison, Frenchy. This has to be developed and it has to be incredibly strong to motivate Cutter and Apollo so intensely. Frenchy has to be one of the best guys they ever knew, someone so high on Cutter's list that he'd consider risking his new life to get revenge. I've been thinking about how Frenchy would be somebody who turned his life around in prison, got off drugs and became a truly helpful, solid and caring guy. One who really escaped The Life and made it for all of them. He could be the one who got Cutter thinking about going straight too. I always saw Cutter as being turned straight by his wife, but Frenchy could have laid the foundation.

Frenchy would have been the most stand up guy on the whole cell block who took care of everybody, negotiated truces among prisoners, and even with prison guards or the warden, if need be. He was trusted by everyone and had become a truly great man. Word on the inside was that Frenchy had gotten a good job back in the real world, but then somehow St. Nick captured him and forced him back onto heroin. He used Frenchy's old breaking-and-entering skills on a huge job, then framed him and murdered him, making it look as though he OD'd. The guys in jail swore vengeance on St. Nick, but he was untouchable and so utterly brutal no one wanted to risk everything to go after him. After that, Cutter, shaken to the core, radically changed his life. He determined to go straight and when he got out he met Margarita and turned his life around.

When he learns of the opportunity to take down St. Nick, part of him explodes with vengeance. But he is mature, not the crazy hothead he used to be. He now has to consider very carefully his vow to never do anything crooked again. This new life he has built cannot be risked, but the vengeance that burns inside him drives him like a rocket engine. His life may be frustrating and he may feel trapped in certain ways, but at least it's solid and stable.

What I'm doing here is to turn the various story ideas over in my mind, seen through the lens of each of these dramatic situations. Sometimes it will open up new possibilities and sometimes it will give me fresh insight into what I've already been wrestling with. Especially at this stage of development, the plot is up for grabs—anything goes and the sky's the limit. There's plenty of fun to be had playing with possibilities. For me, this is the best part of storytelling—pure, wide-open creation. With this tool, I work my way through each of the pertinent 36 Dramatic Situations, like an inventor wandering through an electronics parts store. "Wow, I could use that. I've got to have that. I'm not sure what that is, but it's intriguing and I'm taking it home."

Apollo's sense of Crime Pursued by Vengeance is clearly powerful as well. Even if he's got a hidden agenda, he should still be boiling with rage, and his rage should fuel Cutter's, pushing him, driving him to get involved. Let's play some wild 'What If?' What if St. Nick has done something else to Apollo, either directly or indirectly, that Cutter knows nothing about? What would really piss off Apollo, or any crook for that matter? What are the possibilities?

1. A great robbery that's been painstakingly set up for months and then gets co-opted by St. Nick at the last minute.
2. Getting ratted out to the cops.
3. Some illegal money that was stashed away gets ripped off (and you can't go to the authorities).
4. Murder (but we've already got that).
5. Getting squeezed out of a lucrative territory or enterprise.
6. A daughter being stolen away for a forced marriage.
7. St. Nick tries to kill Apollo.
8. Getting framed.
9. What's the single worst thing that I could possibly think of? How about most of Apollo's gang getting wiped out with poison in retribution for a perceived slight against St. Nick?

I kind of like the first one, but the others have points of interest. One of the things to bear in mind is that I may want St. Nick to not know who Apollo is

(I definitely don't want him to know Cutter at all), and this may complicate that first possibility. I may want to get Apollo involved in Cutter's mission, possibly even injecting himself into the mix to the surprise of Cutter. I may well come up with something that has no relationship at all to this list.

From St. Nick's point of view, is there any way he feels like a crime has been done to him? He's really volatile, so he's probably going to take serious offense at many things. He will see any trouble he's having buying this bank as a crime against him. How *dare* they try to exclude me? If Cutter is playing the part of one of the inspectors, for example, then he'll be taking some heat from St. Nick. Depending on how much trouble the banking industry is giving St. Nick over trying to join their country club, he could be in a towering rage. I like that he has to be on his best behavior at this particular time. Otherwise he might well execute every banking official who gives him the least opposition, and they probably have no idea how close they're coming to sudden and awful death when they challenge him.

The other thing that occurs to me (this is another example of the free-association aspect of this tool) is that St. Nick reminds me of a dictator—someone who is used to getting his way on every little thing. Saddam Hussein is an obvious role model, or his sons. What this brings to mind is that as I toyed with the possibility that Apollo was the son of a dictator from the turn on the century (you'll see this when you get to the Brainstorming chapter). It was just a wild raw idea, something unexpected to add a twist to him. Now that I'm thinking about how like a dictator St. Nick is, it reminds me of what I played around with for Apollo. Could Apollo's background make him react in a certain way to St. Nick? Maybe Apollo's father was cruel to him and Apollo has to prove something to this dictator-like character, St. Nick. Just a thought, which may not amount to anything, but that's what much of this type of brainstorming process is like. You will generate hundreds of possibilities and end up tossing most of them overboard. But if you brainstorm wildly enough, then the ones you keep are likely to be fresh, unusual and stimulating. Really push it. Remember, first and foremost it's the ENTERTAINMENT industry. It's the movies!

I knew the son of a dictator in prep school and he was a very powerful figure, even as a high school senior. He had an aura of power and the stories we heard from him and his cousins were high intensity. If Apollo came from a similar background, it could add a fascinating level to his character, especially if that was his past and he's grown and changed and adapted quite a bit, since I picture Apollo as an amazingly charming, gregarious devil of a fellow who is fun and dangerous and mesmerizing and unpredictable.

I see Apollo not so much as treacherous toward Cutter, but someone who's willing to use him. He and Cutter were close friends, but Cutter is used to Apollo always having something up his sleeve. There is real love between them since they were cellmates for eight years. If Apollo has these deeply buried buttons that get pushed by St. Nick, it could make Apollo act irrational or crazy, and might make him go off the plan. Don't be afraid to take the chain of thought anywhere it leads when playing with the 36 Dramatic Situations. Again, if a situation catalyzes an idea, it's done its job; they're only triggers.

Remember that all of the above ideas came from playing around with *Crime Pursued by Vengeance.* Now let's examine the subheadings:

A. (1) The Avenging of a Slain Parent or Ancestor
    (2) The Avenging of a Slain Child or Descendant
    (3) Vengeance for a Child Dishonored
    (4) The Avenging of a Slain Wife or Husband
    (5) Vengeance for the Dishonor, or Attempted Dishonoring, of a Wife
    (6) Vengeance for a Mistress Slain
    (7) Vengeance for a Slain or Injured Friend
    (8) Vengeance for a Sister Seduced
B. (1) Vengeance for Intentional Injury or Spoliation
    (2) Vengeance for Having Been Despoiled During Absence
    (3) Revenge for an Attempted Slaying
    (4) Revenge for a False Accusation
    (5) Vengeance for Violation
    (6) Vengeance for Having Been Robbed of One's Own
    (7) Revenge Upon a Whole Sex for a Deception by One
C. (1) Professional Pursuit of Criminals

We have already got *Vengeance for a Slain or Injured Friend.* Once Cutter infiltrates St. Nick's circle, if his wife doesn't know what's going on, or even where he is, she is going to feel like a 'slain' wife [A4] and will be seeking vengeance. Cutter's son could be feeling like a 'Child Dishonored' [A3] in his own way. Both Margarita and Mischa will be seeking *Vengeance for Intentional Injury or Spoliation* and *Vengeance for Violation* as well as *Vengeance for Having Been Robbed of One's Own.*

Revenge for a False Accusation is interesting because Cutter is a reformed pathological liar and the truth is very important to him. If he is being falsely accused, then it's a huge deal, even after he has started lying as part of the job. He may still over-react to being accused of something he didn't say or do. The energy of his vengeance can certainly vary from standing up to the accuser all the way to murder (Here I'm exploring the extremes).

If St. Nick is having trouble getting his bank, he might seek vengeance because he feels as though he's being falsely 'robbed.' That brings up *Vengeance for*

Intentional Injury or Spoliation, Vengeance for Violation and *Vengeance for Having Been Robbed of One's Own*. Cutter and Apollo feel these three as well, in terms of Frenchy's loss. These three situations don't necessarily shed any new possibilities or insights that I can see, but it doesn't hurt to look them over and see if they trigger anything new. Often it takes time to notice something, and handling a problem repeatedly, even from mildly different points of view, can shake something loose.

Professional Pursuit of Criminals is intriguing. It's not only Sherlock Holmes, but notice even Michael Corleone is busy with Professional Pursuit of Criminals. He himself happens to be a criminal, but part of his job is to ride herd on other criminals. The same is true here. Not only is it obvious that Cutter and Apollo are trying to take down the master criminal, St. Nick, but they are also presumably involved with other criminals, some of whom probably cannot be trusted or who have agendas of their own. It also suggests the possibility of a lawman who might be after either St. Nick, Apollo or Cutter.

This is entirely new territory which can certainly add a new level of complexity to the plot. Cutter could even join forces with an FBI agent who has been after St. Nick for years and sees him slipping out of reach as St. Nick goes legit. Certainly someone could be after Apollo, since he's got things up his sleeve. This can definitely mess things up, possibly even at a crucial moment for Cutter. I don't know why the law would be after Cutter, since he hasn't done anything illegal since he went straight. Maybe Apollo has someone pretending to be the law to intimidate Cutter. Maybe he told someone about a crime that Cutter did before he went to prison, for which the statute of limitations hasn't expired. Maybe some cop recognizes him from a past run-in and has an eye on him. It opens up a Pandora's box of possibilities that a story like this might naturally generate.

INTERRUPTING THE PROCESS TO BRAINSTORM

Before I go further into this process, I want to stop and regroup and shake things up. What I've done so far with the 36 dramatic situations is making me notice that big sections of the story need to be developed more. At this point I've got what I think is a good beginning, with a good strong dilemma. As I work my way through the 36 I notice that I beginning to feel more grounded in the plot and that I have a foundation, but I want to get some distance from it and do some broader creative thinking. I want to turn things upside down and throw dynamite into the order I've created so far. I want to see story possibilities from different points of view and basically just give myself a good whack in the head. (Speaking of which, check out the book *A Whack on the Side of the Head: How You Can Be More Creative* by Roger Von Oech. It's a great book for shaking up, expanding and freshening your creative process.)

I don't want to get trapped in my earliest view of the plot. I want to really bang on it and make sure there isn't a great plot lurking in here that I haven't thought of. This may sound like a wild goose chase, but I am trying to show my entire process of developing a script using the four tools. If your story doesn't have some real juice to it, all the structuring in the world won't get it off the ground.

I have lots of questions pertaining to the plot which I'll be laying out and exploring. There are big holes in the script as it stands now. I have doubts about how to make it all work. I have wild, out-to-lunch ideas to play with. I have different crazy endings to try on, all of them unformed. I have major research yet to do. I am wondering what business I have trying to write a screenplay in the first place. I have a tiger by the tail and have to figure out what to do with it. Does any of this sound familiar? Each of you, if you write every day, or as close to that as you can get, also have all these questions swirling around in your brain on a constant basis. They're normal, and if you're not challenging yourself as much as you can, then your material can easily turn out mediocre. So right about here is the part of the process where I wrestle with some of the plot problems in the story.

One of the things I'd like to do is to make this script funnier. Give it a bit of an Elmore Leonard twist—a comic edge. I could take this into a savage thriller, and it may end up there yet, but I'd like to try for a satiric edge. What are some possibilities for this? One of the things I stumbled onto is that Cutter could be much more challenged in his straight life. Maybe he feels trapped, is getting old and maybe fat, might be a hypochondriac or might have to stay on mood-altering drugs to deal with reality. What if he needed anti-psychotic drugs to help him stay 'normal' or needs sleeping pills to sleep?

This led to the possibility of him being run down, defeated or broken in some ways. This can be a total contrast to the man about whom we've heard these wild stories—the one who's unstoppable, super, high strung, raving mad, indomitable, fearless, feisty and absolute fun. There can be a side to this new reformed man that's small, broken, boring, pathetic, henpecked and wasting away. That could also provide a great contrast to what emerges when he explodes back into his old self later in the script. What if he's a hypochondriac, susceptible to practically everything—colds, flu, migraine headaches, insomnia, allergies—you name it? This has to be handled well so that it comes across as funny. What I'm trying for is that he can be pathetic at certain levels, laughable. But how do I maximize this without losing the audience? They need to be able to see themselves in him.

Basically he's also unfailingly honest and upstanding (even though he used to be a world class liar), heroic, nose to the grindstone, normal, realistic and clear eyed, without illusions. But he's also trapped, depressed, lifeless, ill and tired. He's got a nice wife, a life, a home, a future free of crime, is in love, goes to church, is stable, is a good father and is happy in his own way. However he's also in debt, is getting old and fat with a bad back and bad teeth, he has settled for what he's got, doesn't like his job and often feels powerless. All of this can make him a more intriguing character and bring more comedy into the mix. You can see how I'm still playing with dilemma.

Crisis and Decision & Action need to be blazingly huge in a story like this, which promises catastrophic disaster. When I get into a story like this in which someone who is a ticking time bomb gets dragged into an explosive situation, I'm rubbing my hands together in glee, saying, "Wow, I can't wait for it to all go crazy!" What I've seen since the first glimmer of this story is that Cutter would explode back into his wild lying and stealing persona in a desperate attempt to make this insane situation work out somehow.

I have hundreds of questions about the raw possibilities for this plot. My head is exploding with them. Let's lay some of them out:

1. How crazy can this story get? I want it to be off the charts! I want it to be so wild that people are jumping out of their seats. I know that this is hard to do, but it's my intention to blow the audience away with Cutter's virtuosity in lying. He should be stunning, astonishing and unbelievably brilliant.

2. It seems inevitable that St. Nick will discover who Cutter is and what he's up to. What are the raw possibilities for this? Is St. Nick fully on to him, or just discovering that he's not who he says he is? What desperate trouble would that put Cutter in?

3. Will Cutter be betrayed by Apollo? I've had it in the back of my mind that Apollo has a bunch of counterfeit money he needs to do something with. Did he steal it? Make it himself? Is it poor quality funny money, so that he needs to palm it off on a sucker? Is the law onto him so that he can't use his normal process of getting rid of it? Is he in huge trouble? How desperate is he? How well planned out is all this? Is it a master plan dating way back?

4. If Cutter is on medications to stay 'normal' what happens when the meds are gone? Does Apollo substitute placebos for them because he needs the old Cutter to come out? Is Cutter such a hypochondriac that he panics when he realizes that his meds are gone? What's he like without them? Dangerous? Crazy? Fun? This can complicate things immensely and be really funny (or sad).

5. Is the bank deal caving in or is it going through? Once St. Nick is legit, then he's home free in the high-flying world of 'legal' theft with its behind-the-scenes politics, corrupt corporations and shady high finance. Either way could spell disaster for Cutter. If it's failing, St. Nick would be after him with a meat cleaver.

6. What's involved with Cutter going crazy, with reverting to his old out-of-control lying self? How does this manifest itself? What kind of struggle does he put up? Does he make a conscious choice to go off the deep end to deal with the catastrophic situation that has emerged? Does he know this is going to cost him everything? This is a big question. It seems like this is going to be a big, big part of the third act.

7. What are some possible ways for Cutter's cover to come unraveled? What could cause St. Nick to find out that Cutter is not what he appears to be? An accident? Does Apollo betray him? His ignorance of banking regulations? Does he get caught up in the complexity of the lies he's been telling? Does an old acquaintance show up out of the blue and ID him or blow his cover? A stupid mistake?

8. What about his son, Mischa? Does he inject himself into the mix and screw things up? Does he get taken hostage? Is he trying to help his dad? Is he trying to prove that he's got the goods to be a player in his dad's world? How much criminal ambition does he have? Has he been spying on Cutter? Did Apollo put him up to it or encourage him?

9. What about Cutter's wife, Margarita, finding out what he's up to? Has he kept her totally in the dark? Does she spy on him? Does she not trust Apollo at all? Does she stumble onto what's going on? Does she ever see Cutter while he's on the job, or does he see her occasionally, maybe daily? These are big questions.

10. What about the two strikes that Cutter has against him? Has he committed new crimes? Is somebody onto him? Is Apollo threatening to turn him in for an old crime that he did before jail, which is still an open case? Is he getting deeper and deeper into criminality, which threatens to send him to jail for life?

11. What about the law? Are they after St. Nick? After Apollo? On to Cutter? What are the craziest possibilities? Are the feds all over St. Nick, trying to take him down before he vanishes into this legitimate enterprise? Is there a crooked cop on the deal who threatens to blow the deal over more money?

12. Is there a crook from St. Nick's past exploding in on the situation like a bull in a china shop? St. Nick may be clean, but he's got a past and that might be catching up with him. Are there people beside Apollo and Cutter who want to destroy him? How would this screw things up? How crazed could it get?

13. What about St. Nick's legitimate connections? Does he have a senator buddy who's shepherding him through this because he needs St. Nick's

skills? How much muscle does the senator bring to the mix? Does this make St. Nick a shoe-in to get the bank? How much pressure is on Cutter as a bank examiner to certify St. Nick?

14. What are some of the outside influences that might help everything go to hell at precisely the wrong moment? A stock market crash? Another huge corporate scandal? A political scandal? War? A terrorist attack? A car accident? New laws? Maybe it rains frogs. Just kidding.

15. Does Cutter get caught searching for St. Nick's assets? Or is St. Nick getting suspicious? In this type of plot, this will be important. What kind of access does Cutter have to St. Nick's finances because St. Nick is so anxious to become legit? What resources does St. Nick have? Wouldn't he be intensely suspicious of anyone who is looking at any part of them? How might some of the secrets involved slip out? How much does St. Nick begin to trust Cutter? Does he bribe Cutter to see things his way? What does Cutter find? This is its own entire mini-universe.

16. What about a love interest? Not every movie has one, but most do and it's a good thing to try on for fit. This type of movie seems to want one. I don't think Cutter's wife will work because he probably has to leave her behind to do this job. There should be somebody hot that Cutter is in daily contact with. What if it's St. Nick's secretary and she's super hot? What if she's St. Nick's daughter? What if Cutter has to pretend to fall in love with her as part of the scam? What if she's totally hot for him but St. Nick will kill him if he lays a finger on her? What if he's delirious for her—insane with lust? How crazy could it get? How complex? How funny? How erotic? How dangerous?

17. What if this whole story takes an Inspector Clouseau twist? Could Cutter be like Clouseau? Would it work if it's that slapstick? How whacked could it get? Does that undermine the intensity of the plot or add to it? It's certainly a sharply different take on the whole thing and has entertaining possibilities.

18. What about his wife, Margarita? She's very underdeveloped so far. Who is she? What's she like? What are some crazy possibilities for her? What if Apollo had originally set her up with Cutter as part of a long term master plan? What if she works for Apollo? Then Apollo has been setting this up for years. That would make for an interesting revelation that could emerge late in the script. She could still outwit Apollo and help Cutter get away in the end, back to a life of his own choosing.

19. What if Margarita turns out to be Apollo's daughter or even his grand-daughter? I've always had it in the back of my mind that Apollo is of

indeterminate age. Maybe he does T'ai Chi and stays young. He could be 70 and look 50 if he takes great care of himself. It makes for an interesting character. Then Cutter would be married into Apollo's family and there'd truly be no escaping him. This makes her much more unexpected as well.

20. What is Margarita's background? She's rather cliché now and just kind of sits there like a lump. The poor little pious wife who beats her fists helplessly on Cutter while he gets dragged back into his old life. What are some wild possibilities for her? Professor? Cat burglar? Rocket scientist? Lawyer? Nun? Revolutionary? Journalist? Banker? Spy? Executive secretary? Maybe most of these are too hackneyed, but it's worth attention and development. What if she had been an actress? A detective? A CEO? A hooker? A PhD? A psychotic? A poker champion?

21. In what way is this the perfect crime? Is it really a perfect crime or did that just serve as a springboard to get the story going? If it is a perfect crime, it implies that Apollo has set something up that cannot fail. All there is at this point is a golden opportunity to disappear with a lot of St. Nick's money or to ruin him. This aspect has yet to be developed. This is the real process of building a story out of an initial premise. It's like mud wrestling, where you're in a slippery medium grappling with things that you can feel but not see—where everything's constantly shifting as you try to pull a story together.

22. What are some opportunities to make this a perfect crime? Is there a foolproof way to take a huge bite out of St. Nick's hidden assets and get away scott free? The more perfect it is, the more tempting it is for Cutter, and the harder it is for him to walk away from the job—which increases his dilemma. Presumably Apollo has a reputation for coming up with great plans. This is absolutely central to the script I'm proposing. I may come up with a hundred possibilities before I find one that works, or I might even discard the idea of it being a perfect crime altogether.

This question must be pursued in depth because it's so central to the plot. To pull off the perfect crime the person robbed has to either (1) Not know he got robbed; (2) Not have any idea who did it; (3) Believe the person who did it is dead and the goods are irretrievably gone; (4) Believe it was someone else who took it and got away clean; (5) The mark gets killed himself, with no suspicion falling on the crook, and therefore no investigation and nobody looking for missing assets; (6) The mark ends up in jail forever, so there's no recourse, especially if the thief is unknown; (7) You can never be caught for the crime; (8) The victim doesn't know they've been robbed; (9) The victim thinks they foiled the crime, but actually didn't; (10) Somebody else takes the blame for it. I'm sure I'm missing dozens of possibilities, but this gets me going.

Within the story construct that I've got going, Cutter is pretending to be a bank examiner which gives him access to St. Nick's assets, so what kind of perfect crime might be possible? Things can obviously be transferred electronically. That can make Cutter and Apollo rich. What if Cutter exposes the hidden funds to the law and to the IRS? Then they get confiscated or complicated in a disastrous way for St. Nick, which is an acceptable form of revenge (although without profit). Another possibility for revenge is to get St. Nick in so much trouble with his superiors (if he has any) that they'll destroy him or put him through a fate worse than death. In that case, assets could disappear in the confusion. Another way is to have the law storming in and everything going crazy, which provides a perfect opportunity to disappear with a large sum. Only St. Nick would ever know the money is gone, but if he's on the run, in jail, or dead, then they get away with it.

One of the problems I've been wrestling with is: How does Cutter get access to St. Nick's finances, even if he is acting as a bank examiner? Why would St. Nick even begin to trust an outsider? It kept sticking in my craw. As I turned the problem over in my mind, it occurred to me that St. Nick would much prefer to have a *crooked* bank examiner. Maybe his books need to be cooked so they'll pass muster. This provides even deeper access. Here's the idea that I came up with.

Suppose that St. Nick and the senator (let's call him Senator Hutchings) set it up to hire this crooked bank examiner (let's call him Shallott) who will shepherd St. Nick through the hurdles of buying this bank. Now suppose that when St. Nick gassed this whole town years ago over the racehorse incident, Shallott's only family, his brother—severely retarded and in a wheelchair—lived in that town because he loved horses above all else. This would give Shallott fierce and undying hatred for St. Nick, but he's had to bide his time because St. Nick is too dangerous to go after. Now this chance opens up, so Shallott goes to his old friend Apollo and tells him about this once-in-a-lifetime opportunity to take down St. Nick, but he needs help. Apollo provides Cutter as the best man for the job. Now I can get Cutter in as an assistant, so that he doesn't have to know everything about banking, and it gives him deep access to St. Nick's books.

I've been turning this problem over in my mind for some time and now it clicks. This also brings up the question: What makes Cutter the right man for this job? He may need to have a few more specialized skills. He should be good with numbers, with computers, maybe a bit of a financial wizard. We've known he's good at thinking on his feet, learns fast, can juggle a complex system of lies, is fearless and a good team player—a consummate operator. Reminiscent of the vintage *Mission Impossible* TV shows, they're working an inside job with access to a corrupt leader's finances, taking an opportunity to topple him.

Now that Shallott and Cutter are invited into St. Nick's world to cook his books, the story is much easier to develop. Shallott can work things so that St. Nick, who's still eager to get approved by the banking commission, will comply, opening up layer after layer of his secret finances. Presumably Shallott and Cutter are helping him find ways to shift his illegal assets around, so as to help him put money into a reserve fund that is required to buy this bank. This has to be done properly and with finesse, so as not to attract undesirable attention from the IRS and other predatory entities.

Now Shallott should be sharp as a razor, able to take a very hard line with St. Nick about what must happen to get approved. This would enable him to push the envelope in dealing with both St. Nick and his top financial experts who help St. Nick oversee this process. But the fact is that since Shallott has been recommended by Senator Hutchings and hired (and presumably heavily bribed) by St. Nick, then Shallott is himself one of St. Nick's financial experts.

Something that can help Cutter and Shallott pull this off is for there to be a fake investigation launched into St. Nick right as the bank buy is nearing completion. Maybe through a crooked FBI official that Apollo has bribed. If Senator Hutchings is mentioned in connection with St. Nick, then he may have to run for cover. It won't stand up for long, but it doesn't necessarily have to. If St. Nick is distracted for long enough, then his full attention won't be on what Shallott and Cutter are up to. It's the basic principle of magic. Get them watching one hand while the other does the disappearing act. This is akin to what they did in *The Sting*, where a fake FBI agent came in on Robert Redford to get the cop from back home off him.

Another possibility that I stumbled onto is: What if Cutter unexpectedly finds himself in awe of St. Nick when he starts working with him? The inspired genius of St. Nick's lying and thieving could very much impress Cutter. This is unexpected for Cutter because he has found someone who can lie circles around him. The adroitness with which St. Nick and his circle maneuver is staggering and dazzling to Cutter, as he learns more and more. This adds a new wrinkle to Cutter's dilemma; he's increasingly less able to quit this operation, because he's 'falling in love' with his worst enemy (An Enemy Loved). Cutter sees a consummate artist at work and realizes that still has a lot to learn. He hates this guy's guts and yet he finds himself in awe of him. His worst enemy has turned out to be a kind of guru.

Another possibility is that St. Nick could be impressed with Cutter and invite him to work for him, rather than just consult. This would give Cutter deeper access to St. Nick, but also render Cutter more vulnerable. If Cutter is taken in, then he might learn about a huge master plan that he needs to stick around for, not only to destroy it, but also because it's fascinating and intoxicating. He could be rubbing shoulders with world bankers, senators, corporate CEOs, big money aristocrats, CIA operatives, Mafia dons and drug dealers all doing a clever mix of legal and illegal business in ways that make Cutter's head spin.

Now we come to the next thing that I hit upon after long hours of thinking and reading and feeling stumped. What I want is for Cutter to be precipitated into the world of the super fat cats, the big time players with their gigantic banks and corporations and hidden agendas. This is the world of legalized theft, manipulation and masterful power brokers who run things behind the scenes. What are some possibilities for this? What I hit on in my research is for Senator Hutchings to have set up a mega-scam in which a government program provides guaranteed agricultural loans to third world countries. Hutchings is on the Senate Banking Committee and has slipped a loophole into a new law at the eleventh hour. This highly specialized loophole, combined with an obscure tax loophole affords them a singular opportunity to make a vast fortune. Hutchings plan is to offer these loans to countries that have dictators in power, which opens up all kinds of under-the-table possibilities.

The catch is that Hutchings needs a bank to do this through, but he has to be behind the scenes as a silent partner. He seeks out St. Nick, his old friend who has never even been indicted. He knows St. Nick wants to go legit and they've worked together successfully before. St. Nick is foaming at the mouth to get out of the troublesome underworld and into the realm of the aristocracy. Senator Hutchings recommends Shallot, this crooked bank examiner, as someone who can rig the process of buying a bank as well as help St. Nick use his hidden assets to do so.

There's an African dictator, let's call him Joseph Umbotha from Mambia (an imaginary country) in particular, who is anxious to do business. The law allows goods, but not money to go to a third world country, in an attempt to cut down on corruption. The bank will issue a loan for several hundred million dollars, possibly even billions, and pay the money to an agricultural corporation for supplies that get shipped to Mambia. St. Nick and Hutchings get a kickback from the corporation for the business—and for the chance to import its genetically modified seeds into Mambia. Umbotha takes delivery and uses the seed, agricultural products and farming equipment to create an immense modern plantation as his own private business, which will bring in a fortune over the years. He will sell none of the food locally, in fact preferring to starve his enemies, but then sells and barters the food for weapons and restricted equipment (some of which Hutchings sets up, again getting a kickback). Payments are made for a while until the loan limit is reached and then Umbotha defaults, causing the U.S. government to repay the loan to St. Nick's bank since it's a government guaranteed loan.

So far St. Nick and Hutchings are not out a dime, but the real kicker is that in exchange for all this extremely profitable agricultural equipment and goods,

Umbotha allows Hutchings and St. Nick to set up a huge manufacturing plant in Mambia. He provides them with virtually free prison labor as well as free raw materials for a ten year period, after which this highly-profitable operating factory reverts to Umbotha. But by then, Hutchings and St. Nick will be fabulously wealthy, and will in fact use the profits to buy more banks around the world and become a banking empire.

St. Nick and Senator Hutchings work out the details of this in a secure room that has just been swept for bugs. Any electronic equipment within 100 feet will set off an alarm. Cutter is hidden behind the wall with two cans and a string stretched taut between them, making a primitive children's toy phone, and hears everything. He also overhears St. Nick tell Hutchings that he is extremely impressed with Cutter and that he's going to offer him a job in the organization because he needs men with balls and brains like him. Cutter had just fought with St. Nick about something and thought he'd ruined the revenge operation, but now learns that St. Nick actually admires him for standing up to him. Hutchings cautions him to not let Cutter know what's really going on, and St. Nick says he certainly won't for quite some time, but in the meantime they need someone who can think on his feet and who wants to make a ton of money. Plus, St. Nick says that if it goes wrong, they can pin it on Cutter and, using their connections, get off scott free. St. Nick stresses that Cutter kicks ass and if they can turn him, he'll be a valuable member of their team.

All of this sets Cutter's brain reeling, and when he reports back to Apollo they realize that they will have to alter their plan. But it also offers them a bigger opportunity to take St. Nick down even more. Cutter will be taken inside their organization and promoted. There's a bigger crime that they can derail, but there's higher risk, especially with the possibility of Cutter being used as a patsy. There's more money involved now but there's also a real crime against humanity in Africa with the sweatshop factory. Cutter may be furious about the American taxpayer getting robbed of billions of dollars through the loans. This might anger Apollo, too, which would make us like him more. They would now want to take down Senator Hutchings as well as St. Nick. Cutter's morals versus his greed are discussed with Apollo. Plus, Cutter's addiction is kicking in—he's got the itch to be involved in this type of high-level, high-stakes operation—and he's even more amazed at St. Nick's and Hutchings' brilliance. He knows it's wrong, but he's got to play the game and get involved in this high-wire adventure. Everything gets ratcheted up another few notches and it all complicates Cutter's dilemma even more.

BACK TO EXPLORING

THE 36 DRAMATIC SITUATIONS

Let's go back to our investigation of the 36 Dramatic Situations. In the first three situations I've shown that you can do quite a lot with each situation. Now, with the plot up and running I can work leaner and faster.

4. VENGEANCE TAKEN FOR KINDRED UPON KINDRED (Intrafamily fighting or infighting)

The possibility of infighting between St. Nick, the Senator, as well as their cabal of international bankers, arms merchants, drug smugglers and CIA operatives. Infighting in Cutter's family.

5. PURSUIT (In pursuit of something or being pursued)

Cutter and Apollo in pursuit of St. Nick (for revenge and wealth), who's in pursuit of legitimacy and gigantic legal profits. Senator Hutchings is after huge profits. Cutter is pursued by his demons, by his son, maybe by his wife. Cutter could be pursued by a cop who spots him and remembers him from way back, and wants to take him down for an old crime or an insult. Apollo can be pursued by the law, maybe by a counterfeiter that he ripped off, maybe by other criminals who find out what he's up to. Apollo is certainly also in pursuit of huge profits through his hidden agenda with counterfeit money. St. Nick might be pursued by a criminal who shows up and wants him dead, or there could be an untimely (or unexpected) investigation into his criminal affairs. Two of the subheadings that click are: *Fugitives from Justice Pursued for Brigandage* (acts of piracy) *or Political Offenses, Etc.*; *A Hero Struggling Against a Power.*

6. DISASTER

Everything starts going wrong at the worst possible moment for Cutter, including possible betrayal (intentional or not) by Apollo. Disaster for St. Nick as he sees his dreams of becoming an 'aristocrat' (a member of the 'club') falling apart. The same for Senator Hutchings, seeing his potential billions disappearing. Margarita, Cutter's wife, seeing their family at risk, or actually falling apart. Mischa being drawn into a life of crime. The reappearance of Apollo in Cutter's life at the beginning of the script is a disaster. Mischa getting caught up in St. Nick's grasp at the crucial moment. Also Mischa not being able to get his dad to talk about his wild old days is a disaster from Mischa's point of view. Disaster can be physical, psychological, imminent or past (St. Nick killing the whole town, including Shallott's brother), as well as the *fear* of disaster. What are the worst types of disaster that could happen to Cutter at the most crucial moment? What are the craziest?

The most unexpected? The funniest? The freakiest? Some good subheadings: *Defeat Suffered; A Monarch Overthrown; A Fatherland Destroyed* (a good metaphorical image*); The Fall of Humanity* (St. Nick and Hutchings making money off the suffering of starving Africans); *An Outrage Suffered; Abandonment by a Lover or a Husband; Children Lost by Their Parents.*

7. FALLING PREY TO CRUELTY OR MISFORTUNE

Obviously this includes the appearance of Apollo in Cutter and Margarita's life. From St. Nick's point of view, it's anything that impedes his ascension into high society and legalized theft. The same for Senator Hutchings with his big money and power. Apollo's betrayal of Cutter. Mischa being left out. Same for Margarita. The appearance of the law on any of the players. The situation blowing up in Cutter's face at the crucial moment. Cutter blowing up in St. Nick's and Hutching's faces at the crucial moment. All the subheadings are useful: *The Innocent Made the Victim of Ambitious Intrigue; The Innocent Despoiled by Those Who Should Protect; The Powerful Dispossessed and Wretched; A Favorite or an Intimate Finds Himself Forgotten; The Unfortunate Robbed of Their Only Hope.*

8. REVOLT

Shallott and Apollo set in motion a revolt against St. Nick. Cutter is in revolt against his old life of crime. His wife is in revolt against his gig with Apollo. Mischa is a troubled teen who rebels against his father. St. Nick and Hutchings are in revolt against their stations in life. Cutter leads a revolt against them when things get troublesome and fall apart. Some good subheadings: *A Conspiracy Chiefly of One Individual; A Conspiracy of Several; Revolt of One Individual, Who Influences and Involves Others.*

9. DARING ENTERPRISE (Doing something brave or adventurous)

Shallott's idea is adventurous, Apollo is daring and enterprising, and Cutter is famous for his sense of adventure, even though at the beginning of the script he is stymied. However, he is involved in a daring enterprise by getting out of a life of crime. Hutchings and St. Nick are both involved in daring enterprises. Cutter will go completely wild late in the script. Good subheadings: *Preparations For War; War; Recapture of a Desired Object; Adventurous Expeditions; Adventure Undertaken for the Purpose of Obtaining a Beloved Woman* (Cutter trying to get back to his wife, or maybe gets tempted by St. Nick's gorgeous secretary).

10. ABDUCTION (Kidnapping, either physical or psychological)

Cutter is abducted by Apollo, blackmailed, pressured, enticed and dragged into this plot against St. Nick. This also suggests the possibility of a literal kidnapping. Mischa could get taken hostage by St. Nick and Hutchings when things get dicey. Could Cutter or Apollo take someone hostage? What about the law swooping in at a critical moment? Useful subheadings: *Rescue of a Captive Friend; Rescue of a Child; Rescue of a Soul in Captivity to Error.*

11. THE ENIGMA (The riddle, the mystery—either external or internal)

Cutter is trying to figure out how to get out of this whole thing, trying to come to terms with why he's secretly enthused about Apollo dragging him into this. Margarita is trying to figure out what's going on with Cutter. Cutter, Apollo and Shallott are trying to figure out the best way to take down St. Nick. St. Nick and Hutchings are trying to work their master plan without any glitches. Mischa is trying to figure out how to get some adventure out of his boring father. How can Cutter use the element of mystery to trick St. Nick? Is there anything mysterious about Apollo and Cutter's past that we don't learn about until late in the script? Useful subheadings: *Search for a Person Who Must Be Found on Pain of Death; A Riddle To Be Solved on Pain of Death; The Same Case, in Which the Riddle is Proposed by the Coveted Woman; Tests for the Purpose of Ascertaining the Mental Condition.*

12. OBTAINING

Pretty straightforward. Everybody's trying to obtain various things in this story. Some of them are tangible, like wealth, and some intangible, like respect, integrity, culture, freedom, revenge, love, power. All the subheadings are useful: *Efforts to Obtain an Object by Ruse or Force; Endeavor by Means of Persuasive Eloquence Alone; Eloquence With an Arbitrator.*

13. ENMITY OF KINSMEN (Hatred or animosity between kin, friends, co-workers etc.)

Between Cutter and Apollo; between St. Nick and Hutchings and any of their underlings; between Mischa and Cutter; between Cutter and Margarita. It can be huge or small, longstanding or momentary. Suggestive subheadings: *Reciprocal Hatred; Hatred Between Relatives for Reasons of Self-Interest; Hatred of the Son for the Father; Mutual Hatred.*

14. RIVALRY OF KINSMEN (Competition between kin or friends, etc.)

Again, between Cutter and Apollo; St. Nick and Hutchings and underlings; Mischa and Cutter; maybe between Cutter and Margarita. Suggestive subheadings: *Rivalry of Father and Son, for an Unmarried Woman* (this suggests a very interesting possibility of Mischa being drawn into St. Nick's secretary, with whom Cutter may be having a fling); *Rivalry of Friends.*

15. MURDEROUS ADULTERY

The possibility of Margarita (who needs to be developed, energized and activated) finding out about an affair between Cutter and the secretary, maybe even trying to kill the secretary, or wanting to. It also suggests the possibility of adultery in St. Nick and Hutching's camp, possibly creating bad blood. Useful subheading (probably entirely metaphorical): *The Slaying of a Trusting Lover.*

16. MADNESS (Any and all varieties of insanity, even totally delightful ones like Jim Carrey or Harpo Marx)

Cutter has recovered from madness and is now being dragged back into it by Apollo. Apollo brings madness into Cutter's house by infecting Mischa, who hangs in the balance, and by bringing discord into Cutter's marriage. St. Nick is criminally insane, as is Senator Hutchings, who has great public stature. The sting will get nutty as things fall apart at the crucial moment. Cutter will go crazy in an awe-inspiring way when he's backed into a corner—the crazier the better. In fact, if he doesn't go off-the-charts wild then I'm going to feel cheated because that's one of the promises of this movie—seeing him snap back into his old self and blowing our minds. There's the possibility that Apollo might have a history of insanity. In the end, if Mischa is scared straight, then he escapes from madness. Also, Cutter could end up telling the truth about everything that St. Nick and Hutchings are up to, overturning the apple cart for many in Washington. Perhaps there is the possibility of cash mailed out to millions of average consumers who have been ripped off by the likes of St. Nick and Hutchings—how's that for a crazy ending? Useful subheadings: *Kinsmen Slain in Madness; Lover Slain in Madness; Slaying or Injuring of a Person not Hated; Disgrace Brought Upon Oneself Through Madness; Loss of Loved Ones Brought About by Madness.*

17. FATAL IMPRUDENCE (Doing something unwise, which has fatal consequences, either literally or metaphorically)

Cutter knows that throwing back in with Apollo is going to ruin his life. Apollo trying to run his hidden agenda with counterfeit money may sink everything. St. Nick and Hutchings may misjudge or underestimate Cutter, Shallott and Apollo. Does Shallott die in the process of revenging his brother? Do Cutter, Apollo, Mischa or Margarita almost die? Does St. Nick die? Does St. Nick suffer a fate worse than death? Does Cutter make a serious mistake in the process of the sting? What's the worst mistake that Cutter could possibly make? That St. Nick could make? All the subheadings are useful: *Imprudence the Cause of One's Own Misfortune; Imprudence the Cause of One's Own Dishonor; Curiosity the Cause of One's Own Misfortune; Loss of the Possession of a Loved One, Through Curiosity; Curiosity the Cause of Death or Misfortune to Others.*

18. INVOLUNTARY CRIMES OF LOVE (Unintentional sex crime or 'love' crime)

Cutter does not intend to hurt or betray his wife or son; nor does Apollo mean to betray Cutter or put him in mortal danger. Cutter may unintentionally mistreat Apollo. Same between St. Nick and Hutchings. In the book, all the sub-headings are explicitly sexual in nature so not of much use to us here.

19. SLAYING OF A KINSMAN UNRECOGNIZED (Killing your brother without recognizing him, or mistreating someone so that they feel 'slain' and 'un-recognized')

Cutter feels like Apollo is 'slaying' him and not recognizing who he is now when Apollo pressures him to join the sting against St. Nick. Mischa feels left out of his father's old life, and also left behind when Cutter goes off with Apollo. Margarita feels left out, betrayed and abandoned. Are there any possible betrayals, partial betrayals, or perceived betrayals between St. Nick and Hutchings? Interesting subheadings: *Being Upon the Point of Killing a Son Unknowingly; The Same Case, Strengthened by Machiavellian Instigations; Being Upon the Point of Slaying a Brother Unknowingly; A Father Slain Unknowingly, Through Machiavellian Advice* (interesting possibility if Mischa is turned and used against his dad); *Involuntary Killing of a Loved Woman; Being Upon the Point of Killing a Lover Unrecognized* (the last two are metaphorical slayings); *Failure to Rescue an Unrecognized Son* (this suggests some potent possibilities).

20. SELF-SACRIFICE FOR AN IDEAL

Cutter owes his life to Apollo and feels the need to pay back the debt. Cutter has sacrificed to be living the straight life because it is his ideal. How much is he willing to risk to take down St. Nick, especially when it gets dicey? Apollo feels very strongly about getting revenge on St. Nick, as does Shallott. Does Shallott sacrifice his life to help Cutter pull off the scam? Doesn't Hutchings feel as though he's risking himself to help the CIA pull off these illegal arms shipments, the way Oliver North did? Suggestive subheadings: *Sacrifice of Life for the Sake of One's Word; Life Sacrifice for the Success of One's People; Life Sacrificed in Filial Piety* (is Mischa willing to sacrifice his life to save his father?); *Life Sacrificed for the Sake of One's Faith* (not literally one's religion, but one's faith, or bond, or word)*; Both Love and Life Sacrificed for One's Faith, or a Cause; Sacrifice of Well-Being to Duty.*

21. SELF-SACRIFICE FOR KINDRED

Cutter and Apollo are willing to put themselves in harm's way to help avenge Frenchy. Cutter is also willing to do anything for his wife or son. His son may be willing to risk everything to rescue his father in the end. Cutter and Apollo are willing to do anything for each other. Is there any of this between St. Nick and Senator Hutchings, or with their underlings for their bosses? Does Shallott risk everything to avenge his brother or to save Cutter so he can complete the revenge? Some useful subheadings: *Life Sacrificed for that of a Relative or a Loved One; Life Sacrificed for the Happiness of a Relative or a Loved One; Ambition Sacrificed for the Happiness of a Parent; Ambition Sacrificed for the Life of a Parent; Love Sacrificed for the Sake of a Parent's Life; For the Happiness of One's Child.*

22. ALL SACRIFICED FOR A PASSION

This is right at the nucleus of the whole script because Apollo is asking Cutter to give up his new life for the chance to destroy St. Nick, who they both hate passionately. Cutter has previously given up his underworld life because of his passion for freedom and love. Cutter gives this new life up for revenge. St. Nick is giving up his underworld life for his passion to be one of the ruling aristocrats and to not only escape from the world of cops and robbers, but to be above the law in many ways. Senator Hutchings is willing to risk everything for the chance to become a billionaire and acquire much greater power. In the end, Mischa may have risked everything to break into his father's exciting new world, as may have Margarita, in an attempt to break Cutter out of this world. When Cutter goes wild in the ending, he is risking everything to take down St. Nick and his entire operation. If he tells nothing but the truth in the very end to destroy them all, then he's again giving up on his underworld life for his passion for freedom, family, solidity, love, happiness and truth. Interesting subheadings: *Religious Vows of Chastity Broken for a Passion* (a nice analogy for Cutter breaking his vow to never lie); *Respect for a Priest Destroyed* (Margarita losing respect for Cutter); *A Future Ruined by Passion; Ruin of Mind, Health, and Life; Ruin of Fortunes, Lives, and Honors; Temptations Destroying the Sense of Duty, of Pity,* etc.

23. NECESSITY OF SACRIFICING LOVED ONES

Cutter is faced with this as soon as Apollo shows up because Apollo needs him to leave his family for the job. If Apollo's hidden agenda with the counterfeit money is in play, then he's faced with the possibility of sacrificing Cutter. Does Mischa contemplate putting his father at risk to fulfill his dreams of breaking into Cutter's criminal world? This is a dark possibility, but it might add more danger to the script. If St. Nick comes to truly like Cutter, then he's going to be faced with the necessity of getting rid of him when Cutter's plan is revealed. Also, St. Nick and Senator Hutchings might each have to consider throwing the other to the wolves. Suggestive subheadings: *Necessity for Sacrificing a Daughter* (or Son) *in the Public Interest; Duty of Sacrificing One's Child, Unknown to Others, Under the Pressure of Necessity; Duty of Sacrificing, Under the Same Circumstances, One's Father or Husband; Duty of Contending with a Friend.*

24. RIVALRY OF SUPERIOR AND INFERIOR

This is interesting because the dynamics in almost all these relationships revolve around who has the upper hand or who is the superior operator. It's active between Cutter and Apollo since Cutter never trusts Apollo, even though they're blood brothers. It's between St. Nick and Hutchings for similar reasons. Between Cutter and St. Nick as Cutter maneuvers to find a way to take St. Nick down. It will especially be true once St. Nick discovers who Cutter really is and what he's up to. It will be there between Mischa and Cutter, in their struggle for dominance, as well as between Cutter and Margarita as she tries to force him to not break his vow. Intriguing subheadings: *Rivalry of a Mortal and an Immortal* (various cases can be made for who is the 'immortal'); *Of a Magician and an Ordinary Man* (interesting—and again, who's the magician in any given scene?); *Of Conqueror and Conquered; Of a King and a Noble; Of a Powerful Person and an Upstart; Of Rich and Poor; Of an Honored Man and a Suspected One; Rivalry of Two Who are Almost Equal.*

25. ADULTERY

There is the possibility that Cutter has an affair with St. Nick's secretary. This raises lots of story options, including what Margarita is going to do if she finds out. Are there other possibilities of adultery that could complicate the plot? With St. Nick or Hutchings and women they know? Are there possibilities of metaphoric adultery? Intriguing subheadings: *A Wife Betrayed For Debauchery; A Good Husband Betrayed for an Inferior Rival; Vengeance of a Deceived Wife.*

26. CRIMES OF LOVE (Sexual crimes, or metaphorically, crimes against a lover)

Cutter seeing himself betray his wife, and she seeing it being done to her. Apollo betraying Cutter. Mischa being abandoned by Cutter and seeing it as a crime of love. All the subheadings are entirely sexual in nature.

27. DISCOVERY OF THE DISHONOR OF A LOVED ONE

Obviously this would be when Cutter finds out he's being betrayed by Apollo, or when Margarita and Mischa learn that Cutter is going off with Apollo, or when St. Nick finds out who Cutter really is and what he's up to. It brings up the question of a betrayal between St. Nick and Hutchings. Dynamic subheadings: *Discovery of a Father's Shame; Discovery that One's Lover is a Scoundrel; Duty of Punishing a Son Condemned Under a Law Which the Father Has Made.*

28. OBSTACLES TO LOVE

There are obstacles to love between Cutter and Margarita, possibly between Cutter and St. Nick's secretary, between Cutter and Mischa and between

Cutter and Apollo. Any other possibilities? One possible subheading: *By the Incompatibility of Temper of the Lovers* (Cutter and Margarita, Cutter and secretary).

29. AN ENEMY LOVED (Love for an enemy, respect for an enemy, fascination)

Cutter's relationship with Apollo, because as tight as they are, Cutter knows that Apollo is simply not to be trusted. Cutter's relationship with St. Nick because if he's astonished by how phenomenally skillful St. Nick is, then he'll discover that his worst enemy is his guru. His passion for the secretary—how much of an enemy is she? Maybe she's a deadly serious one. Cutter's respect for Hutchings as well. Does St. Nick still like Cutter even after he finds out what Cutter is up to, because Cutter is so phenomenal? The only subheading that suggests anything is: *The Loved One Hated by Kinsmen of the Lover* (if St. Nick's secretary is related to him).

30. AMBITION

Everybody's got incredibly huge ambitions, from Cutter and Apollo wanting to destroy St. Nick, to Hutchings' and St. Nick's ambition to make billions, and so on. We've also got Cutter's ambition to be straight and tell the truth. Mischa has powerful ambitions. Apollo never quits. It's interesting to isolate each person's ambition and look at its origins, how it plays out, how it changes, what they'll do to achieve it. All the subheadings are suggestive: *Ambition Watched and Guarded Against by a Kinsman, or By a Person Under Obligation; Rebellious Ambition; Ambition and Covetousness Heaping Crime Upon Crime.*

31. CONFLICT WITH A GOD (Conflict with a great power)

Obviously Cutter versus St. Nick and in a sense, Cutter versus Apollo. But Cutter is a deity in his own right as St. Nick will discover when their fight to the finish kicks in. Mischa against Cutter is a type of this conflict. Cutter trying to escape from his addictions of lying and stealing (these are great and powerful 'gods' that can dominate him). Cutter's conflict with Margarita also is in this category. All the subheadings are useful: *Struggle Against a Deity; Strife with the Believers in a God; Controversy with a Deity; Punishment for Contempt of a God; Punishment for Pride Before a God.*

32. MISTAKEN JEALOUSY (Jealousy arising from a misunderstanding; or an intentional set up)

Is Cutter only having an affair with this stunningly gorgeous nymphomaniac secretary to get some state secrets out of her, so that Margarita's homicidal jealousy is unfounded? Does anyone set up a situation to make someone jealous? Is Mischa envious of what Cutter is doing in this criminal world, but in truth Cutter is having a horrible time? (I've been playing with the possibility that both Mischa and Margarita have separately tracked Cutter down to his secret mission and are spying on him. I may not go there, but it's an intriguing possibility and adds significant complications and could be fun.) Subheadings that may prove useful: *The Mistake Originates in the Suspicious Mind of the Jealous One; Baseless Jealousy Aroused by Malicious Rumors; Jealousy Suggested by a Traitor Who is Moved by Hatred or Self-Interest.*

33. ERRONEOUS JUDGMENT (Making a bad choice or poor judgment—or fear of it)

Cutter knows this is a bad choice from the beginning, but he's blackmailed by Apollo and is raging for a chance to get at St. Nick. Cutter is dealing with Mischa's choices in life. Margarita is questioning Cutter's choice. Then Cutter is getting in over his head and knows it, knows he's going to make a bad choice or a serious misstep. Apollo is also misjudging his enemies. St. Nick misjudges the situation and misjudges Cutter. St. Nick and Hutchings are likewise misjudging each other. Mischa makes a disastrous choice at a critical moment. Interesting subheadings: *False Suspicion Where Faith is Necessary; False Suspicion Aroused by a Misunderstood Attitude of a Loved One; False Suspicions Drawn Upon Oneself to Save a Friend* (this could also be an interesting possibility); *They Fall Upon the Innocent; The Accusation is Allowed to Fall Upon an Enemy; The Error is Provoked by an Enemy; False Suspicion Thrown by the Real Culprit Upon One of His Enemies; Thrown by the Real Culprit Upon the Second Victim Against Whom He Has Plotted From the Beginning* (could be a nice possibility for a reversal).

34. REMORSE

Cutter will feel remorse for abandoning his straight life. Margarita will feel this too, for allowing him to go off with Apollo (even though she really had no choice). Does Apollo feel any remorse? How about Mischa? What about St. Nick? He's a man without conscience, therefore he has utterly *no remorse*. Does Cutter's remorse send him back to telling the truth at the very end? Intriguing subheadings: *Remorse for a Parricide* (if Mischa puts Cutter in harm's way); *Remorse for an Assassination* (keep in mind, this doesn't necessarily have to be a literal assassination)*; Remorse for a Fault of Love; Remorse for an Adultery.*

35. RECOVERY OF A LOST ONE

Cutter re-emerging into his old criminal pathological lying self—recovering his old addictions and Apollo getting his old partner back. Cutter gets his old straight life back in the end, wins his wife back and ends up having his son scared straight. Is St. Nick trying to recover his innocence by escaping the world of crime? Does Senator Hutchings have to get back some old family glory that was lost? There are no subheadings for this situation.

36. LOSS Of LOVED ONES

Cutter is missing his old riotous lying ways. Cutter is being torn away from his family, then is betrayed by Apollo. Shallott, the crooked bank examiner, loses his only family member because of St. Nick. St. Nick and Hutchings lose their gigantic victory at the last minute. Does Apollo lose Cutter in the end? Some useful subheadings: *Witnessing the Slaying of Kinsmen While Powerless to Prevent It; Helping to Bring Misfortune Upon One's People Through Professional Secrecy; Learning of the Death of a Kinsman or Ally* (various people could die or be 'lost').

So you can see I got a lot of mileage out of these 36 Dramatic Situations. In fact, I found a lot of my plot through this in-depth exploration. A scientist could create everything in your room with the Periodic Table of Elements. Your chair is made up of Carbon, Hydrogen, Oxygen and so on. In a similar way drama is made up of Madness, Disaster, Ambition and so on. These 36 elements are the fundamental building blocks of all storytelling—or to switch metaphors—they are the DNA that story worlds consist of, and you can organize them in any way you want to suit your needs. I'll make many passes over the 36 Dramatic Situations before I am done, but each time I find fresh nuance by exploring every crevice. The subtle things, the little differences can often make it work, make it real or add that special magic 'something.' I feel like I have scoured every inch of the world of this story with this tool. I trust you now feel much more at home with the 36 Dramatic Situations, and the more you use it, the more comfortable you'll feel with it. And remember, there are no wrong choices with this tool. If a situation triggers an idea, then it has done its job.

[Note: If you're following the detour from the chapter, *Utilizing the Dilemma*, you should now skip ahead to the chapter, *Utilizing Research and Brainstorming*.]

18
UTILIZING
THE ENNEAGRAM

Let's now explore what the Enneagram has to offer in terms of character development for our script. Looking first at Cutter, I find that I'm probably looking at two different people because he seems to be a 7 (the Enthusiast in the Riso-Hudson system) when his wild side comes out, and yet when we first meet him he might be a 1 (the Reformer) or a 6 (the Loyalist). Two entirely different personalities seems to be a really fun possibility for this movie.

The 7 in the Healthy aspect is "*highly responsive, excitable, enthusiastic about sensation and experience. Most extroverted type: stimuli bring immediate responses — they find everything invigorating. Lively, vivacious, eager, spontaneous, resilient, cheerful.*" This seems to be what I pictured the wild Cutter to be like. A 7 in the Average aspect can "*become adventurous and 'worldly wise,' but less focused, constantly seeking new things and experiences.*" Then there's a gold mine: "*Unable to discriminate what they really need, become hyperactive, unable to say 'no' to themselves, throwing self into constant activity. Uninhibited, doing and saying whatever comes to mind: storytelling, flamboyant exaggerations, witty wisecracking, performing. Fear being bored: in perpetual motion, but do too many things — many ideas but little follow through. / Get into conspicuous consumption and all forms of excess. Self-centered, materialistic, and greedy, never feeling that they have enough. Demanding and pushy, yet unsatisfied and jaded. Addictive, hardened, and insensitive.*"

This is right on the money for how I pictured the wild Cutter. The last two sentences are interesting. I always saw him as addictive, but demanding and pushy, unsatisfied and jaded, hardened, and insensitive—these are interesting traits to contemplate. It definitely makes for a more completely rounded character with more tangible flaws. They definitely sound like a career criminal, however charming Cutter may be. Plus, I want the audience to feel attacked by him (as well as highly entertained) when he goes wild at the end, and this would help do that. I like it. I hadn't thought that far ahead yet with his character.

Now let's look at the Unhealthy aspects of a 7: "*desperate to quell their anxieties, can be impulsive and infantile: do not know when to stop. Addictions and excess take their toll: debauched, depraved, dissipated escapists, offensive and abusive. / In flight from self, acting out impulses rather than dealing with anxiety or frustrations: go out of control, into erratic mood swings, and compulsive actions (manias). / Finally, their energy and health is completely spent: become claustrophobic and panic-stricken. Often give up on themselves and life: deep depression and despair, self-destructive overdoses, impulsive suicide. Generally corresponds to the Manic-Depressive and Histrionic personality disorders.*" That's a fascinating look at the low end and/or dark side of Cutter. It's rich in flaws and broken personality and disorders, all of which I knew I needed for Cutter and saw in him in the abstract, but here's a list of mesmerizing possibilities for him staring me in the face. In this way it's like the 36 Dramatic Situations—it's an intensely valuable resource to draw from and can save a lot of brain racking.

Words like desperate, infantile, excess, depraved, out of control, erratic mood swings and manias are all so rich and intense and varied and deep and suggestive. Then we've got even darker elements of deep depression and despair, self-destructive overdoses, impulsive suicide. These are bad news, and what I like about them is that it goes all the way to the bottom in terms of developing a full-spectrum portrait of Cutter. Looking at these lists is a real eye opener. I'm looking at a real human being, rather than just my take on the character who I've been seeing in my mind's eye as I build the plot and the people. As I develop him further, I'll be paying special attention to these possibilities and keep coming back to them to try and work in as many as are useful.

Now let's look at the other side of Cutter's personality—the sober, honest, ardent husband, father, churchgoer and community man. The first thing that jumps out at me is that this Cutter seems to be a 1. "*Conscientious with strong personal convictions: they have an intense sense of right and wrong, personal religious and moral values. Wish to be rational, reasonable, self-disciplined, mature, moderate in all things. / Extremely principled, always want to be fair, objective, and ethical: truth and justice primary values. Sense of responsibility, personal integrity, and of having a higher purpose often make them teachers and witnesses to the truth.*" This is a rich source of personality traits that he seems to have, and I want to embed them deeper into him. This is the man I want to open the movie with. A truly changed man. We won't know how changed he is until we start to hear about his old wild days, but this is who I want.

I'm also thinking about how I want him to be at the end of the movie. In the Healthy section is the part 'At Their Best': "*Become extraordinarily wise and discerning. By accepting what is, they become transcendentally realistic, knowing the best action to take in each moment. Humane, inspiring, and hopeful: the truth will be heard.*" This suggests some interesting possibilities because he's not just back to where he used to be before Apollo dragged him in, but has actually improved a lot from this ordeal. This is a real hero. I see him at the end of the movie being free from his hypochondria, his need for medication, his claustrophobia and all that.

Then, in the Average aspects a 1 can "*become high-minded idealists, feeling that it is up to them to improve everything: crusaders, advocates, critics. Into 'causes' and explaining to others how things 'ought' to be.*" This is an interesting set of possibilities that I hadn't thought of and it helps flaw the "changed" Cutter, keeping him human. There are also comic possibilities in this if he's a crusader and can get preachy. Also we've got "*orderly and well-organized, but impersonal, puritanical, emotionally constricted, rigidly keeping their feelings and impulses in check. Often workaholics — 'anal-compulsive,' punctual, pedantic, and fastidious.*" This has some obvious comic possibilities as well—the fussy little repressed busybody that people like to laugh at. Plus I want there to be as much contrast between who he starts out as and who he turns into when he goes wild.

There is also comic paydirt in his being "*very opinionated about everything: correcting people and badgering them to 'do the right thing' — as they see it. Impatient, never satisfied with anything unless it is done according to their prescriptions. Moralizing, scolding, abrasive, and indignantly angry.*" These are fun, especially abrasive and indignantly angry. That's giving him some real flaws that can stress the marriage—it's not all hearts and flowers in Camelot. As I look at the Unhealthy aspects I don't see too much that I want to use because I want him to be in pretty decent shape.

APOLLO

I see Apollo as a 7 also with many of the attributes from Cutter. They go together in so many ways. But I would also see him as maybe a 5 (the Investigator or the Thinker). This goes along with him being a good planner—the intense cerebral type. "*possessing good foresight and prediction*" as well as "*make pioneering discoveries and find entirely new ways of doing and perceiving things*" plus "*model building, preparing, practicing, and gathering more resources.*" Also interesting is "*provocative and abrasive, with intentionally extreme and radical views.*"

But I'm also looking at him at a possible 6 (the Loyalist). "*Able to elicit strong emotional responses from others: very appealing, endearing, lovable, affectionate. Trust important: bonding with others, forming permanent relationships and alliances. / Dedicated to individuals and movements in which they deeply believe.*"

But then again, maybe he's got attributes of the 8 (the Challenger or the Leader). "*Self-assertive, self-confident, and strong: have learned to stand up for what they need and want. A resourceful, 'can do' attitude and passionate inner drive. / Decisive, authoritative, and commanding: the natural leader others look up to. Take initiative, make things happen: champion people, provider, protective, and honorable, carrying others with their strength.*" At their best: "*Courageous, willing to put self in serious jeopardy to achieve their vision and have a lasting influence.*" In the Average aspect: "*enterprising, pragmatic, 'rugged individualists,' wheeler-dealers. Risk-taking, hardworking, denying own emotional needs. / Begin to dominate their environment, including others: want to feel that others are behind them, supporting their efforts. Swaggering, boastful, forceful, and expansive: the 'boss' whose word is law. Proud, egocentric, want to impose their will and vision on everything, not seeing others as equals or treating them with respect.*" In the Unhealthy aspect: "*The criminal and outlaw, renegade, and con-artist,*" plus "*develop delusional ideas about their power, invincibility, and ability to prevail: megalomania, feeling omnipotent, invulnerable.*" These are all interesting possibilities for Apollo.

You can see that I'm not just throwing myself into any one of these, but rather, I'm really exploring the raw possibilities. And I may draw from each of these as needed, because while a person will tend to be predominantly one of these types, they can be mixed with other types. Plus, as a screenwriter I have no special loyalty to the science of the Enneagram. I may just pillage and ransack for what I need and end up cannibalizing all the different types for specific character traits that I want to put into one of my characters. I think I predominantly see Apollo as a 7, but I am truly wide open and may build him out of as many of these as I need and want.

ST. NICK

I see him as an 8 (the Challenger or the Leader), straight up. "*The Powerful, Dominating Type: Self-Confident, Decisive, Willful, and Confrontational.*" I obviously see him as "*self-assertive, self-confident, and strong: have learned to stand up for what they need and want. A resourceful, 'can do' attitude and passionate inner drive. / Decisive, authoritative, and commanding: the natural leader others look up to. Take initiative, make things happen.*" One of the things I'm playing with is for Cutter to unexpectedly look up to St. Nick, mostly for his and Senator Hutchings' astronomical ability to lie. But are there any good attributes he might possess? Certainly he has to be somebody that we love to hate, but if he has unexpected good sides, that makes him more multi-dimensional as a character and complicates the plot as well. I'll be looking at those possibilities as I develop his character further.

I clearly want him to have substantial negative character traits since he's the central antagonist. Some of the useful ones that I see are *"swaggering, boastful, forceful, and expansive: the 'boss' whose word is law. Proud, egocentric, want to impose their will and vision on everything, not seeing others as equals or treating them with respect. / Become highly combative and intimidating to get their way: confrontational, belligerent, creating adversarial relationships. Everything a test of wills, and they will not back down. Use threats and reprisals to get obedience from others, to keep others off balance and insecure."* As we get into the Unhealthy aspects, we get great material for a villain: *"Defying any attempt to control them, become completely ruthless, dictatorial, 'might makes right.' The criminal and outlaw, renegade, and con-artist. Hard-hearted, immoral and potentially violent. / Develop delusional ideas about their power, invincibility, and ability to prevail: megalomania, feeling omnipotent, invulnerable. Recklessly over-extending self. / If they get in danger, they may brutally destroy everything that has not conformed to their will rather than surrender to anyone else. Vengeful, barbaric, murderous. Sociopathic tendencies. Generally corresponds to the Antisocial Personality Disorder."*

SENATOR HUTCHINGS

I can totally see him as a 3 (the Achiever). *"The Success-Oriented, Pragmatic Type: Adaptable, Excelling, Driven, and Image-Conscious."* I see him as a highly honored senator so part of his disguise would be *"adaptable, desirable, charming, and gracious. / Ambitious to improve themselves, to be 'the best they can be' — often become outstanding, a human ideal, embodying widely admired cultural qualities. Highly effective: others are motivated to be like them in some positive way."* Some of this can be perhaps mesmerizing to Cutter. At his best he can be *"modest and charitable, self-deprecatory humor and a fullness of heart emerge. Gentle and benevolent."* What great camouflage.

Plus in the Average aspect he can be *"terrified of failure. Compare self with others in search for status and success. Become careerists, social climbers, invested in exclusivity and being the 'best.' / Become image-conscious, highly concerned with how they are perceived. Begin to package themselves according to the expectations of others and what they need to do to be successful."* Then we've got *"premeditated, losing touch with their own feelings beneath a smooth facade. Problems with intimacy, credibility, and 'phoniness' emerge. / Want to impress others with their superiority: constantly promoting themselves, making themselves sound better than they really are. Narcissistic, with grandiose, inflated notions about themselves and their talents. Exhibitionistic and seductive, as if saying 'Look at me!' Arrogance and contempt for others."* This is all great stuff and helps me create a fully dimensionalized personality.

As we get into the Unhealthy aspect, we get *"fearing failure and humiliation, they can be exploitative and opportunistic, covetous of the success of others, and willing to do 'whatever it takes' to preserve the illusion of their superiority. / Devious and deceptive so that their mistakes and wrongdoings will not be exposed. Untrustworthy, maliciously betraying or sabotaging people to triumph over them."* Plus *"relentless, obsessive about destroying whatever reminds them of their own shortcomings and failures. Psychopathic, murder. Generally corresponds to the Narcissistic Personality Disorder."* This is rich material and I'll definitely be looking to other sources as I develop his character, but I've got a lot to work with here.

MISCHA

I can see Mischa as quite possibly a 4 (the Individualist). I see him as rather unhealthy psychologically, so not many of the Healthy aspects look useful. In the Average aspects we've got: *"Heighten reality through fantasy, passionate feelings, and the imagination. / To stay in touch with feelings, they interiorize everything, taking everything personally, but become self-absorbed and introverted, moody and hypersensitive, shy and self-conscious, unable to be spontaneous or to 'get out of themselves.' Stay withdrawn to protect their self-image and to buy time to sort out feelings. / Gradually think that they are different from others, and feel that they are exempt from living as everyone else does. They become melancholy dreamers, disdainful, decadent, and sensual, living in a fantasy world. Self-pity and envy of others leads to self-indulgence, and to becoming increasingly impractical, unproductive, effete, and precious."* All of this is useful. It opens up possibilities and presents me with a good palette of colors with which to paint him.

Let's look at the Unhealthy aspects. *"When dreams fail, become self-inhibiting and angry at self, depressed and alienated from self and others, blocked and emotionally paralyzed. Ashamed of self, fatigued and unable to function. / Tormented by delusional self-contempt, self-reproaches, self-hatred, and morbid thoughts: everything is a source of torment. Blaming others, they drive away anyone who tries to help them. / Despairing, feel hopeless and become self-destructive, possibly abusing alcohol or drugs to escape. In the extreme: emotional breakdown or suicide is likely. Generally corresponds to the Avoidant, Depressive, and Narcissistic personality disorders."* This is all good and again, rich with possibilities.

MARGARITA

I can see her as a 2 (the Helper), *"The Caring, Interpersonal Type: Generous, Demonstrative, People-Pleasing, and Possessive."* She would seem to have great qualities: *"Empathetic, compassionate, feeling for others. Caring and concerned about their needs. Thoughtful, warm-hearted, forgiving and sincere. / Encouraging and appreciative, able to see the good in others. Service is important, but takes care of self too: they are nurturing, generous, and giving — a truly loving person.*" In the Average aspect there are some intriguing possibilities to flaw her a bit: "*Become overly intimate and intrusive: they need to be needed, so they hover, meddle, and control in the name of love. Want others to depend on them: give, but expect a return: send double messages. Enveloping and possessive: the codependent, self-sacrificial person who cannot do enough for others — wearing themselves out for everyone.*" If she's going to find out where Cutter is and discover that he's having an affair with St. Nick's secretary, then she's going to flip out and be insanely jealous. I don't see any of that in this description of a 2, but I absolutely don't need to draw everything from this resource. It's just an interesting set of character traits and I don't need to be a slave to it in the least. I know how to paint a portrait of an insanely jealous woman and will do just fine on my own, thank you very much.

So that was a tour through the Enneagram. You can see how I used it in various ways, taking its strengths, but not being a servant to it. I find it a remarkable resource that exposes me to a fascinating spectrum of possibilities for character development, and I take it wholesale or pick and choose as needed. Obviously in this exercise I'm only working off the one-sheet from the Enneagram Institute's website, but if you go to any of the books you can go quite a lot deeper. It's a great way to supplement what you find in these one-sheets and will expand your journey extensively.

19

UTILIZING RESEARCH AND BRAINSTORMING

In the process of starting to pull this story together I did some preliminary research. This is very much part of exploring the possibilities in a good idea. Who are the great liars in history? In literature? In comedy? Baron Von Munchausen came to mind. He's supposedly the greatest liar in history. I know there are books about him so I went to www.Amazon.com and found new and used copies. I wanted to get out of thinking small and into some unusual possibilities that might not occur to me on my own. As I'm developing a script I like to read and watch things in a similar vein because it puts me in the zone for that type of storytelling.

I checked out my *Golden Retriever,* which is a great video guide. They list all the movies on DVD and video, sorting them into categories, like Roaring 20's, Robot/Androids, Rock Stars on Film, Rodeos, Role Reversal and so on. It's a great resource for finding films in a similar genre to yours. I checked to see if they have a category for Liars, but didn't find it. (*Liar, Liar* comes to mind and I'm sure there are others, which I'll seek out.) I'll also go to one of my video store guys who is immensely knowledgeable and ask him. I just saw *The Italian Job*, and that was good research for this story. I read some of *The Writer's Complete Crime Reference Book* by Martin Roth which has a fascinating and comprehensive cross-section of crimes and crime information that steered me in some interesting directions.

In the Alistair Maclean novel, *Ice Station Zebra*, the main character was the one of the most amazing liars I've encountered in literature. The first time I read that book I was astonished by this spy who, as things heated up, had an elaborate explanation for what was really going on and who he really was. But then as the situation shifted he said he hadn't told the truth because of national security, and the real story was such and such, and that was even more elaborate and intense. Then later it turns out that story was a lie too and he supplies an even more amazing story. When we finally find out what's *really* going on, the truth tops all his incredible lies. It was great.

I walked into a bookstore that specializes in mysteries and asked for any books about phenomenal liars. When I said I was doing research on a caper film I was led to two novels by Donald Westlake, *Nobody's Perfect* and *What's The Worst That Could Happen?* The second one was made into a film with Martin Lawrence and Danny DeVito. *Nobody's Perfect* is one of these crime stories in which everything goes wrong. The wackiness, the stupidity, the ineptitude, the hustling, the complications, the miscommunication, the double crossing—all of these things suggested possibilities and helped me see how a master of the genre works. It got my brain spinning with ideas that could give this plot some comic twists.

Then I went to see the 2003 remake of movie, *The In-Laws*, which was an absolute treat, as well as a gold mine of research. You've got a completely crazed, unpredictable Michael Douglas dragging a hapless, anal Albert Brooks into these adrenaline-fueled adventures; it opened up an entire new universe of possibilities. I had begun to play with having Apollo be a really wild character, possibly in a comic way, but it was just an inkling—an attempt to go against type and not make him the grim, thuggish hard-ass you'd expect in a role like this. As I'm sitting down at *The In-Laws*, it occurs to me that there's a real correlation between it and this script I'm developing. As the movie gets rolling, I see that it's much more than I hoped for because Michael Douglas' character was so crazy and fun.

A BRAINSTORMING SESSION

It made me realize that I could take Apollo out much, much further than I had originally imagined him. I had a spark, but this was a dazzling sunburst in comparison. It got my imagination reeling and triggered an explosive brainstorming session. Apollo could be so off-the-hook crazy, so fun to be with that it lifts the whole film into another dimension. He could be exciting, brilliant, gleeful, fanatical, incredibly perceptive, dangerous, unpredictable, free, adventurous, maddening, inscrutable, intoxicating, energetic, joyous, deadly and giddy, something like Owen Wilson's character, Dignan, in *Bottle Rocket*. Max Bialystock in *The Producers* is also similar. It made me think of other great comic characters who have dragged people into trouble. Maude in *Harold and Maude*, Long John Silver in *Treasure Island* and the list goes on and on.

The main thing is that these characters are total rascals, rogues, mischief-makers and scoundrels. Like Loki, the god of mischief, they are troublemakers, but often also bringers of life. If Cutter is intent on his straight life, but is secretly frustrated with it all, then the more frustrated he is, the more susceptible he is to Apollo's infectious energy. Has Cutter lost his spark, his zest for life, his spirit? Isn't that going to add to his dilemma if Apollo is not just trying to derail his life, but is also an irresistible call to adventure, the call of the wild? Knowing this, he would struggle that much more to fend Apollo off, knowing that once he takes that metaphoric first drink, it's all over.

What this did was to open the lid on this project and I suddenly saw how much more fun I could have with a story like this, with a character like this. I started thinking about who this cellmate could be. Perhaps he's an old con who knows everything and everybody. If Cutter spent years with him, wouldn't he learn Apollo's entire body of knowledge, as often happens with cellmates in prison? What is Apollo's background? What are the craziest *possible* backgrounds? Was he a dictator's son? A race car driver? A spy? A pool hustler? A karate champion? A safecracker? An aristocrat? Does he have a history of insanity? It's fun to explore the wacked-out possibilities in any genre, but this type of story positively *begs* for it. I watched *The Big Lebowski* again, and talk about wacked-out, that put me in the zone to write something *totally* wild. It's so creative and loopy, and it made me realize that I want this script to be *that* much fun.

Remember, it's Saturday night at the movies, so we want to really cut loose. Does Apollo have a hidden agenda with this job he's trying to recruit Cutter for? If he's a trickster, how many hidden agendas *could* he have? How much is he trying to drag Cutter kicking and screaming back into his former ways? Does he see Cutter as a wild tiger locked in a cage, his soul crying to be set free? How much can we emphasize with Apollo's point of view? How much would we mistrust him? How much do we secretly want him to shake Cutter out of his rut? How much do we want Cutter to be able to resist Apollo? This is only a few of the hundreds of questions to be explored in developing a script like this.

My favorite part of writing a script is at the point where there's a premise laid down, but everything is utterly wide open. Watching Michael Douglas's character made me realize how over the top you can go, and the audience just cannot get enough of it. I certainly know that in general, but I had begun to form a picture of Apollo, and *The In-Laws* totally shattered it, or expanded it by a factor of 10,000. The more outlandish Apollo is, the better for this movie. It's like that line in *My Favorite Year* (another great example of an adventurer dragging a shut-down person into trouble and into life) where the kid, Benjie Stone, says to Peter O'Toole, "I need my Alan Schwanns as big as I can get them."

If Apollo sweeps in, already caught up in a full-blown adventure, then he's way ahead of where I pictured him. It's all much less casual. If he's being hunted, or in the middle of a great job, or in disguise, or in huge trouble, then it starts at 100 mph, rather than from a standstill. You're supposed to start a script with an explosion (not necessarily literally). They call it *in medias res*—'in the middle of things.' The great science fiction writer, Alfred Bester, said you should start at white heat and build from there. He also talks about *attack as a storyteller*—the level of energy with which you attack the story and the audience. If you want to see great attack, read his best books *The Stars My Destination* and *The Demolished Man* which are both still in print. They're stunning, astonishing books that are so creative, entertaining and fulfilling.

Has Apollo stolen something amazing and is trying to get away with it? Has he come to hide out? Has he been mowing Cutter's lawn for months without Cutter even recognizing him through his disguise? Does he crash a burning car into Cutter's house? Does he kidnap Cutter from a nice dinner with his family? Does Cutter think that Apollo has been dead, and he now reappears magically alive? Does he just approach Cutter at the grocery store?

Do you see how many different ways we can approach this plot? It's completely wide open and pure fun. What can *you* come up with? What's the single craziest opening you can possibly invent? What's the most unexpected, the least clichéd, the most preposterous, the funniest, the scariest, the most ridiculous, the last thing you'd ever expect? How do you throw a monkey wrench into the audience's expectations? Or into your own pattern of storytelling? How do you get outside your own story or even your own sense of what this story should be? How do you take a crowbar to it? This is attack as a storyteller. Going after the audience, going after the problem as a writer, going after your own expectations and your own limits. You can see that there's a whole outrageous trajectory this type of process can take us on. A big part of the fun of writing is this ride, the joy of creating something that will blow an audience's mind. Think about how you go to the movies begging to have your mind blown. Tear into your story with that level of attack. The audience wants the ride of their life and it's your job to give it to them!

BACK FOR MORE RESEARCH

One of the things that I ran up against very quickly is that I don't know *anything* about banking beyond the normal checking and saving account, loans, ATMs and so on. But as for how to buy a bank and the certification process of buying one, I didn't know the first thing. I did a search on the Internet, looking under "banking," "bank examiners," "bank fraud" and "banking regulations." I spent hours and found much that was interesting and plenty that was boring. I knew so little that I didn't even have much in the way of specific questions yet. I looked up the Treasury Dept., the Secret Service, the IRS and U.S. Customs. I found radical takes on the Federal Reserve, saying that it was a conspiracy to bring the financial power of the United States under a cabal of international bankers. I found tedious material that would put the average reader to sleep in minutes.

I went to the Los Angeles Public Library's website and they had 2,537 books on banks and banking. I looked through more than half of them in the catalog and found an author, Stephen Frey, who specializes in writing banking thrillers the way John Grisham writes legal thrillers. I took out two of his books on tape, *The Insider* and *The Vulture Fund*, which I listened to in my car (a great way to do research in what might otherwise be down time). They were fascinating and useful. I skimmed a book on bank management and another on how to own your own international bank, both of which had points of interest. I also watched a History Channel show on banks.

I asked around to see if anyone knew any bankers and got two hits. One friend's son in law is a bank examiner for the FDIC and he directed me to a government website that has information on what a bank has to do to get certified. That was extremely useful. Now I was getting some specifics. A client of mine works in a bank and he said he could put me in touch with banker, bank examiners and government banking officials. So with a little digging I found somebody who knew somebody. I could obviously just go into a bank and ask someone, but that felt a bit awkward because they seem so busy. However, if I hadn't found these other sources, I would have done it.

EUREKA!

A nice score was a book from the library called *Shell Game: A True Story of Banking, Spies, Lies, Politics—and the Arming of Saddam Hussein* by Peter Mantius (St. Martin's Press, New York, 1995). It was a real find because the book is about a banking scandal in the late 80s in which the Atlanta branch of the Italian Banca Nazionale del Lavoro (this was known as the BNL Scandal) was using a system of bogus agricultural loans to Iraq to funnel more than four billion dollars into Saddam Hussein's weapons programs. The evidence indicates that this was being done with the tacit complicity of the CIA and the White House as a way to do an end run around the American public while providing support to Iraq in their war against fundamentalist Iran. It was a way of doing covert foreign policy in the same way it was done the Iran-Contra Scandal. You can see that I lifted this agricultural material loan straight out of the book and added my own twists, which gave me part of the core of this script. This is an excellent example of good research meeting you halfway. It was my biggest find.

I brainstormed this into something that could connect with a third world dictator, but without it being too political (a studio might not want to touch it then). I'm doing it more as satire, with a tongue in cheek take on it. I range far and wide for research, but most of it is from reading and the Internet. I like to go to the actual place if I am able. Knowing how to use the library is very useful. Buying used books on www.amazon.com can save you a fortune if you need to own them. I will scavenge information from anywhere I can and am always on the lookout for new sources. There are books now that specialize in doing research on the Internet. One of them is *Facts in a Flash: A Research Guide for Writers* by Ellen Metter. The best thing is to find a person who lived it. They'll have stories that you never could imagine.

[Note: If you're following the detour from the chapter, *Utilizing the Dilemma*, then go back to where you left off in that chapter and resume the book's normal flow.]

20
UTILIZING THE
CENTRAL PROPOSITION

In using this tool I find that paying attention to the central conflict between Cutter and St. Nick opens up various kinds of questions and myriad possibilities. There's a difference between knowing that I want something to happen and figuring out *how* to actually do it. The whole thing is like a jigsaw puzzle or an engineering project. If you move this or change that, then how does it impact the rest of the plot that I've already put together, or am planning on? You learn how to hold story possibilities in your head as you wrestle the basic story into shape. If Cutter and St. Nick's conflict builds to a fight to the finish, what does that fight consist of? Can there even be open warfare if the whole script is based on hidden identity? Is it a lying contest? Essentially I see it as two giants locked in mortal combat, but what could that really be?

Cutter's intention is to destroy St. Nick, but he can't be up front about it. In addition I need Cutter to go off the deep end as a wild liar, so he can't be found out or there's no game. Even if we're two-thirds or three-quarters through the movie it still shouldn't break out into open conflict because St. Nick is so deadly that it would end the game instantly. Cutter can be *almost* found out or St. Nick can suspect him. These things would cause Cutter to lie like crazy. I could see the lid coming *all the way* off with maybe five minutes left in the movie.

What I'm seeing is that St. Nick and Cutter get caught up in a deadly dance. It's like two insane genies going at each other. They're both such high intensity characters, especially once the wild Cutter emerges. Much depends on how Cutter comes unhinged. Does he totally lose it, so that his original focus on revenge and theft has been diluted? Does he know what he's doing? Does his fascination with St. Nick impact how he acts? Has he been steered into a different sense of mission? Also, what's happening with the bank? Is it now a legal bank? Is it on the edge of being fully certified? Is the first loan to Umbotha hanging in the balance? Their conflict or covert conflict will have much to do with that.

Cutter would have to be totally cornered to break out so explosively. Before I get into Cutter touching off the fight to the finish I want to backtrack and set it up again, reincorporating new ideas into what is Crisis and Decision & Action. I see Shallott's cover getting blown. I'm not quite sure how, but I've got a couple possibilities. One is that the FBI is now investigating St. Nick, who may have reason to suspect that Shallott had something to do with it—maybe good reason. Shallott is in a state of thinly disguised rage, seeking revenge over St. Nick murdering his brother and is not the seasoned pro that Cutter is, so he may slip up. The FBI investigation should come out of nowhere and Senator Hutchings would be working behind the scenes to quash it, but hasn't gotten rid of it yet.

I also see Umbotha in the mix. So far he has come into this country to see the first round of loans released by the bank and has hit it off with Cutter. I also see one of St. Nick's old mob friends showing up trying to blackmail a piece of St. Nick's action. I see Mischa having found where Cutter is and spying on him, trying to inject himself into his father's life. Remember that Mischa is from Cutter's first marriage and Cutter was in jail or off on benders for much of Mischa's childhood. Mischa is a borderline criminal and has the 'gift,' like his dad. His mother had forbidden him to be around Cutter, but once he turned eighteen, Mischa had been spending a lot of time with his father. Cutter was working hard to be a good role model to him, trying to steer him into a good life. It was having a good effect until Apollo showed up and turned their whole world upside down.

I also want to inject Apollo into the mix. He's not in it enough so far to suit me. I always figured to have him involved more, even if he's the janitor in the building, working in disguise. He's too great a character to lose for a long period. I see that Umbotha's deal is in trouble, but I'm not sure why. I also want the CIA to come out of the woodwork, as well as drug money, arms dealers, sheiks, former KGB, generals and billionaires. I'm playing mad scientist and it's all up in the air at this point. I want to keep Cutter's secretary in the mix in a tantalizing way and I need to keep Margarita active.

Let's say that Shallott's cover gets blown during a meeting at which Umbotha, whose deal is on the table, is present. If Shallott slips up and gets badly roughed up by St. Nick, he could be collapsing under the pressure. Cutter, who is there too, is immediately under suspicion since Shallott brought him in, so Cutter has to counteract this suspicion or die and lose the mission against St. Nick. I would need a scene earlier between Shallott and Cutter in which they discuss the eventuality that one of their covers might be blown. They agree that each will disavow the other for the good of the mission, and they're deadly serious. We could see that in Cutter when he totally distances himself from Shallott in St. Nick's office. He'd say that Shallott got him through a friend or a temp agency and that he'd worked with him a few times, then got this offer to be his assistant on this job. But, he says, "Hey, I don't know him and I don't give a rat's ass about him. Kill him, what do I care?" You can see that the earlier scene in which they discuss this possibility is crucial, otherwise we'd lose sympathy for Cutter.

So Cutter would cut him loose and Umbotha is there as St. Nick is exploding on Shallott. St. Nick could execute Shallott with an injectable drug that makes it look like he's had a heart attack. Umbotha watches, casually amused as he reads a magazine. Cutter is on the spot and can show almost no emotion. Then the phone rings and it's the FBI agent who's investigating St. Nick, wanting new information about an IRS irregularity for the money that's been placed in reserve. St. Nick has to take the call. He's got Shallott's body on the floor and his whole operation hanging in the balance. He could send Cutter to get an ambulance which would buy Cutter a few minutes.

I see Cutter making the call and then going into the bathroom and freaking out, throwing up, looking at himself in the mirror, telling himself that he's hit bottom, he's going to die, that he's useless and doesn't know how to even begin to pull this off. If he's only getting two hours of sleep a night because he's reading banking books every night to solidify his cover, then he's ready for a nervous breakdown too. The thing I want to do here is to have Mischa, whose been spying on his dad a lot by this point, hidden in the air vent and he would see this whole thing. Then I want Cutter to start to pull himself together, doing what I call the 'Judy Garland transformation' that I talked about in the chapter on Decision and Action. This is the cornered wild animal coming out fighting. It's the lump of coal being turned into a diamond by intense pressure. Mischa would see him completely transfigure into this legendary wild man he's heard about his whole life but never seen. The Cutter that emerges is ready for absolutely *anything*.

He goes back into St. Nick's office 'loaded for bear.' He'll be arguing for his job and his trusted position. I want conflict between Cutter and St. Nick, but it has to be carefully controlled. Umbotha is still there and is still impressed with Cutter's fearlessness and drive. If St. Nick's old mob buddy barges in the office demanding his cut or else, Cutter could turn on this brutal looking Mafia executioner, cook up a lie, and threaten to have him shipped off to Mambia with Umbotha where he will never be seen again. Umbotha laughs and picks up on it, saying he has a special prison for his political enemies for whom death is too easy a punishment. It has tiny cells where you can never lay down, intense prison labor, torture, bad food and erratic sleep. But he says not to worry because they have excellent health care... and it can take decades to die. The mobster turns white and runs out, never to be seen again. Cutter and Umbotha smile gleefully at each other.

Umbotha is taken even more with Cutter and declares to St. Nick that if Cutter does not negotiate his deal, then there won't be a deal. St. Nick is still not necessarily convinced and Cutter pressures him, conjures up lies and works to earn his respect. This insistence by Umbotha that Cutter do the deal is the strongest thing I can come up with at this point to create conflict between St. Nick and Cutter. St. Nick is caught in a tough spot, but he's no pushover. He has gotten to like Cutter and wants someone that sharp on his team, but Shallott's betrayal has set off his internal alarms. He's got Cutter in his sights.

A CIA agent could show up to get Umbotha out of there because of Shallott being killed. He has heard about it from Senator Hutchings who got the word from St. Nick on a secure line. Umbotha brushes him off, saying he's having fun and besides he has an old friend stopping by for lunch, so he's not going anywhere. The CIA agent can be really aggressive and demand that he get out, saying too much can be compromised, but Umbotha won't budge and scares the agent off. Cutter could also help drive him off with another extravagant lie.

Then one of St. Nick's guys comes in with Mischa, saying he found him lurking in the hall. Everything grinds to a halt. Our new wild Cutter turns on Mischa and, without missing a beat, slaps him hard in the face and then kisses him full on the lips. He says that Mischa is his bitch and is a jealous freak. Cutter tells St. Nick that Mischa is his boyfriend and he'd heard so much about St. Nick's super hot secretary that he got all jealous and came in to sneak a look at her. Mischa catches on instantly that their survival depends on this and drops into character. He's a natural and after all, he wanted in—he just didn't want in *this* way. But he's lucky to be alive and so is Cutter. Cutter is totally non-plussed. Umbotha thinks this is hilarious, saying he loves young guys, which throws St. Nick a little. Umbotha sweeps up Cutter and Mischa and insists that they come out to lunch with him, and he tells St. Nick to bug off.

They go out to eat and who should walk in but Apollo! Umbotha leaps up and hugs him, introducing him to Cutter and Mischa as his oldest friend. Cutter is stunned, but cannot show it. Mischa plays it cool. Umbotha says that their fathers used to both be the presidents of their own countries and when they visited, which was often, the kids got together and raised holy hell. Apollo sits down and is off-the-hook wild. He and Umbotha immediately start partying it up and our new wild Cutter matches them pound for pound and drink for drink. Umbotha asks Apollo what he's up to these days and Apollo says he's into counterfeiting, child pornography, drugs... you know, the usual. To Cutter's astonishment, Apollo reaches into his bag and pulls out a stack of counterfeit hundreds. Umbotha is delighted. He says he's got diplomatic immunity and just loves this stuff. They end up at Umbotha's suite at a super ritzy hotel in a high stakes poker game, which degenerates into a wild party. Cutter is the life of the party and tells lie after lie to Umbotha who roars with laughter.

I need to complicate things here and get them into a more headlong rush toward the ending, so I might see something like St. Nick calling Cutter for an emergency down at the bank. He might have to go back and cook up some massive lie to a sheik who will not take no for an answer on some banking business. Cutter could tell him an elaborate lie about the IRA and MI6 and how this is not the right time for this bank to get involved with him, apologizing profusely to the sheik. Senator Hutchings would be using the White House to help get the FBI off St. Nick's back. Cutter could eavesdrop with his cans and string again on St. Nick and Hutchings, and use what he learns to weave more elaborate lies. It's all unformed at this point, but I want it to get as crazy as possible. I'm just trying to get the wild Cutter launched with an element of conflict between he and St. Nick. All of these ideas came from looking at possibilities of conflict between them. In general it's a fight to the finish, but in this type of story it has to be somewhat different. Cutter is still trying his damndest to take down St. Nick, and he can't blow his cover.

Bear in mind that half the stuff I just came up with could get tossed. I'm struggling to come up with a wild finale, and at this point I'm only getting into the first part of the ending. I still need ways for Cutter to be lying his ass off and helping take down St. Nick in the process. It has to be satisfying, complete, entertaining, dangerous, and funny. I may have bitten off more than I can chew, but I'm working it as hard as I can and I'm using the power of the tools to help me shape the material. This tool focuses on setting up a potential fight and then touching off a fight to the finish, with a question arising in the mind of the audience as to how it's going to turn out. But look at how much I have to create, and experiment with, and turn upside down, and throw away, and stretch my concept of the plot in order to properly use this tool.

Having done this wild brainstorming session, let's now take this material and go back to the tool, the Central Proposition. Now I have some raw material on which to use it. What I first want to do is *Visualize the Fight to the Finish*. I can see Cutter and St. Nick going at each other to the maximum degree that they can in this story. I feel that it still needs more, but if you're ambitious with a story, then you're going to get stumped regularly. I'm in over my head, but that's where I live as a writer. Get used to it. If you're not in over your head with your script then you're probably turning out material that is too simplistic or has already been done to death. I can see Cutter in the fight of his life, trying to make this whole thing come together. He has to attack everything as hard as he can, not just St. Nick. That's a big chunk of the conflict that gets touched off—Cutter versus everybody and everything—but it's St. Nick he's after, and who is in his face as much as I can make that happen. The proposition keeps the protagonist versus antagonist focus strong. He doesn't trust Cutter after Shallott's cover gets blown, and that battle isn't over until St. Nick is finished off in the end or Cutter fails totally.

Now I want to know: ***What's the question in the mind of the audience once the fight to the finish has <u>only just started</u> and they don't know how it's going to turn out?*** Essentially we're wondering if Cutter can pull off this revenge on St. Nick. But we want to get as highly specific as possible on the Central Dramatic Question. The audience is watching a highly specific set of events and these will give rise to a highly specific question in their mind once the whole conflict goes beyond the point of no return. If the situation changes and we're looking at a more complex or different state of affairs, then the question may well change. What we're really talking about is Cutter declaring war, mostly on St. Nick, but also on those who are conspiring to derail his revenge. Cutter's the genie who gets let out of the bottle at this crucial moment. His old addictions have kicked in and he's in attack mode. I understand this and try to steer the conflict onto St. Nick as much as possible, but I'm not a slave to that. So what would be the question that would arise in the mind of the audience once Cutter launches his attack?

Can Cutter possibly pull this off and take down St. Nick?

This pretty much sums it up. Now the important question is: Is this question powerful enough to drive the whole movie? It will be a factor of how much opposition St. Nick brings and how bad the situation really is. In other words, a weak situation could give rise to the same question, but on a scale of 1 to 10 it would rate very low. How intensely is the audience on the edge of their seat at the point when Cutter goes wild and declares war? The more trouble he's in and the more powerful an enemy or enemies he's up against, the more powerful the question will be. The more we utterly loathe St. Nick, the more powerful the question will be. I'm noticing that things could definitely be worse for Cutter. What are the various ways? How can I make it a more life or death showdown? How can I make it crazier? How powerful can St. Nick and Hutchings be? How much in doubt is Umbotha's deal? How brutally insane is Umbotha? How crazy and fun is he? How slimy? Is the bank on the edge of going under before it really gets going? What about the CIA, the FBI, the IRS, Customs, the Federal Reserve, the White House, drug runners, organized crime, the Senate? These are all possible players in the mix. I've probably got tunnel vision right now; it's easy to get trapped in narrow sets of possibilities. It takes time to get outside certain entire types to thinking. It takes time for the obvious to become apparent. There's no substitute for time. But I also have to work it, pound it, beat it up, shake it out, violate where it's heading, see more clearly the possibilities that are lurking in there waiting for me to notice them. This is the creative process.

What action by the protagonist touches off the fight to the finish, giving rise to the Central Dramatic Question? Cutter snaps into his old wild self and explodes into the situation as an out-of-control liar. He's going after St. Nick, Hutchings, the thieves, hustlers, billionaire bankers and arms dealers who are trying to drag this revenge operation down. I'm still carrying a lot of possibilities as I wrestle it into shape. The basic answer to this question is that he snaps and goes on the attack against St. Nick to try to keep St. Nick's trust and keep the deal together so that he can complete his revenge.

What action by the protagonist sets up the potential fight? Remember in our proportion diagram that the set up of the fight usually comes much earlier in the plot.

Here we're talking about the first X. We're trying to incorporate the complete action of the script. So here we're looking at a situation in which Cutter and St. Nick could cross swords earlier in the plot. What I've been thinking about is that St. Nick might challenge Cutter on the veracity of something Cutter has said. If Cutter, who is struggling to stay honest in this bad situation (this is half of his dilemma) gets called a liar, then he might come back at St. Nick really hard. They could get into it with some real energy. Getting called a liar really pushes his most central button, especially by his number one enemy. Cutter soon learns, when he eavesdrops on St. Nick and Hutchings, that St. Nick was impressed by how ballsy Cutter was in standing up to him. I'm not sure what the argument between Cutter and St. Nick will be about at this point.

Is there anything in common between the setting up and the touching off of the fight that can tie them together? What I do is to look at both these points and see if there's anything in common, in and around them. The first thing I notice is that Cutter is bent out of shape each time he gets called a liar. This really pushes his buttons. He's also intensely dedicated to taking down St. Nick. In the first instance, he is freshly undercover in St. Nick's organization and is seething with vengeance against him because of Frenchy's death. In the second instance, he has just seen Shallott murdered. I think the first one feels more like the common element that ties them together. There isn't really a rule of thumb for the common term except that we want there to be some kind of linkage between the set up and the touch off so that there's a valid logical connection between them. I know this process can be taxing, but the best thing I can say is to just try to find something to tie together the set up and the touch off because it will reinforce the structural unity of the plot.

Now let's take a whack at putting together the proposition. Remember that we will be including a little more information so that a stranger to the story can make sense of it.

CONDITION OF THE ACTION (Setting up the Potential Fight)

Cutter, a reformed pathological liar who vowed to his wife never to lie again, gets blackmailed into a revenge-oriented perfect crime by his former cellmate, Apollo. Cutter poses as a bank examiner and starts lying again to try to take down St. Nick, a legendary savage crime lord who's in the process of going straight by buying a bank in collusion with a corrupt Senator Hutchings. When St. Nick challenges Cutter for supposedly lying to him when in fact he isn't, Cutter, refusing to allow himself to be called a liar, attacks St. Nick and defends his integrity.

CAUSE OF THE ACTION (Touching off the Fight to the Finish)

Cutter gets drawn into this complicated situation much deeper when he learns of St. Nick's and Hutchings' secret plan to make a fortune using government guaranteed agricultural loans in a crooked deal with a brutal African dictator, Umbotha. The plan changes when Cutter unexpectedly gets taken deeper inside St. Nick's organization and he now has a chance to destroy St. Nick more thoroughly and expeditiously, and also to derail a deadly criminal conspiracy. Cutter sees one of his partners murdered and, again being accused of lying to St. Nick (which he in fact is), refuses to be accused of being a liar, kicks into his old lying self and goes on a wild attack against St. Nick and the others to try and pull off the scam and destroy St. Nick.

RESULTING ACTION (Dramatic Question)

Will he pull off this scam and take St. Nick down?

You can see how proposition tells the core of the story. It's actually a great pitching tool because it forces you to go right to the nucleus of your plot and to present it clearly and logically. You're focusing on the pure drama in your story. It does help pull a plot together from a diverse collection of possible story elements. I've seen this work over and over in my classes. I often find that I resist this tool when I'm working on one of my own scripts because it forces me to get clear and logical when I may be in another type of creative zone and don't want to give up that expansiveness. But then once I've done it, I find that the plot has not only improved, but is cleaner and clearer.

The next step is to stand back from this proposition and evaluate it. How strong is the Central Dramatic Question? How much on the edge of their seats is the audience? Is it measuring up to what I intend for the film? These are all potent questions and are very much part of this process. I've structured the argument and now I want to step back and see if it's worth a damn.

I find that after taking some time off from doing the above proposition, a flood of realizations, ideas, possibilities, oversights and recognition of blind spots are coming to me. This is entirely organic to the process. It can be really hard to hold everything in your head at one time, and if you direct your thinking at one aspect of the plot, other things can get eclipsed. One of the first things that comes to mind is that I want more conflict. I found that I had been leaning too much in the direction of comedy. Earlier I had been getting too much into the thriller aspect and started developing the comic take on it. This back and forth process is normal. Basically you go from system to system strengthening each as you go. Now I want to get back more to the savagery of the story and make sure that part is properly spun up. I love the phrase 'to spin a yarn' by the way. I like to spin a story up.

The wild and crazy stuff is entertaining and truly needs to be in this plot, but it hit me after I did the above proposition that St. Nick is a brutal monster and the stakes are huge. He and Hutchings are plotting to rob the American taxpayer of billions, and are conspiring with a genocidal dictator. Cutter can hear them planning this and his outrage should be explosive. I want the audience to *hate* St. Nick with absolute intensity. I was thinking of the great screen villains and how fiercely we hate them. I had always talked about St. Nick being *that* bad, but hadn't established it very well yet. I want him to be diabolical, malignant, treacherous, psychotic, demonic and depraved. All of this will fuel the audience intensity and will upgrade the power of the dramatic question. Umbotha is not hard to get into that category and Senator Hutchings can certainly go there.

As soon as I recognize the need to go darker a whole raft of ideas that I've been playing with float up, including some possibilities that open up new worlds. One of them is the whole arena of CIA, arms dealers, money laundering, drug smuggling, covert foreign policy and shadow government. There's plenty of fun and intrigue to be had here, but it's also dangerous territory. Wrapping all this in with a character like Umbotha makes a lot of sense and can really go places.

The main new thing that came to me is that the situation could change dramatically in Africa if the country next to Mambia is in the throes of a Communist revolution. It may have been brewing for a while, which made Umbotha a useful asset to the CIA, but now it has exploded. This would put Umbotha in the catbird seat because he immediately goes from being useful to being absolutely indispensable. This would change everything because all of a sudden the CIA needs to covertly funnel a lot of money to Mambia so that Umbotha can arm himself with all the latest weapons against this threat.

Notice that by choosing Communism I sidestep the whole minefield of using terrorism in a comic way at this point in world history. Terrorism and the various takes on our defending ourselves against it is such a politically sensitive hot button that a movie studio would run the other way. I'm paying attention to marketability, which you always have to consider unless you're independently wealthy and are going to not only make the movie yourself, but market and distribute it as well.

I can see Umbotha suddenly the toast of the town, being escorted to high level meetings with the CIA, the White House, arms merchants, covert ops, more Senators and so on. I can also see the CIA coming to St. Nick and saying that they would like to use his bank as a cover for CIA money because it already has a solid relationship with Umbotha and also because it's new and clean—untouched and unaffiliated. The lid could be taken off the agricultural loan program, with government guarantees being extended from two billion to eight billion dollars, so that 'free' money flows like champagne. The loans will be made, all disguised as agricultural loans, but certain banking regulations will be waived so that a big chunk of the money goes straight to arms purchases from American defense industries. The original plantation and factory deal (in which Umbotha provides free labor and raw material to St. Nick's and Hutchings' sweat shop factory in Africa) will still be in place, but it will just be one of many deals, rather than the centerpiece. All of this will be done through St. Nick and Hutchings' bank, so they will get the fees on every transaction as well.

St. Nick and Hutchings would be delighted. Hutchings, who could also be on the Senate Intelligence Committee, could have even steered the CIA to the bank. This would make any pending investigations of St. Nick or the bank vanish immediately and permanently. Immunities could be issued, subpoenas quashed and investigators told that it's a matter of national security. St. Nick is now in the 'club.' He's untouchable and no cop in the world is looking for him, nor will any be in the future. He's home free!

This is all going to put much, much more pressure on Cutter, who is overhearing this with his primitive listening device. His opportunity to catch St. Nick and destroy him is evaporating before his eyes and his window of opportunity is being slammed shut. Look how much more we've just ratcheted up the pressure on the audience. They're going to be coming up more on the edge of their seats. There's still a certain tongue in cheek aspect to it, but the danger and intensity factor has been ratcheted way up, therefore the power of the Central Dramatic Question goes way up.

One of the things I did in this process is to go back and review my notebook for this script, which caused some of these ideas to pop. I also laid out the bare basics of the plot on cards. It's the standard 3x5 card work, but I've found a nice twist on that over the years. I noticed that about thirty to fifty 3x5 cards would cover my desk, so I started cutting them in half. Then I realized that I had hundreds of out-of-date business cards around and I started using them. I write on them with a Sharpie marker and take the extra time to write neatly. This way I can lay out well over a hundred cards on a regular desk and I can read the ones in the corner because the Sharpie ink is fat and the writing is neat. This helps me get an overview.

I did this because I needed to collect my wits to take the plot to the next level. When I did the central proposition for this plot I found that it was missing big chunks of story. I knew it needed lots of work, but once I applied this tool I was able to see what I had and what I needed. The cards enabled me to put down what I've already got, lay out the new ideas that came to me, and then incorporate them into the mix. It also helped me to see the whole script, including the gaps in what I'd figured out so far, and they were huge. I've been trying to show you my entire process as much as possible, so I'll show you what the cards say on the list below. You can recreate them on index cards if you want to work with them.

1. Cutter is living straight life with wife and son
2. Apollo appears and blackmails him into job
3. Cutter meets Shallott, the crooked bank examiner
4. Senator is setting up bank with St. Nick as front
5. St. Nick's illegal money will go into reserve account
6. Cutter & St. Nick fight – Cutter called a liar and he's furious
7. Cutter hears plan – govt. guaranteed loans to dictator
8. Cutter learns they're ripping off taxpayer's money to get super rich
9. Apollo's revenge plan put on hold – Cutter gets promoted
10. Cutter moving crooked money into reserve account
11. Cutter awed by St. Nick and Hutchings' lying skills
12. Stock market nosedives – messes things up for St. Nick
13. Complications on moving illegal money
14. FBI & IRS investigate St. Nick – Cutter tells stunning lie, which helps
15. St Nick goes psycho in private – Hutchings chills him out
16. Hutchings helps get money into reserve acct. – bank is open for business
17. Old mob pal of St. Nick wants a cut or he spills on St. Nick
18. Umbotha shows up – sees Cutter deal with old mob pal and likes Cutter
19. Umbotha – limos, parties, diplomatic immunity, girls, drugs & money
20. Umbotha wants St. Nick to launder drug money for him
21. Hutchings nervous about drug money – says no
22. Communist revolution in African country next to Mambia
23. CIA needs Umbotha big-time now
24. Umbotha meets senators, arms dealers, White House, drug smugglers
25. CIA wants St. Nick's bank to be a CIA front bank
26. All limits taken off agricultural loans – now eight billion
27. Investigation goes away – immunity – citing National Security
28. St. Nick is now in the 'club' – celebrating with Hutchings – above the law
29. Shallott freaks out and blows his cover
30. St. Nick flips and murders Shallott – turns on Cutter
31. Cutter does Judy Garland transformation & turns wild – Mischa watches

32. Cutter emerges and scares St. Nick's mob pal away permanently
33. Umbotha loves Cutter and won't allow deal to happen without him
34. Mischa gets found and brought in
35. Cutter pretends Mischa is his gay lover to cover for him
36. The wild Cutter goes after St. Nick to keep his trust

The thing to bear in mind is that these are my notes to myself, so I'm not over-explaining them to myself. I like my note cards to be very stripped down. It keeps it simple and clear. I'm starting to see a whole plot, rather than clumps of clever ideas and partially formed possibilities. Notice that these cards don't emphasize the beginning because I have a decent grasp of that, nor does it get into the ending, because that has yet to be made up. I've only just cobbled together a middle and I'm mighty glad to have that at this point. Notice that I'm ranging over the entire plot.

Now let's take another whack at the proposition. Notice that I have changed the common term because as I looked at it this time, the idea of him being hung up on being called a liar in a situation of this magnitude no longer held up for me. I've italicized the common term in each of them.

CONDITION OF THE ACTION (Setting up the Potential Fight)

Cutter, a reformed pathological liar who vowed to his wife never to lie again, gets blackmailed into a revenge-oriented perfect crime by his former cellmate, Apollo. Cutter finds himself posing as a bank examiner and being forced to lie again to try to take down St. Nick, a legendary savage crime lord who's in the process of going straight by buying a bank in collusion with a corrupt Senator Hutchings. When St. Nick challenges Cutter for supposedly lying to him, Cutter *refusing to lose this opportunity to take down St. Nick*, stands up to him angrily and lies his way out of it.

CAUSE OF THE ACTION (Touching off the Fight to the Finish)

Cutter eavesdrops and learns of their secret plan to legally rob the U.S. taxpayers of billions and make a fortune by using government guaranteed agricultural loans in a crooked deal with a brutal African dictator, Umbotha. Cutter is unexpectedly taken deeper inside St. Nick's organization, and when a Communist revolution in Africa puts Umbotha in driver's seat with the CIA, the CIA comes to St. Nick and offers to make the bank a CIA front, with unlimited money flowing and immunity to prosecution. Cutter sees one of his partners murdered and, *unable to let this evil go unchecked*, he snaps and kicks into his old lying self, launching a wild attack to stop the plan and destroy St. Nick.

RESULTING ACTION (Dramatic Question)

Can Cutter stop this huge plot and take down St. Nick in the process?

You can see how the power of the Central Dramatic Question has altered because both the stakes and the situation have changed a lot. Bear in mind that this proposition is subject to change if I stumble into something even better. One of the habits of mind of a trained dramatist is to be flexible and plastic. I'm wide open to change and I'm always looking.

TAKING ANOTHER PASS AT THE PROPOSITION

In the spirit of being open and flexible, I have been wrestling with the proposition more, still not being satisfied with it and have come up with something further. What's been chewing at me is that I'm not happy with Cutter's action that touches off the fight to the finish. In general, the Cause of the Action is a real declaration of war, much like the attack on Pearl Harbor or destroying the World Trade Centers. Those are real acts of *war*, and are not indirect or preparatory or weak. My instinct is to have the touch off of the fight to the finish be an attempt at a killing blow. This obviously depends on the type of material because in a comedy it is scaled down in intensity (only in certain ways because the protagonist is usually taking the situation very seriously).

This is one of the principles that I bear in mind in terms of working with the proposition. I keep feeling as though Cutter's attack is weak. I know it's because he is boxed in and can't blow his cover, especially now that St. Nick suspects him. His hands are really tied, and yet it's *still* weak. I spent hours wrestling with this and tried many different options. Cutter and Apollo are very smart and we expect a powerful attack from them in this type of movie, so I felt increasingly that I had to do better. Finally I hit upon something that had some real energy.

At the point when the 'wild Cutter' comes out and goes on the attack, he arranges for the delivery of a fabricated communiqué that claims to be from the Communist group in the country next to Mambia. They claim to know that the CIA is smuggling weapons disguised as agricultural shipments into Mambia through a U.S. bank, and they denounce the capitalist dogs for their blatant criminal acts. This is a strong act by Cutter, touching off a hornet's nest of panic in St. Nick, Hutchings, Umbotha and the CIA's camp. St. Nick's paranoia would flare up and they would search for a leak. It would seem utterly unlikely that Cutter has even the remotest thing to do with it, since as far as anyone knows he has absolutely no knowledge of the inner workings of the bank's secret agenda.

This attack has some real clout and it's a true declaration of war within the confines of Cutter's limitations. From my point of view it is 10,000 times stronger than what I had before. Let's now revise the proposition yet again (which is very much part of this process—you set up a proposition, evaluate it and try again if you're not happy with it).

CONDITION OF THE ACTION (Setting up the Potential Fight)

Cutter, a reformed pathological liar who vowed to his wife never to lie again, gets blackmailed into a revenge-oriented perfect crime by his former cellmate, Apollo. Cutter finds himself posing as a bank examiner and being forced to lie again to try to take down St. Nick, a legendary savage crime lord who's in the process of going straight by buying a bank in collusion with a corrupt Senator Hutchings. When St. Nick challenges Cutter for supposedly lying to him, Cutter *refusing to lose this opportunity to take down St. Nick*, stands up to him angrily and lies his way out of it.

CAUSE OF THE ACTION (Touching off the Fight to the Finish)

Cutter eavesdrops and learns of their secret plan to legally rob the U.S. taxpayers of billions and make a fortune using government guaranteed agricultural loans in a crooked deal with a brutal African dictator, Umbotha. Cutter is unexpectedly taken deeper inside St. Nick's organization, and when a Communist revolution in Africa puts Umbotha in driver's seat with the CIA, they offer to make St. Nick's bank a CIA front, with unlimited money flowing and immunity to prosecution. Cutter sees one of his partners murdered and, *unable to let this evil go unchecked*, he snaps and kicks into his old lying self, launching into a wild attack by fabricating a communiqué from the Communist revolutionaries, claiming to know about the weapons being smuggled in as agricultural shipments, with the money coming from a U.S. bank.

RESULTING ACTION (Dramatic Question)

Can Cutter destroy this operation and topple St. Nick in the process?

Now this is hitting pretty hard and I'm satisfied with it. You can see that it took quite some doing, but I tinkered with the core of the plot and proposed several different takes on it. I found weaknesses in each of them and kept banging on it until I came up with something that had much more power than my first take. I hope this example helps you acquire a full working understanding of this tool.

21
UTILIZING
SEQUENCE, PROPOSITION, PLOT

Now let's pull this script together with Sequence, Proposition, Plot. The first thing I have to do in order to do reverse cause and effect is to figure out the ending. That's very daunting when you truly have no ending. I have some ideas and a few half-baked possibilities, but they're a set of unconnected ideas that have the luxury of floating free and unbothered. I sat down and stared at the empty page in my notebook where the ending is supposed to appear and I drew a total blank. Again I'm in way over my head. I didn't panic, but I knew I was up against it. If you want a hard-core exercise in screenwriting, then right now try to come up with an ending for this script based on what you've got so far in this book. It will keep you busy. You'll almost certainly create something entirely different than I come up with. And remember that I am actually writing this screenplay. It's not just a demonstration for this book.

After thinking about it for some time, one of the things I came up with was a stronger start of the fight to the finish—Cutter fabricating the communiqué from the Communist rebels. How are St. Nick, Hutchings, Umbotha and the CIA going to react to this communiqué? I see them panicking, with St. Nick's paranoia flaring up and with lots of finger pointing going on both in their group, and inside the CIA, since someone in there might have passed along this secret. I see the possibility of a spy being found within the CIA—somebody who's being thrown to the wolves.

The bank office would be swept again for bugs, but nothing would be found. St. Nick and crew panic and decide to move ahead quickly with the loan operation before anything else goes wrong. They also decide to do as much of it in cash as possible, to make it all less traceable. Umbotha has had a huge shipment of drugs smuggled into the country and the resulting mountain of cash that he launders through the bank gives them trucks full of money. Now that they're a CIA sanctioned operation, it's all smooth sailing. However, some of the weapons manufacturers get greedy and want kickbacks and cash up front. Also a U.N. fact-finding commission is looking into Umbotha's human rights record.

Cutter and Apollo are still raging with hatred for St. Nick and want to stir up more trouble for him to try and crash the deal. They make some phone calls, pretending to be Hutchings and arrange for a covert delivery of a weapons system. But the delivery site is a food bank where members of the press have been summoned, and when this Dept. of Agriculture crate is opened, it's full of Stealth Missiles. That stirs up a hornet's nest of trouble. St. Nick will burn down an entire block of buildings in response. I want him *that* vengeful. Cutter leaks some crucial information to a Congressional Investigative Committee, steals some of the cash from St. Nick's stash and takes great joy in turning several random people into instant millionaires with gifts of cash, just for a lark.

Cutter and Apollo's identities are then discovered and Mischa is taken hostage. I'm not sure how—it's probably Mischa's fault. St. Nick and Hutchings throw someone from the bank to the wolves, which enables the CIA to make the rest of the investigation go away. It's all swept under the rug by citing National Security.

Cutter is trapped in his web of contradictory lies and sees no way out. Margarita, his wife, convinces him to go back to telling the truth. He agrees but he's got to rescue Mischa and settle a few things. Umbotha, who occupies the top five floors of his luxury hotel, is having a giant bash, which has turned into a block party. Cutter has a group of protesters show up and create havoc, protesting Umbotha's human rights record and, in the resultant confusion, Apollo sends in a band of pickpockets to spirit Mischa out of the room where he's being held under guard.

Cutter has found out that St. Nick and crew have the entire amount of money—eight billion dollars worth—in semi-trucks ready to be shipped out as payment to arms manufactures and agricultural corporations. Cutter and Apollo manage to steal the trucks and in a wild chase scene, elude St. Nick and crew by throwing bales of cash into a crowd and creating chaos. They might burn a bunch of the counterfeit money to confuse things too. Cutter takes the trucks to a Democratic mailing center where they break in, bribe the night watchman and spend the night having the mailing machines package, address and stamp overnight envelopes.

The next day Cutter arranges a press conference in which he tells the truth about everything on live national TV. He announces that St. Nick had a change of heart and has sent the money that was stolen from the taxpayers back to them. Packages of $50,000 dollars in cash were sent to many of the country's poorest—to those who make less than $20,000 a year. Pandemonium erupts, the reporters point out this will create a lot of chaos. Cutter can only agree, but what can you do? It's a done deal.

Senator Hutchings is arrested and given a major sentence. St. Nick is grabbed by Umbotha and taken back to Africa, where he will become a personal prisoner of Umbotha for the remainder of his days. Cutter goes back to his simple little life, now truly free and happy. Several packages of cash manage to find their way to Cutter's home. His son Mischa is scared straight and Apollo runs off to Rio with Honey, St. Nick's secretary, along with several bags of cash.

This gives us something to work with. It has some fun elements and has real danger. It's an ending that I can begin to shape. Much of it can still be revised or thrown away. Let's start doing reverse cause and effect. I included the new material about the Communist communiqué as well.

1. Cutter is living straight life with wife and son
2. Apollo appears and blackmails him into job
3. Cutter meets Shallott, the crooked bank examiner
4. Senator is setting up bank with St. Nick as front
5. St. Nick's illegal money will go into reserve account
6. Cutter & St. Nick fight – Cutter called a liar and he's furious
7. Cutter hears plan – govt. guaranteed loans to dictator
8. Cutter learns they're ripping off taxpayer's money to get super rich
9. Apollo's revenge plan put on hold – Cutter gets promoted
10. Cutter moving crooked money into reserve account
11. Cutter awed by St. Nick and Hutchings' lying skills
12. Stock market nosedives – messes things up for St. Nick
13. Complications on moving illegal money
14. FBI & IRS investigate St. Nick – Cutter tells stunning lie, which helps
15. St Nick goes psycho in private – Hutchings chills him out
16. Hutchings helps get money into reserve acct. – bank is open for business
17. Old mob pal of St. Nick wants a cut or he spills on St. Nick
18. Umbotha shows up – sees Cutter deal with old mob pal and likes Cutter
19. Umbotha – limos, parties, diplomatic immunity, girls, drugs & money
20. Umbotha wants St. Nick to launder drug money for him
21. Hutchings nervous about drug money – says no
22. Communist revolution in African country next to Mambia
23. CIA needs Umbotha big-time now
24. Umbotha meets senators, arms dealers, White House, drug smugglers

25. CIA wants St. Nick's bank to be a CIA front bank
26. All limits taken off agricultural loans – now eight billion
27. Investigation goes away – immunity – citing National Security
28. St. Nick is now in the 'club' – celebrating with Hutchings – above the law
29. Shallott freaks out and blows his cover
30. St. Nick flips and murders Shallott – turns on Cutter
31. Cutter does Judy Garland transformation & turns wild – Mischa watches
32. Cutter emerges and scares St. Nick's mob pal away permanently
33. Umbotha loves Cutter and won't allow deal to happen without him
34. Mischa gets found and brought in
35. Cutter pretends Mischa is his gay lover to cover for him
36. Umbotha takes Cutter to party with old friend and it's Apollo!
37. Cutter fabricates false communiqué from Communists
38. Communiqué knows about weapons smuggling and U.S. bank

These are the cards that I added for the ending.

39. St. Nick gets paranoid and suspects everyone
40. 'Traitor' found inside the CIA
41. St. Nick & crew panic – move operation at full steam – all cash now
42. Umbotha brings in big drug shipment – launders tons of cash – in trucks
43. Weapons manufacturer gets greedy, kickbacks, cash up front
44. Umbotha is a spoiled brat – can't be told anything
45. U.N. fact-finding crew – human rights violations in Mambia
46. Cutter & Apollo rage in their hatred against St. Nick
47. Cutter has weapons system delivered to food bank
48. St. Nick burns down an entire block
49. Crucial info leaked to congressional investigation committee
50. Cutter steals money & is turning random people into millionaires
51. Cutter & Apollo discovered – Mischa taken captive
52. St. Nick plants evidence against Cutter in plan to frame him
53. CIA quashes new investigation of bank, citing Nat'l Security
54. Time running out for Cutter
55. Cutter trapped in all his contradictory lies
56. Margarita convinces him to go back to telling the truth
57. Protesters converge on Umbotha's block party – chaos ensues
58. Apollo's band of pickpockets get Mischa out of Umbotha's hotel
59. Cutter & Apollo steal eight billion dollars of St. Nick's money
60. Some money thrown into crowd to create confusion and help escape
61. They mail 8 billion out in $50,000 chunks to poor people around country

62. Cutter tells truth about operation on live national TV press conf.

63. Hutchings gets arrested for drugs, robbery, murder, etc

64. Umbotha takes St. Nick back to Africa as his prisoner

65. Cutter goes back to his normal life, happy and now truly free of his demons

66. Mischa is scared straight

SEQUENCE, PROPOSITION, PLOT FOR THE WHOLE SCRIPT

I work off these index cards as I build the reverse cause and effect. Remember, I'm trying to tie the script as a whole together; I'm working on the macro picture, so I will be skipping over details and dealing only with the general, not the specific. If the big picture doesn't work, then the details won't matter. I'll be working my way backwards, each time asking: "What is the cause of that?" rather than: "What comes before it?" In this way I separate the Necessary from the Unnecessary, so certain cards won't be used on this pass.

First I want to know: *What is the Object of the script?* My objective as the writer is that by the end of the script I want to have Cutter dismantle St. Nick's entire operation and go back home to an honest life, free of his demons.

Now: *What is the Final Effect that demonstrates that Object onscreen with real actors?* Cutter, now truly free and happy, goes home with Margarita and Mischa, who has been scared straight.

What is the Immediate Cause of that Effect? The whole operation gets busted, Umbotha takes St. Nick back to Africa as a prisoner, and Hutchings goes to jail.

What's the cause of that effect? Cutter tells the whole truth about the entire operation on live national TV.

What's the cause of that? Cutter, Apollo and Mischa steal St. Nick's trucks containing eight billion dollars and mail it out to many of the poorest people in the country.

What's the cause of that? St. Nick and Apollo create chaos with human rights protesters and rescue Mischa by using a band of pickpockets.

What's the cause of that? Margarita convinces Cutter to go back to telling the truth instead of trying to lie his way out of this. He agrees and sets up a plan to accomplish this.

What's the cause of that? Cutter is totally trapped in an interlocking set of lies and it looks like he's going to prison for life because it's now three strikes against him. (This is why Margarita can now convince him to tell the truth.)

What's the cause of that? St. Nick has framed Cutter with trumped-up charges, and the CIA makes the new investigation against St. Nick go away by citing National Security.

What's the cause of that? Cutter and Apollo's identities are discovered and Mischa is captured. They torture key information out of him.

What's the cause of that? Cutter overextends himself when they arrange to have a weapons system delivered to a food bank, and he leaks crucial evidence to a Congressional Investigating Committee. Cutter turns people into instant millionaires by handing out cash that he stole.

What's the cause of that? Cutter knows he's got St. Nick and crew reeling, and now is the time to strike. Cutter steals some of St. Nick's hidden cash assets.

What's the cause of that? St. Nick and crew panic, lashing out in paranoid ways. They decide to move ahead full steam with the operation, changing it to all cash so nothing's traceable. Umbotha brings drugs under CIA protection and launders the proceeds at the bank.

What's the cause of that? Cutter emerges as a wild man, completely reverting to his old lying raging self, and goes on the attack against St. Nick, sending in a fabricated communiqué from the African Communist rebels claiming to know all about the weapons shipments disguised as agricultural crates, and that a U.S. bank is behind it.

What's the cause of that? Shallott's cover gets blown and St. Nick murders him, and then turns his suspicions on Cutter.

What's the cause of that? (I don't know. What *could* cause Shallott's cover to be blown? Did Shallott do something stupid? Did Shallot get so mad at St. Nick that he flips out? Does something happen that tips St. Nick off? Does Cutter make a mistake? These are all possibilities. One of the nice things about this tool is that I don't need much in the way of detail on the first pass. I can sketch something in and then figure it out in more detail on the next pass.) Let's say that Shallott slips up because he's so angry.

What's the cause of that? St. Nick and Senator Hutchings are celebrating because they're now above the law. St. Nick is slipping out of Shallott and Cutter's grasp.

What's the cause of that? The investigation against St. Nick is dropped and the limits on how much can be loaned to Mambia through the agricultural program are unofficially lifted.

What's the cause of that? The CIA wants St. Nick's bank to be a purely CIA bank because it's already in business with Umbotha and is unencumbered by other clients.

What's the cause of that? The CIA very much needs Umbotha now; he's escorted all over DC for meetings with senators, spies, the White House and arms dealers.

What's the cause of that? Umbotha is partying it up and trying to force St. Nick and Hutchings to launder drug money at the bank, when they hear there's been a Communist overthrow in the country next to Mambia.

What's the cause of that? Umbotha shows up in America, comes to the bank and sees Cutter deal with St. Nick's old mob pal. He immediately takes to Cutter and brings him along to wild parties.

What's the cause of that? Senator Hutchings pulls some strings and gets the rest of the money through the red tape and into the reserves. The bank is officially open for business.

What's the cause of that? St. Nick goes psycho on Hutchings and says it's all getting too complicated—he can't take it, he's going to flip out and blow the deal.

What's the cause of that? There are complications moving St. Nick's illegal assets into the reserves, the FBI starts investigating him and the stock market drops precipitously.

What's the cause of that? Cutter is promoted in St. Nick's organization and works on moving hidden assets into the legal system.

What's the cause of that? Cutter tells Apollo what he heard, namely that St. Nick and his crew are robbing the U.S. taxpayers. Because he knows he's going to be promoted, he and Apollo put their original plan on hold to see if a better opportunity to destroy St. Nick emerges.

What's the cause of that? Cutter eavesdrops on St. Nick and Hutchings as they discuss their plan to use government guaranteed agricultural loans to get filthy rich. St. Nick says he really likes Cutter's fighting spirit and will promote him.

What's the cause of that? Cutter reacts furiously to being called a liar by St. Nick and then is freaked out, thinking that he has blown his revenge operation.

What's the cause of that? There's a legal glitch with the IRS, and St. Nick's paranoia flares up and he accuses Cutter of being a liar.

What's the cause of that? Hutchings sees a way to use the Uruguayan tax shelter in their operation and they start doing it to bring in St. Nick's offshore money.

What's the cause of that? Apollo shows up in disguise and turns out to be an old acquaintance of the Senator's. Apollo turns out to actually be a retired ambassador from Uruguay and Cutter is stunned, but doesn't show it. Apollo tells Hutchings on the sly that his country is offering some unique tax shelters. (I just made this up. It isn't in the cards. I wanted more Apollo in this story. He's been around for a long time and his father was the dictator of a South American country, so he could have been an ambassador at one point, even if it was only an honorary one.)

What's the cause of that? Cutter and Shallott start working to bring St. Nick's illegal assets into the legal system.

What's the cause of that? Shallott takes Cutter into the bank as his assistant, telling St. Nick that Cutter is solid and that he needs Cutter's help to pull off bringing St Nick's hidden assets into the system legally.

What's the cause of that? Shallott tells Cutter about how Senator Hutchings created a loophole and needs St. Nick to front this new bank so that they can use the loophole to make incredible sums of money.

What's the cause of that? Apollo blackmails Cutter into being part of this operation. Plus Cutter utterly loathes St. Nick, so he agrees to talk to Shallott.

What's the cause of that? Cutter is living a straight life, having forsaken lying forever, when Apollo reappears in Cutter's life with a job he has to do. (Notice that it wouldn't work to say that the cause of Apollo showing up is that Cutter is living a straight life, so I joined them together. His living a straight life comes *before* Apollo's arrival, but doesn't cause it.)

Now let's see how Proposition, Plot lines up for the overall script: (Note that St. Nick killing Frenchy is not the Initial Act of Aggression because that doesn't happen in the movie itself (it happened before the movie started—what's known as the Conditions Precedent). Here we're dealing with the meat of the story, and fairly early on, Cutter and St. Nick cross swords, so we're setting up a potential fight.)

PROTAGONIST	*ANTAGONIST*

| | **INITIAL ACT OF AGGRESSION**
St. Nick gets paranoid when Cutter and Shallott are moving illegal assets and accuses Cutter of being a liar. |

JUSTIFIED RETALIATION
Cutter stands up to St. Nick and fights, saying that he didn't lie and will absolutely not be called a liar.

AGGRAVATION OF THE ISSUE
St. Nick murders Shallott and comes after Cutter, sure that he's in on Shallott's operation.

PRECIPITATING ACT
Cutter snaps into his old wild self and goes on the attack, fabricating a communiqué from Communist rebels in Africa, saying they know all about the weapons shipments.

DRAMATIC QUESTION ARISING
Will Cutter smash the operation and take down St. Nick
or will St. Nick destroy them?
[From here down is 'Plot']

St. Nick and crew panic and rush ahead with the operation, using only cash, much of it being drug money.

Cutter has a weapons system delivered to a food bank, leaks info to a Congressional committee.

St. Nick figures out who Cutter is, captures Mischa, and has the CIA stop the investigation, citing national security and then frames Cutter.

Cutter rescues Mischa, steals eight billion dollars and gives it all away. He tells the truth on live TV, taking down St. Nick and Hutchings.

Remember that the section we call 'Plot' answers the dramatic question and completes the action, wrapping up the plot.

DIVIDING THE SCRIPT INTO ACTS

Now let's do division into acts. The way I do that is to look at the reverse cause and effect and try to find the act breaks. Notice that if you read the cause and effect from the bottom up, you'll be reading the story in its correct order. As I read up I am looking for natural breaks that could divide the acts. The best rule of thumb for division into acts is that you're finishing up one major chapter and starting another. I see Act I ending when, after overhearing St. Nick and Hutchings' plan, Cutter goes to Apollo and they put their original plan on hold, awaiting a better opportunity to destroy St. Nick, and stop he and Hutchings from robbing the American taxpayers in the process. Here we are finishing one major chapter in the story and starting another. I see Act II ending with Shallott's murder, with Act III beginning with Cutter's Judy Garland transformation as he clicks into his old wild self.

Now let's do Sequence, Proposition, Plot for Act I. We'll be working our way through reverse cause and effect from the point where Cutter and Apollo put their old plan on hold and decide to go with the new flow. For clarity's sake I have copied that section below. I'll be going back through this section, using it as a map, and expanding upon the detail as I work backwards through it, adding in just a little more detail as it becomes necessary.

Here's the section from the previous cause and effect that we will be working from:

Cause: Cutter tells Apollo what he heard, namely that they're robbing the U.S. taxpayers. Because he knows he's going to be promoted, he and Apollo put their original plan on hold to see if a better opportunity to destroy St. Nick emerges.

Cause: Cutter eavesdrops on St. Nick and Hutchings as they discuss their plan to use government guaranteed agricultural loans to get filthy rich. St. Nick says he really likes Cutter's fighting spirit and will promote him.

Cause: Cutter reacts furiously to being called a liar by St. Nick and then is freaked out, thinking that he has blown his revenge operation.

Cause: There's a legal glitch with the IRS, and St. Nick's paranoia flares up and he accuses Cutter of being a liar.

Cause: Hutchings sees a way to use the Uruguayan tax shelter in their operation and they start doing it to bring in St. Nick's offshore money.

Cause: Apollo shows up in disguise and turns out to be an old acquaintance of the Senator's. Apollo turns out to actually be a retired ambassador from Uruguay and Cutter is stunned, but doesn't show it. Apollo tells Hutchings on the sly that his country is offering some unique tax shelters

Cause: Cutter and Shallott start working to bring St. Nick's illegal assets into the legal system.

Cause: Shallott takes Cutter into the bank as his assistant, saying that Cutter is solid and that he needs his help to pull off bringing St Nick's hidden assets into the system legally.

Cause: Shallott tells Cutter about how Senator Hutchings created a loophole and needs St. Nick to front this new bank so that they can use the loophole to make incredible sums of money.

Cause: Apollo blackmails Cutter into being part of this operation. Plus Cutter utterly loathes St. Nick, so he agrees to talk to Shallott.

Cause: Cutter is living a straight life, having forsaken lying forever, when Apollo reappears in Cutter's life with a job he has to do.

To work backwards through Act I, we can refer to this section above as a map to guide our process below.

SEQUENCE, PROPOSITION, PLOT FOR ACT I

What's the object of Act I? Cutter and Apollo see an expanding opportunity for revenge and also a chance to stop a major theft of the American public, so they put their original plan on hold.

What's the final effect that demonstrates the object onscreen with real actors? (What I'm doing here is to visualize the last scene in this act in more detail than I did at the macro level.) Cutter and Apollo realize that a gift may have dropped in their laps. St. Nick wants to promote Cutter and they know what his secret plan is. This gives them a great chance to take down St. Nick in a more spectacular way and also to stop the robbing of the U.S. taxpayer, which unexpectedly infuriates them.

Immediate Cause: Cutter goes to Apollo and tells him what he just learned.

Cause: Cutter hears St. Nick and Senator Hutchings discussing their plan to use government guaranteed agricultural loans to run a scam with an African dictator in which they loan him the money, he defaults on the loan and the U.S. government repays St. Nick and Hutchings. They get a factory in Mambia for ten years with free labor and free material, which will make them an additional fortune.

Cause: Cutter eavesdrops on them in their bug-proof room using two cans and a string. He hears St. Nick say that he likes Cutter's fighting spirit and is going to promote him.

Cause: St. Nick flips out at Cutter, and Cutter doesn't take one inch of crap off him. St. Nick gets a grip on himself and cools down, but Cutter is scared that he has ruined the revenge operation.

Cause: St. Nick gets paranoid and accuses Cutter of lying. Cutter, who isn't lying, reacts furiously and lashes out in his own defense.

Cause: The IRS challenges one of the tax deals through Uruguay and Cutter says that he and Shallott can handle it. It's not a problem.

Cause: They start using the Uruguayan connection that Apollo provided them with and it's working well. (Here it becomes necessary to expand some the details of the Uruguayan tax shelter that Apollo introduces.)

Cause: Hutchings wants to try it and Shallott okays it.

Cause: Apollo takes Hutchings aside and tells him about this new tax shelter that Uruguay has put in place, and Hutchings thinks it might work for them.

Cause: Apollo shows up at the office with Hutchings, and Cutter, to his surprise learns that they are old acquaintances. Apollo is a retired ambassador from Uruguay.

Cause: Cutter and Shallott begin the complex and illegal work on bringing St. Nick's hidden illegal assets into the system so they can be put into the reserve fund that allows the bank to do business.

Cause: Shallott brings Cutter in as his assistant and convinces St. Nick and Hutchings that he is solid and reliable, and that he cannot do this without him. They agree.

Cause: Shallott explains to Cutter that St. Nick's part in the deal is that he has to put up the reserve fund that any bank has to post, and to do that he has to bring hidden illegal assets in from hiding, which makes him vulnerable. Cutter reluctantly agrees to work on it.

Cause: Shallott tells Cutter that Senator Hutchings came to him because he needed a crooked bank examiner to help set up a bank, fronted by St. Nick, to take advantage of a banking law loophole that Hutchings slipped into a bill.

Cause: Shallott says he has a once-in-a-lifetime chance to destroy St. Nick. Shallott says he has waited for just such an opportunity because St. Nick killed his only family in the world when he gassed the whole town over the racehorse cheating incident.

Cause: Cutter reluctantly goes with Apollo and is introduced to Shallott.

Cause: Apollo tells Mischa the story about when Cutter stole the Rolling Stone's limo and Mischa gets all hopped up; Cutter caves in because he can't let Mischa learn more of his past as it will tilt Mischa into a life of crime.

Cause: Cutter won't have anything to with Apollo, no matter what, even though he despises St. Nick thoroughly.

Cause: Apollo springs himself on Cutter, pretending to be a sex offender who just moved into the neighborhood. He threatens Cutter with blackmail if he doesn't come in with him on a job to take down St. Nick.

Cause: (The fact that Cutter has gone straight doesn't cause Apollo to appear, but I'm casting around for a way to create some cause and effect. I don't need it, but if I can create cause and effect, then the script is tied together tighter.) What if Cutter has just had a fight with his wife because he's unhappy and she knows he's itching for the old life, even though he swears he isn't? (This brings some element of cause and effect into the equation, even if it is indirect.)

Cause: He opens the community center he helped organize and reconstruct, and to his surprise he's depressed when it's over. He takes anti-depressants, and Margarita sees him in this slump.

Cause: He's a solid churchgoing family man, a good husband and an upright role model to his estranged son. They head off to the grand opening of the community center.

Notice how much we expanded upon the reverse cause and effect section from the script as a whole. I thought it through more and visualized the next level of detail. I'm literally making this up on the spot, but I have also been marinating this story in my brain for months, so I have good material to draw on. I'm still not into too much detail (which keeps me free)—*just enough for a little more of the story to come into focus.* I'll develop more when I break the act down into sequences and do reverse cause and effect again for each of them. Also notice that as I add a little more detail, I am grooming, revising, rethinking, shaping and developing the plot. I'm not a slave to what I already had—that was just a rough map. If that still works, that's fine, but if I stumble onto something new then I'll run with it.

Here we do Proposition, Plot for Act I. Notice that the Initial Act of Aggression for the Act is not what it was for the whole script because we're dramatizing a smaller section of the script.

PROTAGONIST	ANTAGONIST
	INITIAL ACT OF AGGRESSION Apollo reappears in Cutter's life, blackmails him into being part of this revenge scam on St. Nick and takes him to meet Shallott, who explains the job. (St. Nick, our central antagonist is not in the mix yet, so Apollo is doing his job here.)
JUSTIFIED RETALIATION Cutter reads Apollo and Shallot the riot act, saying that this absolutely must be a watertight operation or he will have their heads. (I just invented this because he didn't have much in the way of retaliation except trying to refuse, and that wasn't a very strong action for our protagonist at the act level. In other words, the tool suggested something stronger was needed and I agreed and created something.)	
	AGGRAVATION OF THE ISSUE St. Nick gets paranoid about the IRS and accuses Cutter of lying about the handling of Uruguayan tax shelter.
PRECIPITATING ACT Cutter stands up to St. Nick fiercely, saying that he is not a liar and he absolutely will not be called one.	

DRAMATIC QUESTION ARISING
Will Cutter make St. Nick back down
or will St. Nick throw him out or even kill him?
[From here down is 'Plot']

St. Nick flips out at him and saying who the hell does he think he is; he wants to kill Cutter, but he manages to cool down, although he's still dangerous.

Cutter panics, sure that he has just ruined the revenge project with his temper and then eavesdrops on St. Nick and Hutchings in their bug-proof room.

St. Nick and Hutchings talk about their plan to use government guaranteed agricultural loans to make a fortune. St. Nick says that Cutter has guts and that he's going to promote him. Hutchings agrees.

Cutter is unexpectedly furious that they're going to rip off the American taxpayers and he goes to Apollo. They decide to put their original plan on hold and see if Cutter's promotion gives them more opportunity to take down St. Nick in a bigger way and stop the crime.

DIVIDING THE ACT INTO SEQUENCES

It's instructive to see how to divide an act into sequences. Remember that there are generally two to five sequences in an act as in our previous example of the *planning sequence*, the *robbery sequence* and the *getaway sequence*. A sequence in turn, usually consists of two to five scenes. Let's divide this act into sequences, then I'll do Sequence, Proposition, Plot on one of them, the next step in this process.

When I look at the reverse cause and effect for Act I, I find four sequences. First we have the (1) *opening sequence* with Cutter doing good around town and then arguing with his wife. Then we've got the (2) *appearance of Apollo* and the meeting with Shallott. Next is (3) *Cutter going to work at the bank* with Shallott, up through where the IRS challenges the Uruguayan tax deal. Next is the (4) *fight between Cutter and St. Nick*, with the overheard plan and Cutter reporting to Apollo. For our exercise, I'm going to do Sequence, Proposition, Plot for the second sequence, the *appearance of Apollo*.

Below, I've copied the section from Act I (above) that I'll be expanding upon. I use this, as well as Proposition, Plot as my map to developing reverse cause and effect for Sequence 2:

Cause: Shallott explains to Cutter that St. Nick's part in the deal is that he has to put up the reserve fund that any bank has to post, and to do that he has to bring hidden illegal assets in from hiding, which makes him vulnerable. Cutter reluctantly agrees to work on it.

Cause: Shallott tells Cutter that Senator Hutchings came to him because he needed a crooked bank examiner to help set up a bank, fronted by St. Nick, to take advantage of a banking law loophole that Hutchings slipped into a bill.

Cause: Shallott says he has a once-in-a-lifetime chance to destroy St. Nick. Shallott says he has waited for just such an opportunity because St. Nick killed his only family in the world when he gassed the whole town over the race horse cheating incident.

Cause: Cutter reluctantly goes with Apollo and is introduced to Shallott.

Cause: Apollo tells Mischa the story about when Cutter stole the Rolling Stone's limo and Mischa gets all hopped up; Cutter caves in because he can't let Mischa learn more of his past as it will tilt Mischa into a life of crime.

Cause: Cutter won't have anything to with Apollo, no matter what, even though he despises St. Nick thoroughly.

Cause: Apollo springs himself on Cutter, pretending to be a sex offender who just moved into the neighborhood. He threatens Cutter with blackmail if he doesn't come in with him on a job to take down St. Nick.

SEQUENCE, PROPOSITION, PLOT FOR ACT I, SEQ. 2

What's the Object of this Sequence? Cutter is starting to get caught up in his dilemma because part of him really wants to do this job against St. Nick.

What's the Final Effect that demonstrates this object onscreen with real actors? Cutter is ready to go in with Shallott, part of him wanting to take down St. Nick so much, but he is also very scared of St. Nick and doesn't trust Apollo.

Immediate Cause: Shallott reassures him that things will work out. This is a golden opportunity and their odds are extremely good to destroy St. Nick and get rich for life.

Cause: Cutter reluctantly agrees, saying he hates St. Nick's guts, but threatens Apollo and Shallot that this better be airtight or he will come after them—if St. Nick doesn't kill them. (I took this from the proposition for Act I.)

Cause: Shallott says he needs somebody with Cutter's skills to help pull their operation off.

Cause: Shallott sees that Cutter's interest has been sparked and continues on, saying that St. Nick is vulnerable in a way that he will never be again, and that in fact if St. Nick's plan works out, he will become absolutely untouchable.

Cause: Shallott tells how St. Nick's part of the deal is to put up the reserve fund that any bank must have to operate, and that the money will come from St. Nick's illegal hidden assets. This gets Cutter's attention.

Cause: Shallott says that Senator Hutchings came to him because he needed a crooked bank examiner who could manipulate the situation to get this bank up and running, and Shallott's job is to help St. Nick buy the bank.

Cause: Shallott says that the Senator, who is on the Senate Banking Committee, slipped a loophole into a law that could make him incredibly rich if he owned a bank. He got his old friend St. Nick, who is anxious to go legit, to buy the bank with the Senator as a silent partner. This was Shallott's way in.

Cause: Shallott explains his connection to this deal is that he had known Senator Hutchings, and when he learned that Hutchings had a connection with St. Nick, he cultivated the relationship with Hutchings further for possible access to St. Nick.

Cause: Shallott says he was on the lookout for a way to get even with St. Nick because years ago St. Nick got caught trying to cheat with his racehorse, so he staged an 'accidental' chemical spill which killed an entire town in Kentucky on Christmas Eve. Shallott's only family member, a retarded brother who loved horses, lived in that town and was killed.

Cause: Apollo takes Cutter to meet Shallott, who says he has a once-in-a-lifetime chance to utterly destroy St. Nick, and that he, Shallott, absolutely *must* take this opportunity.

Cause: Cutter caves in and agrees to listen to what Apollo wants.

Cause: Mischa shows up and Apollo tells him about how Cutter stole the Rolling Stones' limousine with them in it and went on a legendary rampage that the Stones still remember as the best party they ever went to. Mischa is thrilled.

Cause: Cutter says he will not do it, period—especially since he doesn't trust Apollo, no matter what he says.

Cause: Apollo threatens to tell the police about a crime Cutter did that is still an open case if he doesn't help Apollo. Cutter knows if Apollo turns him in that it will be his third strike and he'll go to jail for life.

Cause: Apollo says he has the perfect way to utterly destroy St. Nick, the guy who betrayed and murdered Frenchy, their best buddy from prison. Cutter is moved, but refuses to have anything to do with it.

Cause: Cutter answers the door and it's a new neighbor saying that he's a registered sex offender who is required by law to tell the neighborhood. Cutter tries to be civil, but the guy breaks out laughing and it turns out to be his old cellmate, Apollo.

A SIDEBAR ON SEQUENCE, PROPOSITION, PLOT

Notice how I have visualized the sequence in a little more detail, using what I had already figured out as a map. Hopefully it's becoming clearer how this tool is used and how useful it can be for developing and building a screenplay. I have taught Sequence, Proposition, Plot to many film studio development executives and they consistently say it's the most advanced development tool in the film industry.

After reading Price and Krows for almost three years, I finally hit on this key tool and I can still feel the original electricity of that eureka moment. When I hit the sentence in Price's book (when I was reading it yet again back in 1984) in which he tied together Sequence, Proposition, Plot I literally saw a light bulb. I had to piece it together with what Krows said about double proposition and then I added some to it, but this is very much what Price described in 1908. It's a genuine pleasure to share it with you.

BACK TO USING THE TOOL ON ACT I, SEQ. 2

On to Proposition, Plot for Act I, Sequence 2. As I look at it, I see that it will be a good instructive example of the use of Proposition, Plot. One of the things that I notice is that the level of conflict in this sequence could be higher. When I look for a possible Precipitating Act (an action by the protagonist that touches off the fight to the finish) I find that Cutter doesn't have too much. He resists Apollo at the beginning and at the end, but there isn't a real fight (and there *could* be one— I'm not trying to force it). One of the things I do when I start in with this tool is to say: "What's the fight?" In other words, does *this particular sequence* build to a fight, that erupts two-thirds or three-quarters of the way through?

When I looked at the reverse cause and effect, lo and behold, there was no real conflict from Cutter. It's all Shallott explaining things. They're *interesting* things, but it needs more conflict, which would make this sequence much more dramatic. In other words this sequence is Story, not Drama. If it's only narrative, then it's not necessarily gripping to the audience, because even if it's *really* interesting information, it's still just *information*. I need something strong from Cutter at the point of the Precipitating Act. Cutter isn't going meekly along, but he should be fighting harder for his life. It ups the amperage of the whole sequence. This is fairly routine with this tool—creating conflict where the tool 'points out' that it *could* be.

Now let's map out Proposition, Plot for Act I, Seq. 2:

PROTAGONIST	*ANTAGONIST*

<table>
<tr><td></td><td>

INITIAL ACT OF AGGRESSION
Apollo shows and says he has a way
to destroy St. Nick, threatens
blackmail and tells Mischa about
Cutter stealing the Stones' limo.
</td></tr>
<tr><td>

JUSTIFIED RETALIATION
Cutter refuses to have anything to do
with Apollo and tries to make him
stop telling Mischa the story.
</td><td></td></tr>
<tr><td></td><td>

AGGRAVATION OF THE ISSUE
Apollo takes Cutter to Shallott, who
tells him about this chance to destroy
St. Nick, and demands Cutter's help.
</td></tr>
<tr><td>

PRECIPITATING ACT
Cutter gets furious and tells them
St. Nick is so treacherous that they'll
get their all their families killed.
</td><td></td></tr>
</table>

DRAMATIC QUESTION ARISING
Will Cutter get rid of Shallott and Apollo
or will they somehow drag him into this job?
[From here down is 'Plot']

<table>
<tr><td></td><td>

Shallott says that St. Nick already
killed his family and he wants
revenge. Shallott says it's the only
opportunity to destroy St. Nick.
</td></tr>
<tr><td>

Cutter says he hates St. Nick's guts
too, but he just cannot do this job.
</td><td></td></tr>
<tr><td></td><td>

Shallott tells him about how St. Nick is
vulnerable because he has to move illegal
hidden funds in order to go legit. Apollo
says it won't work without Cutter.
</td></tr>
<tr><td>

Cutter knows they're right and
reluctantly agrees, but says he will
kill them both if it messes up.
</td><td></td></tr>
</table>

Do you see how Proposition, Plot enhanced this sequence dramatically? Do you see how it went from being Story to being Drama? This scene has Dramatic Action now! It's got real kick. The actors have so much more to do than merely relay information for the benefit of the audience. Now it's a gripping, actable scene that will get the audience on the edge of their seats. This sequence just became stageworthy. The scenes inside the sequence will also be rendered stageworthy when I do Sequence, Proposition, Plot to them next. This sequence is part of a tight and dramatic act, and the whole script itself has a coherent and compelling dramatic structure.

Notice also that when I did the Reverse Sequence of cause and effect, the events had a specific order, but when I got to Proposition, Plot I changed their order because I found a better way to do them. I took what I did in Reverse Sequence and *revised* it in Proposition, Plot, because Proposition, Plot challenged me to create more conflict. To do that, the order of events that I laid out in the reverse cause and effect (which was properly done) needed to be revised. I'm free-floating, always on the lookout for a way to make the material more dramatic.

As you work your way down the levels of the script, from the whole script, to each act, to each sequence and finally to each scene, doing Sequence, Proposition, Plot for each level, you are constantly grooming each one of them, changing, revising and refining. It gives you a chance to keep developing your material as you go. You're not just robotically using this process—you're an artist who takes the opportunities it affords to improve your plot at every pass. Plus, when I was writing the reverse cause and effect I didn't specifically notice it was flat dramatically because I was concentrating on expanding the detail a little more and tying it together with cause and effect. It wasn't until I got to Proposition, Plot that the tool itself had a different set of requirements and challenged me to revise what I'd laid out.

It clearly needed to be dramatized. I created conflict in Proposition, Plot because I noticed it wasn't there. I tried the conflict a few different ways (with thumbnail sketches) and found something that seemed to work, then filled it in, above. It's got Cutter and Shallott at each other's throats. They're acting more like desperate criminals than accountants or wimps. Take a moment to understand how I got this sequence to work and you will get how all three steps of Sequence, Proposition, Plot make whatever you're working on tight and dramatic. If it is merely tight, then it can still be Story. In the simplest terms, the conflict wasn't there in this sequence, and the tool, Proposition, Plot challenged me to create it. When I did that, it brought the material to a new level of Dramatic Action.

SEQUENCE, PROPOSITION, PLOT AT THE SCENE LEVEL

Now let's do Sequence, Proposition, Plot for two of the scenes in this sequence. At first I thought it might be one scene, but I think I'll do two. We're meeting a major new character and Mischa is learning about his dad's past. Here again, I have copied that section from above that we'll be working with as a map to doing reverse cause and effect for the scenes, as well as Proposition, Plot.

Cause: Cutter caves in and agrees to listen to what Apollo wants.

Cause: Mischa shows up and Apollo tells him about how Cutter stole the Rolling Stones' limousine with them in it and went on a legendary rampage that the Stones still remember as the best party they ever went to. Mischa is thrilled.

Cause: Cutter says he will not do it, period—especially since he doesn't trust Apollo, no matter what he says.

Cause: Apollo threatens to tell the police about a crime Cutter did that is still an open case if he doesn't help Apollo. Cutter knows if Apollo turns him in that it will be his third strike and he'll go to jail for life.

Cause: Apollo says he has the perfect way to utterly destroy St. Nick, the guy who betrayed and murdered Frenchy, their best buddy from prison. Cutter is moved, but refuses to have anything to do with it.

Cause: Cutter answers the door and it's a new neighbor saying that he's a registered sex offender who is required by law to tell the neighborhood. Cutter tries to be civil, but the guy breaks out laughing and it turns out to be his old cellmate, Apollo.

SEQUENCE, PROPOSITION, PLOT FOR ACT I, SEQ. 2, SCENE 1

What's the Object of the scene? Cutter is trapped by Apollo.

What's the Final Effect that demonstrates that Object onscreen with real actors? Apollo has Cutter handcuffed to the wall (something I just came up with) and his blackmail is having some effect.

Immediate Cause: Cutter tries to throw him out, but Apollo clicks handcuffs on him, then threatens to turn him in for an old robbery that's still open. He also reminds Cutter that he owes him his life (Apollo saved his life in prison).

Cause: Apollo will not go away and seems to know a lot about Cutter's life.

Cause: Cutter is moved by the opportunity but says that he has sworn off all that.

Cause: Apollo says he has a once-in-a-lifetime chance to destroy St. Nick.

Cause: Apollo takes his disguise off and Cutter panics.

Cause: Cutter is furious and Apollo is having so much fun that he can't keep up the act and starts laughing.

Cause: Cutter is stunned and doesn't know what to do, and then Apollo starts asking if he has any kids.

Cause: Apollo comes to Cutter's door in disguise and pretends to be a registered sex offender who has just moved into the neighborhood and is required by law to tell each neighbor.

Cause: Apollo has been watching Cutter and decides to make his move now.

Now I have visualized this scene in even more detail—enough detail to be able to write the scene, but first I'll do Proposition, Plot to develop the scene's conflict. The first thing I want to know is: What's the fight? (Is there one, and if not, why not? Can the scene benefit from conflict or opposition at some level?) It's obviously between Cutter and Apollo, especially once Cutter realizes who it is.

PROTAGONIST	ANTAGONIST
	INITIAL ACT OF AGGRESSION A stranger shows up at Cutter's door, saying he's a registered sex offender who is required by law to tell the neighbors. He inquires if Cutter has any kids.
JUSTIFIED RETALIATION Cutter is in shock, then gets furious and tries to get rid of this weirdo.	
	AGGRAVATION OF THE ISSUE It turns out to be his old cellmate, Apollo, playing a practical joke.
PRECIPITATING ACT Cutter flips out and tries to throw him out before he starts talking.	

DRAMATIC QUESTION ARISING
Will Cutter be able to get rid of Apollo
or will Apollo make his move?

	Apollo says he's got a way to destroy St. Nick. A once-in-a-lifetime chance.
Cutter is moved, but totally refuses, saying that he's sworn off all that.	
	Apollo snaps a pair of handcuffs on Cutter and threatens to turn him in for an old crime which would mean life in jail.
Cutter says he'll kill him, but he is powerless.	

SEQUENCE, PROPOSITION, PLOT FOR ACT I, SEQ. 2, SCENE 2

Object: Cutter gives in to Apollo's demand.

Final Effect: Cutter freaks out and says he'll do it, but to shut up and leave Mischa alone.

Immediate Cause: Mischa is ecstatic and has all these questions. He's getting wild.

Cause: Apollo tells him about all the damage they did, the people who got pregnant and had to leave the country and all that, and says the Stones still say it was the best party they've ever been to.

Cause: Cutter yells at Apollo to shut up. When he won't, Cutter breaks a vase over Apollo's head, but it doesn't faze him.

Cause: Apollo offers the joint to Mischa, who wants some but is stared down by his father.

Cause: Apollo is having a blast telling his stories and lights up a joint.

Cause: Apollo says that at one point Cutter was naked on roller skates being pulled down the street by seven naked women on roller skates.

Cause: Mischa is stunned that his dad is *that* wild and asks Apollo about him.

Cause: Apollo tells Mischa that his dad is the world's greatest liar, and would steal anything. One time he even stole the Rolling Stones' limo—with them in it—and took them on a legendary three-day bender through five states before the National Guard cornered them at the Canadian border.

Cause: Mischa, who has strong criminal tendencies, wants to know about his father's wild side. He says he's heard rumors but Cutter will never tell him anything.

Cause: Mischa walks in on them and Apollo introduces himself as his father's old friend.

PROTAGONIST	*ANTAGONIST*

ANTAGONIST

INITIAL ACT OF AGGRESSION

Mischa walks in and Apollo tells him what a legendary liar and thief his dad used to be. He tells him that one time he stole the Rolling Stones limo—with them in it and took them on a wild three-day bender.

PROTAGONIST

JUSTIFIED RETALIATION

Cutter panics, tries to force Apollo to shut up, and orders Mischa to not listen.

AGGRAVATION OF THE ISSUE

Apollo gets all excited telling his story, lights up a joint and offers some to Mischa, who looks at it hungrily.

PRECIPITATING ACT

Cutter orders Mischa to not smoke that and then beans Apollo in the head with a vase to try to stop him.

DRAMATIC QUESTION ARISING

Will Cutter get Apollo to shut up, or will Apollo tell all to Mischa?

Apollo says that Cutter was so wild that at one point he was going down the street naked on roller skates being pulled by seven naked girls.

Cutter is screaming and ripping his plumbing apart trying to get free.

Apollo tells Mischa how much damage they did on the bender, and so on, and how Cutter lied his way out of it. Mischa is gassed and his wild side is emerging.

Cutter gives in and says he'll do it, but to stop talking to Mischa.

WRITING TWO SCENES, BASED ON ALL THE ABOVE STRUCTURING

Now I'll write the actual scenes. I am not a slave to this structure, but it gives me a shape that is tight and dramatic. There won't be anything in this scene that is unnecessary or flat dramatically, but I can also let it breathe. It's like in jazz; you know the chords that you'll be playing, but you can improvise on them. Bear in mind that I'm looking at a print-out of Sequence, Proposition, Plot for each scene as I write it.

Remember, this is not the opening scene, but comes after we've met Cutter, Mischa and Margarita. Cutter has just had a fight with his wife about her suspicions that he's longing for his old ways, and he has sworn that he isn't. He took some anti-depressants and went for a bike ride to clear his head.

EXT. CUTTER'S HOME – DAY

Cutter bikes down the tree-lined street and pulls into his driveway. He waves to the neighbor's Mexican GARDENER who works among the roses. Taking off his bike helmet, Cutter runs up the steps and goes inside.

The gardener squats down behind a rose bush, and with a furtive look around, strips off his grubby shirt. Underneath is a maroon silk shirt. He steps out of his green work pants and is wearing pleated linen slacks.

He slides off the straw hat and replaces it with a Yankees baseball cap, the brim pulled low. He slips on a pair of sunglasses, and with another glance around, applies a fake bushy moustache.

The gardener stands up and crosses the driveway, then climbs the steps and rings Cutter's doorbell, holding a rose in his hand.

INT. CUTTER'S LIVING ROOM – CONTINUOUS

Cutter has just tossed his shirt down the basement stairs when the bell rings. He looks down at his tiny biking shorts and then up at the door. With a last look downstairs he goes over and opens the door.

Standing there is a strange looking man with a forced smile. He's wearing garish clothes and his posture is terrible. He gazes at Cutter's bare chest uncomfortably, his orange rose held in front of him like a talisman.

Cutter stares at him for a moment too long, then shakes it off.

> CUTTER
> Yes, can I help you?

> MAN
> Um, yes... I ah...
> (smiling bigger)
> I'm, ah, new in the neighborhood.

> CUTTER
> (checking out this weirdo)
> That's... that's good. Hello, I'm Cutter
> Haywood.
> (holding out his hand)
> Pleased to meet you.

> MAN
> Yes, yes.
> (taking his hand)
> My name is Jasper Sullivan.

He continues holding onto Cutter's hand.

> JASPER
> I... I am required by law to inform
> you that I am a... a... registered sex
> offender.

Cutter's eyes go blank, then he looks down, sees that he's hardly got anything on and tugs his hand out of Jasper's.

> JASPER
> I'm so sorry. The police make me do
> this whenever I move somewhere new.

Cutter is totally thrown off and he stares like deer caught in the headlights.

> CUTTER
> I, um... that's...

> JASPER
> I know how you must feel. Trying to
> imagine the things I must have done to,
> uh... for me to end up standing here
> like this.
> > (his smile fading)
> Um, do you mind if I ask you something?

> CUTTER
> What? Yes... OK.

> JASPER
> Do you have any children?

> CUTTER
> WHAT?!

> JASPER
> > (his eyes twinkling)
> Any teenagers?

Cutter is caught between disbelief and rage.

> CUTTER
> Who... what did you...

He steps up to Jasper, but Jasper doesn't pull back and they stand face to face. Jasper is intensely aware that Cutter is wearing practically nothing and it's intoxicating for Jasper.

> CUTTER
> Get... out!

> JASPER
> I'd just like to speak to your son. Is he
> here?

Cutter stares in shock.

> CUTTER
>
> I don't know who the hell you are, mister,
> but you get your ass off my property or
> I'm calling the cops.
>   (glaring furiously)
> Fact is, I'm calling them anyway.

The other man stares at him dizzily.

> JASPER
>
> Why? I... just want to play with Mischa.

Cutter is thunderstruck and looks around for something to hurt him with. He grabs a vase of flowers and turns back to find Jasper giggling.

> CUTTER
>
>   (hefting the vase)
> I'm warning you, mister!

The other guy bursts out laughing and can't stop. Cutter stares warily at him, now really not knowing what to think.

As Cutter watches, the guy peels off the moustache, removes the glasses, pulls off the baseball cap and straightens up.

CLOSE ON Cutter's face as his pupils dilate instantly and he draws in a sharp breath.

> JASPER
>
> You guessed it, buddy boy.

Cutter cannot speak, but a full spectrum of emotions flicker cross his face, most of them related to fear.

> JASPER
>
> I know what you're gonna say.

                    CUTTER
          Apollo...
               (snapping out of it)
          NO, NO, NO, NO, NO!! GET OUT!!
          Get out of my house this INSTANT!!
               (shoving him toward the door)
          I don't want to hear it!

                    APOLLO
               (laughing again)
          Man, the look on your face! It was priceless!

He screams with laughter and Cutter can't help but crack a smile. He recovers
quickly and glares at Apollo, who turns serious.

                    APOLLO
          Listen, I got a way to take down St. Nick,
          big time. Payback for Frenchy.

That gets Cutter's attention and it stops him. He sets the flower vase down on a
shelf, and wrestles with his emotions. Then his eyes harden and he turns coldly on
Apollo.

                    APOLLO
          He's trying to go straight and buy a bank.
          He's vulnerable right now and we could
          finish him off. This kind of opportunity
          only happens in fairy tales.

                    CUTTER
          Every word out of your mouth is a friggin'
          fairy tale! Listen, I loved Frenchy as much
          as anybody... more, but I DO NOT do that
          stuff anymore. I've sworn off it... straight
          and true. You don't have the least idea what
          my life is like now.

> APOLLO
> (chuckling)
> Sure I do... you survive on Prozac, sleeping
> pills and allergy medicine. You're tired,
> depressed and feeling trapped. You got
> therapy, you got hives... hell, you used
> to be Superman himself. Now look at—

> CUTTER
> Goddamn you! I will not—

He goes to raise his hand to make a point but there's a clicking sound at his wrist and his arm stops short.

Cutter looks down and finds himself handcuffed to the radiator pipe. He yanks hard, but he's trapped. Apollo strides to the mantle and pours himself a shot of brandy.

> CUTTER
> I'll kill you! I swear I will!

> APOLLO
> Good... then we're in agreement. Now
> maybe we can have a civilized
> conversation.

> CUTTER
> Once upon a time you were one of my
> best friends, but I never trusted you and
> I don't now. The answer is no. N-O.

> APOLLO
> Look, we can do this the hard way where
> I call Detective Henries and remind him
> about a certain missing super computer.
> The statute of limitations still hasn't run
> out on that sucker, you know? Something
> about it being government property.
> Three strikes and you're a lifer... pally.
> (smiling expansively)

                Or we can do it the easy way... the good
                old way, you know? Besides, you still owe
                me your life, remember that, dickwad?

Cutter's eyes go wide. As he contemplates this, the door opens and Mischa enters.

                      MISCHA
                Hi. Who are you?

He spots his dad handcuffed to the wall in tiny red spandex shorts and stares in amazement.

                      MISCHA
                Dad?

                      APOLLO
                I'm an old buddy of your pop's. We
                were just catching up on old times.
                    (smiling big)
                You must be Mischa. I'm Apollo
                Marseilles. Damn glad to meet you.
                    (they shake)
                I've heard a lot about you, sonny.

                      MISCHA
                Where do you know dad from?

                      APOLLO
                We were cellmates.

                      MISCHA
                    (cringing; not sure he heard right)
                Soul mates?

Apollo laughs out loud and shoves Mischa playfully.

                      APOLLO
                No man... CELL mates. In the
                joint for eight years. Federal
                prison.

Cutter cringes as Mischa's eyes go wide and a mischievous grin lights up his face.

> MISCHA
>
> *Really?* Oh my god...what was he like
> back then? He'll never tell me *anything*.
> I've heard rumors and—

> CUTTER
>
> DON'T! Mischa don't! You don't want
> to know.

Apollo puts an arm around Mischa and they face Cutter.

> APOLLO
>
> Now I think it's important for a son to
> know about his daddy. Especially when
> you were in stir for so much of his
> childhood. This is what he missed out on.
>   (pulling Mischa around)
> Now your old man is flat-out the wildest
> mother... he was CRAY-ZEE! He could
> lie like a rattlesnake and steal the stripes
> off a zebra.
>   (laughing)
> Hell man, one time he even stole the
> Rolling Stones' limousine... with
> THEM in it!

> CUTTER
>
> Shut up! Mischa, NO!

> MISCHA
>
> Oh my god. The Stones are my favorite
> band of all time!

> APOLLO
>
>   (slapping him on the shoulder)
> Well they're your dad's too.
>   (winking at Cutter)
> See? You're bonding already, pally.

> CUTTER
> You shut the hell up!

> APOLLO
> (laughing; to Mischa)
> They all went off on this legendary
> three-day bender through five states
> before the National Guard finally
> cornered them at the Canadian border.

> MISCHA
> I can't believe it. Dad?

Cutter stares daggers at Apollo, whose eyes glitter like sparklers. He pulls out a fat joint and lights it up, then takes big hit and offers it to Mischa.

> APOLLO
> (holding his breath)
> It's killer.

> CUTTER
> NO, NO! DON'T! Goddamn you
> Apollo! Mischa don't smoke that!

He frantically searches for anything to murder Apollo with and finds the vase. He throws it and it smashes on Apollo's head, but that doesn't even faze him. Apollo turns and shoots a demented look at Cutter.

> APOLLO
> Come on partner. Trying to tell a
> story here.
> (back to Mischa)
> At one point on that trip they found
> your old man roller-skating down
> Chicago Avenue buck naked being pulled
> by seven naked girls on roller skates.
> Cutter had a Zorro mask on, with a
> whip in one hand and a bottle of Jack
> in the other. The police couldn't catch—

Cutter screams like a trapped animal. He's ripping the iron pipe down through the ceiling, but he can't get free. Apollo takes another hit and blows the smoke at Mischa, who breathes it in, smiling.

> APOLLO
> When it was all over they had done
> twenty-six million dollars worth of
> damage, nine girls got pregnant, six
> people had to leave the country,
> including Keith Richards, and the
> Mayor of Cleveland quit his job and
> ran off with Keith to be his assistant
> guitar tech.
> (taking another hit)
> The Stones still claim it was the single
> wildest party they've ever been to.

An expression of criminal glee fills Mischa's face and he looks over at his dad in awe.

> MISCHA
> WOW! And dad went to jail for that?

> APOLLO
> Hell no! He lied his way out of it. Weren't
> you listening? He is *way* the best liar ever.
> That's why I need him now.

Cutter is bashing his head through the sheetrock.

> APOLLO
> But that was a harmless stunt. You want
> to hear about the really bad stuff he—

Cutter screams bloody murder, cutting Apollo off.

> CUTTER
> OK, OK! I'll do it! Goddamn it, Apollo!
> Just stop! I'LL DO IT!!

> APOLLO
> Tell me you love me and I'll take off the
> handcuffs.

> CUTTER
> Just get me out of here! I'll do whatever
> you friggin' want!

> APOLLO
> Tell me you love me.

Cutter stands there in his tiny red spandex shorts, his head covered with white plaster. Tears stream down his face, cutting tracks through the white powder.

> CUTTER
> OK... I love you.
> (furious)
> Now get me the hell out of here!

Apollo slips the joint to Mischa and grabs a raincoat off a hook behind the door. He unlocks the cuffs, slips the raincoat around Cutter and escorts him outside as a grinning Mischa takes a hit.

> CUTTER
> Mischa, go to church!

EPILOGUE

I sincerely hope that this book has taken your screenwriting to another level. I have been working with these tools since 1981 when Irving Fiske taught me the basics of Aristotle and then started me reading Price and Krows. I read them for three years to the exclusion of everything else, which ensured having a solid craft at my disposal before I started writing. I'm glad to be able to pass this knowledge along to you and I can say with confidence that if you apply yourself diligently to mastering these tools they will truly give you the habits of mind of a trained dramatist.

It takes hard work to master them, but I've tried to lay this book out so that you can pursue a course of in-depth study and learn how to create, develop and structure screenplays that will tend to work. I present a lot of additional material in conjunction with these tools, so I want to clarify again what the four tools themselves are. I call the first one 'Aristotle' and it consists of Dilemma, Crisis, Decision and Action, and Resolution. The second is the 36 Dramatic Situations; the third tool is the Central Proposition; and the fourth is Sequence, Proposition, Plot.

Pay particular attention to learning the *principles* behind the tools, as well as how to use them. Remember that Price said that the tools create certain distinctions; keep these distinctions in mind even if they become inconvenient, then you won't compromise the power of the tool. Use them as precisely as you can, taking special care to learn the full specifics of what the tool does and how to use it properly. This gives you the sharp edge of the tool, which will cut through the innate slipperiness of dramatic writing.

Keep your sense of proportion and direction. They will help if you get lost. Think about where you are in the story and what you're up to. Make a quick chart of the script—are you halfway through, three quarters? Always remember that it's the protagonist's story, so you will want to keep making your way back to his or her trajectory. That can help give you a compass. Your map is the structural work that you do and it offers you a lifeline when you're overwhelmed. Remember that one of the key points with this approach to screenwriting is that you can take all the energy that goes into rewrites and put it into engineering your script properly before you write it.

Constantly evaluate and adjust as you go. Stand back from what you are creating and give it an objective look. Is it any good? On a scale of one to ten how strong is it? What story are you trying to tell? How is it shifting and taking on a life of its own? Is this shift a good thing or not? Use the wild animal in you to charge off the deep end and get into as much trouble as possible. Don't make safe choices. Attack the audience and attack the story. Chaos can be your best friend as a creator. Use your tools to create order out of what you've created, but don't edit yourself to death as you're brainstorming. If inspiration grabs you then run with it. If your script wants to morph from a thriller into a silly comedy, see what it's got in mind. The worst that can happen is that you've now got two scripts. With these tools you can wade into a quagmire and create order. And don't let anyone tell you to think small. It's the movies!

Work with confidence. Work to develop your craft. Go back and forth between intuition and logic, between rapture and control, between total fearlessness and absolute attention to detail. Keep using your map and your compass to orient yourself and to get a handle on where you are and where you're going. Pay attention to what you as an audience member want when you're at the movies and bring that home to your writing. I read about a playwright who, when he was going to read a script, would take a hot bath and dress up in a tuxedo as though he were going out for a night at the theatre, and then read the play in that frame of mind. *Always* read a script in one sitting. It's the only way to evaluate the thing as a whole.

Soak yourself in storytelling. Read as much as you can. I'm always listening to books on tape while I drive. They're free at the library and I go through them by the dozens, by the hundreds. Read the best screenwriters, playwrights, novelists and other great writers. Think about studying acting, even if you just audit a class. I learned a lot from doing that. You're writing for actors in a performance medium, so learn that aspect of your craft. But also live a real life. The best stories are out there in the world looking for a writer to happen to, so get out there and live life with everything you've got.

I tried to make this book an entertaining read and I hope that sweetens the hard work needed to acquire a solid working knowledge of this craft. Now that you have these tools under your belt and have gained a greater expertise in the craft, go back to why you are involved in this business of writing a screenplay to begin with. Why do you want to write the movie you're writing? What hunger does it satisfy? How does it reflect your deepest passions, your understanding and your peak experiences in life? What's the fire you want to bring to the world as a storyteller? Answering these questions will help you keep on target with not only the 'how' of writing a great movie but also the 'why.' I hope looking over my shoulder as I've worked with these tools in the actual creative process has been useful. Persevere in perfecting your craft and, once again, just keep writing.